Beiträge zur Praxeologie / Contributions to Praxeology

Series Editors

Bruno Karsenti, Paris, France
Erhard Schüttpelz, Siegen, Germany
Tristan Thielmann, Siegen, Germany

Die „Beiträge zur Praxeologie / Contributions to Praxeology" setzen sich zum Ziel, die Praxis allen anderen Erklärungsgrößen vorzuordnen, und die theoretischen Grundbegriffe aus dieser Vorordnung zu gewinnen, zu klären oder zu korrigieren. Sowohl die Arbeiten von Wittgenstein als auch die von Schütz und Garfinkel verweisen auf eine gemeinsame mitteleuropäische Genealogie der „Praxeologie", die bis heute allerdings weitgehend unbekannt geblieben ist. Die Reihe will sich daher in drei Stoßrichtungen entfalten: durch philosophische Theoriearbeit, durch empirische Beiträge zur Theoriebildung und durch Beiträge zur Revision der Wissenschaftsgeschichte.

Die Bände der Reihe erscheinen in deutscher oder englischer Sprache.

Christian Erbacher

The Happy Afterlife of Ludwig W.

The People that Made Wittgenstein's Books and Turned Him into the World's Most Popular Philosopher

J.B. METZLER

Christian Erbacher
University of Siegen
Siegen, Germany

Funded by the Deutsche Forschungsgemeinschaft (DFG, German Research Foundation) – Project-ID 262513311 – SFB 1187.

ISSN 2946-0158   ISSN 2946-0166   (electronic)
Beiträge zur Praxeologie / Contributions to Praxeology
ISBN 978-3-662-66154-3   ISBN 978-3-662-66155-0   (eBook)
https://doi.org/10.1007/978-3-662-66155-0

This J.B. Metzler imprint is published by the registered company Springer-Verlag GmbH, DE, part of Springer Nature.
The registered company address is: Heidelberger Platz 3, 14197 Berlin, Germany

Introduction

Literary Means for a Tale of Philosophical Inheritance

This book tells a great philosophical tale. The backstory of this tale is simple: the philosopher Ludwig Wittgenstein published only one philosophical book during his lifetime: the *Tractatus Logico-Philosophicus*. He left the lion's share of his philosophical writings to posterity in the form of unpublished manuscripts and typescripts amounting to more than 18,000 pages. In his will, Wittgenstein entrusted three of his former students—Elizabeth Anscombe, Rush Rhees and Georg Henrik von Wright—with the task of publishing from his writings what they thought fit. During the subsequent decades, these literary heirs edited the volumes that the learned world has come to know as the influential works of Wittgenstein. Now, the essays in this book tell about Wittgenstein's literary heirs in their ambition to publish the writings of their beloved teacher.

Historically speaking, there are a number of cases in which great philosophers have not published and disseminated their thoughts themselves; it happened instead through students who were deeply affected by discussing with their teacher. One thinks particularly of Plato's dissemination of the thoughts of Socrates. What is exceptional in the case of Wittgenstein, however, is that we can study in detail the mediating processes that have taken place to transmit his philosophy. The reason for this exceptional opportunity is that much of the written correspondence between Wittgenstein's literary heirs has been preserved.

When I read parts of the correspondence between Anscombe, Rhees and von Wright for the first time at the National Library of Finland in spring 2010, I was intrigued by two things: first, the detailed account of decades of editorial work on Wittgenstein's writings which these letters contained, and second, the human story of three philosophers and how their relationships developed through many years of collaboration. On one hand, the letters promised to let facts replace legendary anecdotes and suppositions that have grown around the history of editing Wittgenstein's papers. On the other hand—and this was at least as important to me—the voices in the correspondence and the manner of their conversation created a sense of the editors' personalities and the spirit of their conduct, insights into their commonly shared views and their conflicts. In their correspondence, the literary heirs contributed their individual tones and colours to the 50-year-long conversation in editing—a conversation between three philosophers who were, despite great personal differences, devoted to a common aim, namely to fulfil the task given by Wittgenstein's last will.

Reading the literary heirs' correspondence opened my eyes to a realm of intertwined actions, non-philosophical motives and lines of reasoning that can enter into the transmission of a philosophy through the philosopher's students' editions. Different factors came to the fore at different times: personal acquaintance, the involvement of Wittgenstein's family and friends, cultural and biographical changes during editorial processes, as well as material, technological and business-related aspects, and repeatedly—of course—the literary heirs' understanding of Wittgenstein's philosophy and their attitudes concerning the then-current scholarly reception. The latter incited the literary heirs more than once to publish a certain volume which then, in turn, influenced the scholars' reading of Wittgenstein. The literary heirs' correspondence allows insight into the roles of such contextual factors when the left-behind writings of a philosopher are canonized. Sometimes this insight is explicit, at other times implicit. The letters that Wittgenstein's literary heirs sent to each other are thus not only a quarry to be mined for minute philological details, but a detailed documentation of aspects that can enter the rise of a paradigm in the humanities. They can give the reader an experience of what philosophical inheritance can mean.

My reading experience from the spring of 2010 became the starting point for a decade of research. The essays in this book are revisions of articles that have been published during that decade (a complete list of the publications resulting from my research is at the end of this introduction). While compiling the essays for this book, I can now clearly see that my studies of Wittgenstein's literary heirs' work were, for me, not only an adventure in reading new archival sources and an adventure of research into what they mean—they were also an adventure in finding and forming adequate literary means to present the episodes of the great philosophical tale.

Chapter 1 (previously published as Erbacher 2015c) uses the form of a scholarly article to summarize the scholarly debate around the Wittgenstein editions and to create a structure of their historization. Chapter 2 (previously published as Erbacher 2016b) employs the literary form of a parallel lives story that reveals how the literary heirs became acquainted with Wittgenstein and their interaction with him over time. These are three historically parallel yet different experiences of being with and learning from Wittgenstein, experiences that created the motivation to carry out the Herculean task of editing Wittgenstein's writings. Chapter 3 (previously published as Erbacher et al. 2019) expresses the insight that, after all, the best way to see the literary heirs' perspectives is to listen to their own voices. This chapter's adequate form is thus that of the edited archival source, namely a radio broadcast from the time when Anscombe had just finished translating the *Philosophical Investigations*. Chapter 4 (previously published as Erbacher 2019c) may be read as a hermeneutical tracking of a hermeneutical tracker's editorial methods. Likewise, Chap. 5 (previously published as Erbacher 2017c) explores how von Wright's involvement in his cultural times led him to edit the volume that was supposed to show Wittgenstein's involvement in his cultural times. For this I use the form of a cultural essay. Finally, Chap. 6 (previously published in German as Erbacher 2019a) presents the tragic deterioration of a promising research project in the form of a classic drama.

All these literary formats that I have tried out during my research are essays in the literal sense: attempts or experiments. Experimenting with adequate literary means in philosophy is, for me, part of the research adventure that is documented here. Remembering that finding an adequate form was also paramount to both Wittgenstein and the editors of his writings, the struggle to find adequate literary formats in philosophy seems to be one of the great underlying themes of this book.

I have had the good fortune to be supported by a number of institutions that enabled me to travel to libraries and archives across Europe and to conduct interviews with those who cooperated with Anscombe, Rhees and von Wright. Consequently, in addition to reading the mentioned letters preserved in Helsinki, I was able to gain access to more sources and information that helped me draw an increasingly complex picture of the literary heirs' work. In particular, my early pilot-studies were funded by Nordforsk as part of the project "Joint Nordic Use of WAB Bergen and VWA Helsinki" (2010 and 2011); the Norwegian Research Council funded the three-year research project "Shaping a Domain of Knowledge by Editorial Processing: The Case of Wittgenstein's Work" (NFR 213080, 2012–2015); the Academy of Finland supported my basic research on the sources and my cooperation with researchers who, through the project "The Creation of Wittgenstein" (2016–2020), investigated the philosophical relevance of the literary heirs' editorial practices; the Humboldt Foundation, through the Research Centre for Analytic German Idealism (2018), supported my research on Anscombe's role in editing and translating Wittgenstein's texts; and the German Research Foundation funded my work at the Collaborative Research Centre "Media of Cooperation" (Sonderforschungsbereich SFB 1187), in particular my research in the centre's subprojects "Wissenschaftliche Medien der Praxistheorie: Harold Garfinkel und Ludwig Wittgenstein" (2016–2019) and "Digital Network Technologies between Specialization and Generalization" (2021). In addition to the institutional funding, many individual scholars have supported my work by providing documents and memories and by participating in oral interviews. The specific acknowledgement of their help may be found in the chapters of this book. The book's production was funded by the Collaborative Research Centre "Media of Cooperation" (SFB 1187). For help in making the essays fit for publication in this book, I owe special thanks to Sebastian Gießmann, Julia Jung and Erhard Schüttpelz.

Bibliography of Publications on the History of Editing Wittgenstein Resulting from the Above-Mentioned Research Projects

Erbacher, Christian. Forthcoming. The Letters which Rush Rhees, Elizabeth Anscombe, and Georg Henrik von Wright Sent to Each Other. In *The Creation of Wittgenstein*, ed. Thomas Wallgren. London: Bloomsbury.

Erbacher, Christian. 2020. *Wittgenstein's Heirs and Editors.* Cambridge: Cambridge University Press.

Erbacher, Christian. 2019a. Das Drama von Tübingen. Eine Humanities and Technology Story. In *Working Paper Series des Sonderforschungsbereichs (SFB) 1187* No. 13: 1–44.

Erbacher, Christian. 2019b. Ways of Making Wittgenstein Available – Towards Studying Infrastructures and Publics in the History of Editing Wittgenstein's Writings. In *Infrastructuring Publics – Making Infrastructures Public*, eds. Matthias Korn, Wolfgang Reißmann, Tobias Röhl and David Sittler, 265–284. Berlin: Springer.

Erbacher, Christian. 2019c. 'Good' Philosophical Reasons for 'Bad' Editorial Philology? On Rhees and Wittgenstein's *Philosophical Grammar. Philosophical Investigations*, 42(2): 111–145.

Erbacher, Christian. 2018. Philosophy – Therapy – Culture – On a Triangulated Analogy in the Philosophy of Ludwig Wittgenstein. *Curare. Journal of Medical Anthropology* 41: 130–136.

Erbacher, Christian. 2017a. Brief aus Norwegen. *Deutsche Zeitschrift für Philosophie* 65(3): 574–588.

Erbacher, Christian. 2017b. "Gute" philosophische Gründe für "schlechte" Editionsphilologie. In *Textologie – Theorie und Praxis interdisziplinärer Textforschung*, eds. Martin Endres, Alois Pichler and Claus Zittel, 257–297. Berlin: De Gruyter.

Erbacher, Christian. 2017c. "Among the omitted stuff, there are many good remarks of a general nature" – On the Making of von Wright and Wittgenstein's *Culture and Value. Northern European Journal of Philosophy* 18(2): 79–113.

Erbacher, Christian. 2016a. Die Wittgenstein-Editionen im Kontext – Über editorische Defizite und ihre konstruktive Kontextualisierung. *Editio* 30: 197–221.

Erbacher, Christian. 2016b. Wittgenstein and His Literary Executors. Rush Rhees, Georg Henrik von Wright and Elizabeth Anscombe as Students, Colleagues and Friends of Ludwig Wittgenstein. *Journal for the History of Analytical Philosophy* 4(3): 1–39.

Erbacher, Christian. 2016c. Der gestaltete Gestalter. Die Editionsgeschichte der Schriften Ludwig Wittgensteins und das Medien-Problem des Philosophierens. *Diagonal* 36: 13–26.

Erbacher, Christian. 2015. The Social Construction of Wittgenstein: How a History of Editing Wittgenstein's Nachlass May Contribute to the Social Studies of the Humanities. In *Realism – Relativism – Constructivism, Papers of the 38th*

International Wittgenstein Symposium, eds. Christian Kanzian, Josef Mitterer and Katharina Neges, 80–85. Kirchberg: ALWS.

Erbacher, Christian. 2015a. Editionspraxis, Philosophie und Zivilisationskritik: Die Geschichte von Wittgensteins Vermischten Bemerkungen. *Wittgenstein-Studien* 6: 1–25.

Erbacher, Christian. 2015b. Friedrich August von Hayeks unvollendete "Skizze für eine Biographie über Ludwig Wittgenstein". *Mitteilungen aus dem Brenner-Archiv* 34: 83–100.

Erbacher, Christian. 2015c. Editorial Approaches to Wittgenstein's Nachlass: Towards a Historical Appreciation. *Philosophical Investigations* 38(3): 165–198.

Erbacher, Christian. 2014. Das Medienproblem des Philosophierens und Wittgensteins Nachlass. In *Analytical and Continental Philosophy – Methods and Perspectives, Papers of the 37th International Wittgenstein Symposium*, eds. Sonja Rinhofer-Kreidl and Harald Wiltsche, 79–81. Kirchberg: ALWS.

Erbacher, Christian. 2012. The History of Editing Wittgenstein's Nachlass – Die erste Runde der Nachlassedierung als interdisziplinäres Forschungsprojekt und Geschichte eines philosophischen Erbes. In *Ethics, Society, Politics, Papers of the 35. International Wittgenstein Symposium*, eds. Martin Weiss and Hajo Greif, 66–68. Kirchberg: ALWS.

Erbacher, Christian. 2011. Unser Denken bleibt gefragt: Web 3.0 und Wittgensteins Nachlass. In *Wissenschaftstheorie, Sprachkritik und Wittgenstein*, eds. Sascha Windholz and Walter Feigl, 135–146. Heusenstamm: Ontos.

Erbacher, Christian. 2010. A Note on the History of F.A. von Hayek's Unpublished "Sketch of a Biography of L.W.". In *Image and Imaging in Philosophy, Science and the Arts, Papers of the 33. International Wittgenstein Symposium*, eds. Richard Heinrich, Elisabeth Nemeth, Wolfram Pichler and David Wagner, 76–79. Kirchberg: ALWS.

Erbacher, Christian, Anne dos Santos Reis, and Julia Jung, eds. 2019. "Ludwig Wittgenstein" – A BBC radio talk by Elizabeth Anscombe in May 1953. *Nordic Wittgenstein Review* 8(1–2): 225–240.

Erbacher, Christian, Julia Jung, and Anne Seibel. 2017. The Logbook of Editing Wittgenstein's "Philosophische Bemerkungen". *Nordic Wittgenstein Review*, 6(1): 105–147.

Erbacher, Christian, and Sophia Krebs. 2015. The First Nine Months of Editing Wittgenstein – Letters from G. E. M. Anscombe and Rush Rhees to G. H. von Wright. *Nordic Wittgenstein Review*, 4(1): 195–231.

Hayek, Friedrich A. 2019. *F. A. v. Hayek: Unfinished Draft of a Sketch of a Biography of Ludwig Wittgenstein*, edited and introduced by Christian Erbacher, with an epilogue by Allan Janik. Paderborn: Mentis.

Rhees, Rush. 2017. On Continuity: Rush Rhees on Outer and Inner surfaces of Bodies. Edited and introduced by Christian Erbacher and Tina Schirmer. *Philosophical Investigations*, 40(1): 3–30.

Contents

Editorial Approaches to Wittgenstein's Nachlass

Towards a Historical Appreciation

1.1 The Seven Rungs of Editing Wittgenstein

The *Tractatus Logico-Philosophicus* (*TLP* 1922)[1] was the only philosophical book that Ludwig Wittgenstein published during his lifetime, but he left to posterity about 18,000 unpublished pages, which were written from 1929 to 1951. In his will from January 1951, Wittgenstein gave three of his friends the task of publishing from those writings what they thought fit. Following this desire of Wittgenstein, the three literary heirs—Rush Rhees, Elizabeth Anscombe and Georg Henrik von Wright—edited the books (referred to as editions) that made Wittgenstein's later philosophy available to all interested readers (see Table 1.1). It is generally known that the literary executors' editions differ considerably in the degree of editorial intervention. On one hand, the material itself demanded different editorial approaches, since Wittgenstein's way of working led to collections of raw remarks as well as to more finished selections and arrangements from several stages in his own editing process. On the other hand, the literary executors had different experiences in editing and developed different editorial policies as they proceeded with their task. The different condition or status of the sources and the different editorial approaches make it impossible to identify general characteristics of how the books relate to the sources in Wittgenstein's Nachlass. Moreover, as of today, the literary executors' volumes are not the only editions available: there are also the *Vienna Edition*, the *Bergen Electronic Edition* and critical editions of

---

[1] All references to editions of Wittgenstein's writings in this chapter follow: Pichler, Biggs and Szeltner 2011, 249–286.

This chapter is a revised version of Erbacher 2015.

© The Author(s), under exclusive license to Springer-Verlag GmbH, DE, part of Springer Nature 2023

C. Erbacher, *The Happy Afterlife of Ludwig W.*, Beiträge zur Praxeologie / Contributions to Praxeology, https://doi.org/10.1007/978-3-662-66155-0_1

Table 1.1 The first round of editing Wittgenstein's Nachlass

Year of publication	English edition (Oxford: Blackwell)	German edition (Frankfurt a. M.: Suhrkamp)
1953	*Philosophical Investigations*, ed G.E.M. Anscombe and R. Rhees (*PI*)	
1956	*Remarks on the Foundations of Mathematics*, ed. G.H. von Wright, R. Rhees and G.E.M. Anscombe (*RFM*)	
1960		*Schriften Band 1. Tractatus logico-philosophicus, Tagebücher 1914–1916, Philosophische Untersuchungen*
1961	*Notebooks 1914–1916*, ed. G.H. von Wright and G.E.M. Anscombe (*NB*)	
1964		*Schriften Band 2. Philosophische Bemerkungen*
1967	*Zettel*, ed. G.E.M. Anscombe and G.H. von Wright (*Z*)	
1967		*Schriften Band 3. Wittgenstein und der Wiener Kreis*
1969	*On Certainty*, ed. G.E.M. Anscombe and G.H. von Wright (*OC*)	
1969	*Philosophische Grammatik*, ed. R. Rhees (*PG*)	
1969		*Schriften Band 4. Philosophische Grammatik*
		Schriften Band 5. Das Blaue Buch, Eine Philosophische Betrachtung, Zettel
1971		*Über Gewissheit*, ed. G.E.M. Anscombe and G.H. von Wright
1974	*Philosophical Grammar*, ed. R. Rhees (*PG*)	
1974		*Schriften Band 6. Bemerkungen über die Grundlagen der Mathematik*
1975	*Philosophical Remarks*, ed. R. Rhees (*PB*)	
1977		*Vermischte Bemerkungen*, ed. G.H. von Wright and H. Nyman

(continued)

Table 1.1   (continued)

Year of publication	English edition (Oxford: Blackwell)	German edition (Frankfurt a. M.: Suhrkamp)
1980	*Remarks on the Philosophy of Psychology*, Vol. 1., ed. G.E.M. Anscombe and G.H. von Wright (*RPP 1*)	
1980	*Remarks on the Philosophy of Psychology*, Vol. 2, ed. G.H. von Wright and H. Nyman (*RPP 2*)	
1982	*Last Writings on the Philosophy of Psychology*, Vol. 1, ed. G.H. von Wright and H. Nyman (*LW 1*)	
1982		*Schriften Band 8. Bemerkungen über die Philosophie der Psychologie*
1992	*Last Writings on the Philosophy of Psychology*, Vol. 2, ed. G.H. von Wright and H. Nyman (*LW 2*)	
1993		*Letzte Schriften über die Philosophie der Psychologie*

Table 1.2   Later rounds of editing Wittgenstein's Nachlass

1989	*Logisch-philosophische Abhandlung. Tractatus logico-philosophicus—Kritische Edition*, ed. Brian McGuinness and Joachim Schulte, Frankfurt a. M.: Suhrkamp (*TLP 1989*)
1994–2000	*Ludwig Wittgenstein, Wiener Ausgabe*, Vol. 1–5, *Register, Synopse, Big Typescript*, ed. Michael Nedo, Heidelberg, New York: Springer (*WA*)
2000	*Wittgenstein's Nachlass—The Bergen Electronic Edition*, ed. The Wittgenstein Archive, University of Bergen, Oxford: Oxford University Press (*BEE*)
2001	*Philosophische Untersuchungen. Kritisch-genetische Edition*, ed. Joachim Schulte in cooperation with Heikki Nyman, Eike von Savigny and G.H. von Wright, Frankfurt a. M.: Suhrkamp (*PU 2001*)

Note: The tables present only books/CD-ROM in their first edition. Editions based on lecture notes are not presented. For a comprehensive bibliography, see Pichler, Biggs and Szeltner (2011, 249–286)

Wittgenstein's two main works, the *TLP* and *Philosophical Investigations* (*PI*) (Table 1.2).

To clarify this somewhat confusing situation, this paper begins by presenting a perspicuous reconstruction of the editions from Wittgenstein's Nachlass (Fig. 1.1). As a structuring device, the metaphor of ladder rungs has been chosen. The rungs are roughly rather than strictly chronological, and for the sake of perspicuity, not all editions are discussed. For example, even though editions of letters and

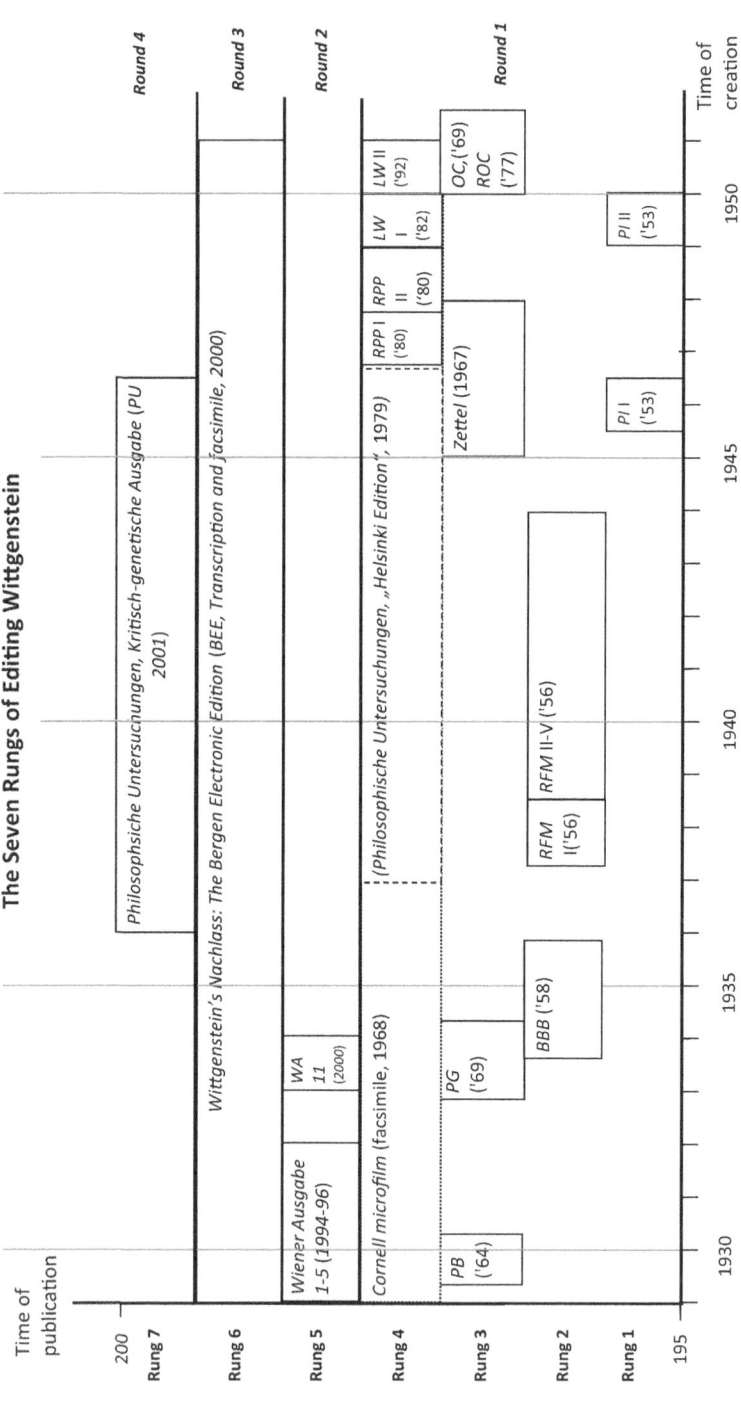

Fig. 1.1 The diagram displays significant steps in the history of editing Wittgenstein's Nachlass by plotting the time of creation and the time of posthumous editions. The first four rungs serve also as a more detailed structuring of what von Wright (2001, 158–168) called the first round of editing Wittgenstein. Abbreviations of editions (e.g. *PI, RFM, BBB, PB, PG*) follow Pichler, Biggs and Szeltner (2011:249–286)

diaries and editions based on lectures notes are important for the history of editing Wittgenstein, they have been excluded from Fig. 1.1. Nevertheless, the seven rungs represent significant steps in the development of editing Wittgenstein's Nachlass. They correspond to von Wright's suggestion to distinguish several 'rounds' of editing Wittgenstein (Von Wright 2001, 158–168).[2] With the phrase 'first round', von Wright referred to the book editions published by Wittgenstein's original literary executors. The ambition at that time was to make Wittgenstein's writings available in readable books without scholarly commentary. By contrast, the subsequent rounds are characterized by the aim to provide more scholarly editions. This chapter focuses largely on what von Wright called round one, distinguishing within it four rungs that represent the different editorial approaches of the three literary executors.

Rhees, Anscombe and von Wright did not conceal their editorial interventions, but scholars have criticized how the brevity of their prefaces and the uniform appearance of the books make it difficult for readers to recognize which Nachlass sources were used and how they were used to create some of the editions (cf. Stern 1996, 442–476). Although several editorial issues will be addressed while discussing the various rungs, the main purpose of this chapter is not to trace editorial details but to show how new archival materials may change the angle from which the editorial history of Wittgenstein's Nachlass is viewed. Exploring the editors' reasons and motives for their unique ways of editing may shed light on the history of editing Wittgenstein's Nachlass—not only as a field for editorial-philological questions, but as a human story of philosophical inheritance. Encouraging this perspective, this chapter offers glimpses into the hitherto unpublished correspondence between Wittgenstein's literary executors with the aim of sketching how their editorial approaches developed historically.

1.2   Rung One: Wittgenstein's Chef D'ouvre: *Philosophical Investigations (PI)*

After Wittgenstein's death in April 1951, the appointed literary executors immediately wanted to make available what they considered to be the book Wittgenstein envisioned: *Philosophical Investigations (PI)*. As students, friends and colleagues of Wittgenstein, they were already aware of significant parts of this book. Rhees had witnessed its development from the first version, written in 1936, through Wittgenstein's last efforts to finish it. Anscombe, with Wittgenstein's consent, had committed herself to translating the *PI* by the turn of 1949/50. Wittgenstein discussed questions about editing with both Anscombe and Rhees, thus the literary executors were in no doubt that the latest version of the *PI* was to be the first posthumous publication. They quickly found a publisher: Blackwell. Yet

---

[2] See Fig. 1, right side.

the company director was unsuccessful in gaining permission for a reprint of the *Tractatus* alongside the *PI*, which was what Wittgenstein envisaged when he considered publishing his book with Cambridge University Press in 1944. Although Routledge and Kegan Paul had given Cambridge University Press such permission, Blackwell was not offered a similar agreement. Accordingly, *PI* had to appear without the *Tractatus*.

The contract for publishing the *PI* (*PI* 1953) was signed in November 1951. Using Wittgenstein's original typescript, Anscombe and Rhees prepared the printer's copy of the German text by the end of 1951. Anscombe's translation of what is known today as Part I (§§1–693) may have been finished by that time as well (Geach 1988, xii: editor's preface to Wittgenstein 1988). However, she continued working on her translation until it was sent to the printer in the summer of 1952. She also continued revising and proofreading pages until the actual printing finally got underway in 1953. In the process of translating and typesetting, other friends and pupils of Wittgenstein, such as Georg Kreisel and Pierro Sraffa, were also consulted. After publication, Anscombe further scrutinized the translation and published a list of corrections in the journal *Mind* (Anscombe 1953, 521–522). Her devotion to the project resulted in a translation that has contributed to the popularity of Wittgenstein's philosophy, also beyond the English-speaking world. For 50 years, scholars around the world have quoted Anscombe's text almost on par with the German original (Kenny 2005, 341–342).

Nevertheless, critical questions have arisen in the wake of Rhees and Anscombe's edition of the *PI*, particularly regarding their decision to include what they called 'Part II'. While the typescript for Part I (Ts227, dating from 1945/46)[3] is usually regarded as *the* extraordinary item in Wittgenstein's Nachlass, coming close to what could be called a finished work by Wittgenstein himself (Schulte 2005, 397–404), Anscombe and Rhees attached a typescript on the philosophy of psychology as Part II to the *PI* (Ts234, dictated in 1949). They decided to merge that fragment with the relatively finished and composed typescript under the one title *Philosophical Investigations*. The division of sections and section headings within Part II were also made by Anscombe and Rhees. These interventions were subsequently questioned, not least because the original typescript that was used for printing was eventually lost (as was the typescript from which Part I was printed). In their preface, Anscombe and Rhees did not conceal that it was their decision to include Part II, but scholars have later criticized this decision, partly encouraged by von Wright's study on the 'troubled history of Part II' (von Wright 1992, 181–192).

While editing the *PI,* Anscombe, Rhees and von Wright thought it was uncontroversial to include the typescript of Part II. Anscombe and Rhees—on separate occasions, but both at the turn of 1948/49—had visited Wittgenstein and received corresponding information. In a letter to von Wright, Anscombe recalled moments

---

[3] Numbering of items in Wittgenstein's Nachlass follows von Wright (1969, 483–503).

of her visit which were important for her understanding of Wittgenstein's intentions:

> My contribution to the belief that Wittgenstein 'would have inserted this, with further material, into the alas considerably expurgated last 30 pages or so of the Investigations['], was based purely on what he said to me when I visited him in Dublin: What he pointed to was not indeed the MS or TS of Part II (which as you remark didn't exist at that time) but those big—or that big—MS volume which contained, as I realized later, the material in the MS of Part II. I realized this because of what Wittgenstein was discussing with me, which was the context of his pointing to that big MS volume (I think in fact he was pointing to only <u>one</u> volume, and thought of 'those volumes' because they go together.[)] (Anscombe to von Wright, 15. April 1991)

Rhees made a similar report:

> The main '<u>revision</u>' on which he was working in the latter part of 1948 and the beginning of 1949 was <u>Part II</u> (as we have called it). He was working <u>very</u> hard on this when I visited him in Dublin in the Christmas vacation 1948/49 (roughly from December 20th to January 10th). He spoke about those parts he had finished a,d [sic] read some of them to me. But he did not explain just which parts of the "Part I" manuscript they were to replace. (Rhees to von Wright, 10. August 1972)

Even today, the status of Rhees and Anscombe's Part II generates controversial discussion amongst scholars. In light of the stylistic differences between Part I and Part II, Rhees noted that 'the question of how Teil I and Teil II belong together, is a question of their <u>internal</u> relations' (Rhees to von Wright, 7. May 1974). The critical-genetic edition of the *Philosophical Investigations* (*PU* 2001) informs in detail about the origins of both Part I and Part II. It replaces Part II with the last existing pre-version of it (Ms 144). In the German reading edition that is based on the critical-genetic edition (*PU* 2003), Part II no longer appears. In the revised English translation (*PI* 2009), Rhees and Anscombe's Part II is still included, but under the heading 'Philosophy of Psychology—A fragment [previously known as 'Part II']'.

1.3   Rung Two: Early Editorial Dispositions

Wittgenstein himself had almost finished the text of the *PI*, but subsequent books published from his Nachlass have required more editing. Thus, the second rung marks the beginning of the literary executors' process of selecting passages and fragments from the Nachlass and composing them into readable volumes. Three editions—*Remarks on the Foundations of Mathematics*, the *Notebooks 1914–1916* and *Blue and Brown Books*—are considered here as belonging on one rung, despite the considerable differences in how they are edited. They belong on the same rung because they represent the literary executors' first experiences of creating books out of Wittgenstein's Nachlass, and their different conclusions resulting from those experiences. Taken together, this prepared the ground for the different editorial approaches they developed later on.

1.3.1   Remarks on the Foundations of Mathematics

Even before the *PI* was published, the literary executors decided to proceed with publishing further selections from Wittgenstein's Nachlass. They knew they would produce a significantly incomplete picture of Wittgenstein's life-work if they left out his work on the foundations of mathematics. Wittgenstein worked intensively on his remarks on the foundations of mathematics until 1945, and his lectures dealt with this theme for several years. Rhees had attended many of these lectures, and von Wright had attended two (Klagge and Nordmann 2003, 340–359). Moreover, Rhees knew, from his own attempt to translate an early version of the *PI* (Ts222, Überarbeitete Frühfassung, 1937 or 1938; Rhees' translation: Ts 226, 1938),[4] that Wittgenstein had once intended that the *PI*'s second part was to consist of remarks on the foundations of mathematics. Thus, the literary executors wanted to publish a volume on the foundations of mathematics in order to create a more complete picture of Wittgenstein's philosophy. Their problem was that they did not yet know what exactly they ought to publish to complete this picture.

While Anscombe was still translating the *PI*, Rhees and von Wright considered that the next publication should be what they called the 'Moore-Volume' (Ts209, later published in *PB*) or the second part of what is known as the 'Big Typescript' (Ts213). However, in December 1951, before reaching a conclusion, Rhees received a surprise: a box from Trinity College that did not contain the expected books from Wittgenstein's library but a great number of handwritten manuscripts. While the literary executors were studying the new manuscripts, Rhees began to think that it would be wrong to publish the Big Typescript next, because it could encourage misunderstandings of Wittgenstein's philosophy. This concern proved to be decisive for Rhees' way of handling Wittgenstein's Nachlass:

> I am going through the big typescript now, and I cannot give a considered judgment yet. I think it is obviously an important work—he has not left anything else quite parallel—and it should be published sometime. But I am not sure that it ought to be the first thing we publish on the philosophy of mathematics. In many ways its method of treatment is unlike the way in which he wrote about mathematics later. […] I have an idea that people will expect to find Wittgenstein's later views in whatever we first publish on the subject. And this work would give a false impression. (Rhees to von Wright, 2. March 1952)

By the time Rhees wrote this in a letter, von Wright had resigned from his chair at Cambridge and had returned to his native country, Finland. This of course complicated communication between the literary executors. Since the photographing of

---

[4]The differentiation of different conceptions of *PI* into *Urfassung, Frühfassung, Bearbeitete Frühfassung, Zwischenfassung* and *Spätfassung* follow the critical-genetic edition (*PU* 2001).

documents was expensive in the early 1950s, the three had to organize meetings where they could jointly study the original documents and reach decisions about publications. This being the case, a grant for working on Wittgenstein's Nachlass from the Rockefeller Foundation came as a great help. It allowed Anscombe to work on translation and it covered costs for travelling and duplicating manuscripts. The first conference of sorts between the literary executors took place in Austria in the summer of 1952. Here they became acquainted with members of Wittgenstein's family and some of his friends. During ten days of their stay, they read through a selection of Wittgenstein's manuscript on the foundations of mathematics and discussed their next editorial project.

After the meeting in Austria, von Wright, along with Anscombe's husband Peter Geach, advocated publishing the so-called Moore-Volume, but Rhees had second thoughts:

> I had been re-reading the Moore Volume myself, although I did not know that either you or Peter Geach were giving any attention to it. And I had written to Elizabeth that I was strongly in favour of publishing certain parts of it, at any rate. [...] But I am doubtful, all the same. About making it the next thing, I mean. I agree with you that "Much in M-V is certainly considerably weaker than anything in the Tractatus or the Untersuchungen". It often expresses views which will seem to foster current misunderstandings of Wittgenstein, and will hinder an understanding of his later doctrines. [...] It will certainly be illuminating for those who have really got hold of the later teaching. But I hesitate to publish it before more has been done to make the later position better known. And I am more in favour of trying to carve something from the manuscripts we were reading last summer. (Rhees to von Wright, 22. April 1953)

Von Wright agreed that there might be such a danger, thus they turned to editing the manuscripts that would eventually be published in the *Remarks on the Foundations of Mathematics* (*RFM* 1956; von Wright to Anscombe, 7 May 1953).

The first edition of *RFM* has five parts: Part I consists of the remarks that Wittgenstein had once considered the second part of the early *PI*. The remarks in Parts II-V were selected from typescripts and manuscripts that originated between 1937 and 1944. The edition presents these different sources in sequential divisions under a common title. This splicing together of relatively finished and composed parts with less finished fragments and selections was problematic for the subsequent reception and also for the production process: the literary executors had agreed that Rhees and von Wright should divide the editorial work amongst themselves, while Anscombe was supposed to translate the remarks. However, it was not before 1954 that von Wright actually typed out the selections that were assigned to him. At that time he was a visiting scholar at Cornell University, on the invitation of Norman Malcom. The geographical distance made correspondence more difficult, not to mention the possibility of consulting the originals. Von Wright wrote from Ithaca:

> Perhaps it was foolish of me not to ask for the originals. For, when one has to ponder over each word and comma, one soon realizes that there are a number of places, where one

would wish to consult the "Urtext" [...] I am often very uncertain about the right way of dividing the text into numbered paragraphs. (von Wright to Anscombe, 2. January 1955)

Also problematic was that it had been more than a year since they had discussed what exactly to include and what to omit in their edition. Von Wright could not recall every detail, as the following passage suggests:

> Could you answer the following question: Did we decide to omit from publication the sections 26.IX–23.XI 1940 and 27.V–6.VI 1941? Which is W's last manuscript of mathematics and logic, and what did we decide about it? (von Wright to Anscombe, 6. November 1954)

Anscombe, as she translated the selected passages, began doubting the rightness of their editorial decisions:

> I have just finished translating the MS (Vol XVIII) written at the turn of 1939–40 &[5] feel rather dubious about it—both in our not having cut it down more, it is so repetitive and dreadfully boring; and in respect of one or two of our very few cuts in it, which seem to me to have been of things essential to some that we have left in. (Anscombe to von Wright, 4. July 1954)

Similarly, when facing the difficulties of composing selections of Wittgenstein's remarks, von Wright began to question their approach on a more general level:

> I have "done" the 1940 manuscript. [...] As expected, the work was <u>awful</u>. I am constantly tormented by the question: Do we do the right thing, or not? (von Wright to Anscombe, 2. January 1955)[6]

In addition to these difficulties, von Wright and Rhees employed different styles in preparing their parts, especially in headings and indexing. This required many subsequent corrections that took more than one year to complete. *RFM* was finally published in 1956.

In contrast to the great amount of work put into the *RFM*, the result was not very favourably received. Kreisel's review, for instance, concluded with the words: 'I did not enjoy reading the present book. Of course I do not know what I should have thought of it fifteen years ago; now it seems to me to be a surprisingly insignificant product of a sparkling mind' (Kreisel 1958, 158). Also the editors themselves, as their insight into the interrelations of remarks in Wittgenstein's Nachlass grew, became increasingly aware of the shortcomings of their selection. According to Anthony Kenny, the first edition of *RFM* even embarrassed von Wright in later years (Kenny 2005, 342). For this reason, Rhees and von Wright heavily revised

---

[5] Anscombe, in her letters, often uses an abbreviation for 'and'. Henceforth it is transcribed as '&'.

[6] And earlier: 'Making the selection has been an <u>agonizing</u> job.' (von Wright to Anscombe, 19 November 1954).

and extended *RFM* some 20 years after their first edition (*RFM* 1978). Yet despite the immense labour of twice shaping the *RFM*, their efforts could not completely resolve the problems affecting the edition, and it is still criticized today (for recent articles, see Mühlhölzer 2012, 19–44; Nedo 2008, 79–105).

The editorial story of the *RFM* shows the difficulties of posthumously publishing the complex material that Wittgenstein had worked on for many years but never published himself. These difficulties were exacerbated as Rhees and von Wright began developing different editorial approaches: von Wright would increasingly question the attempt to create a unified whole from selections of Wittgenstein's remarks; Rhees maintained precisely this ambition. Perhaps their diverging editorial positions contributed to the fact that *RFM* was the only book edited by all three literary executors. Although they regularly corresponded and met, the actual editorial work was more and more divided amongst them. While Rhees worked on his editions mostly on his own, von Wright edited volumes which Anscombe translated. In retrospect, the diverging editorial approaches may already be recognized in the volumes that followed the *RFM*, namely the *Notebooks 1914–1916* (*NB* 1961, edited by von Wright and Anscombe) and the *Blue and Brown Books* (*BBB* 1958, edited by Rhees).

1.3.2 *Notebooks 1914–1916*

While editing the *RFM*, von Wright was giving a course on the *Tractatus* at Cornell University and was experiencing the book in a new way:

> I give seminars in which I try to explain the Tractatus. I have learned a lot from them and I have the feeling that now I am beginning to understand the book. It is even more wonderful than I had thought. And one of the most wonderful things about it is that it is absolutely straightforward. No metaphors, no allusions, no mystery. The difficulty is to avoid twisting his words, to avoid putting an "interpretation" on them. (von Wright to Anscombe, 6. June 1954)

Anscombe too was teaching courses and writing on the *Tractatus* at Oxford. In their letters, the two philosophers passionately discussed individual passages of the *Tractatus*, especially 4.464 and 5.62. This lively exchange about the book that was published in Wittgenstein's youth stands in striking contrast to the practical problems of editing the *RFM* that are addressed in the same letters. Also worth noting is that von Wright and Anscombe's mutual interest in the *Tractatus* was refreshed at a time when the book was enjoying a general re-discovery. Besides Anscombe's own introduction, von Wright's colleague Erik Stenius wrote another introduction, and a little later Max Black's companion appeared (Anscombe 1957; Stenius 1960; Black 1964). In addition, Brian McGuinness and David Pears prepared a new translation of the *Tractatus* that was to be highly regarded by Anscombe:

> I have often tried to translate the <u>Tractatus</u>, and my attempts have always fallen dead to the ground. I now understand why. In some way, I was influenced by the English. It never occurred to me to aim at putting something different from Ogden if possible.
>
> Now you have done a wonderful thing: you have broken the spell. Your draft provides a basis, or a big piece of counter-ballast, if you see what I mean, which will make it possible to produce a really excellent translation. (Anscombe to McGuinness, without date [presumably 1959])

The literary executors' refreshed interest in the *Tractatus* was spurred by three notebooks (Mss 101–103) which Wittgenstein's sister showed them during their stay in Austria in the summer of 1952. These pre-war notebooks document the work that led to the writing of the *Tractatus*. Anscombe had them photographed and sent duplicates to von Wright. After *RFM* was published, von Wright and Anscombe considered their next task to be to edit these notebooks. Already at a very early stage of editing, von Wright suggested an editorial policy that contrasted with their approach to the *RFM*:

> I think the notebooks should be published more or less as they are—with some minor omissions and a slight amount of "editing" only. Not everything in them is of equal interest and quality, but to anyone who is seriously interested in the Tractatus they will be an immense help. For the benefit of scholarship too, it seems to me to be our duty to make them public. (von Wright to Anscombe, 19. April 1957)

Anscombe and von Wright supplemented their edition of the *Notebooks* (*NB* 1961) with notes by Russell (Ts201; cf. Costello 1957, 230–245; McGuinness 2002, 243–258) and Moore (Ms 301), as well as with relevant parts of Wittgenstein's correspondence with Russell. Though it may not be justified to call von Wright's approach regarding the *NB* an editorial policy, the published work shows his disposition to opt for minimal editorial intervention whilst providing additional historical documentation. Consequently, von Wright was much more satisfied with the *NB* than with the *RFM*. Having received the first proofs from the printer, he shared his enthusiasm with Anscombe:

> It was a very exhilarating experience to read the proofs. This is an exciting, most important book which we are publishing. (von Wright to Anscombe, 30 April 1960)

But the *NB* still required some editing, since Anscombe and von Wright considered it their duty to cut the passages Wittgenstein had written in his personal code. This was a matter of reverence and loyalty to the friend who had entrusted them with his writings. Nevertheless, a pirate edition of the excluded passages was later published and aroused much curiosity (*Geheime Tagebücher, GT* 1985, 1991). Another issue regarding the editing of the pre-war notebooks concerned copyright laws. Given that many parts of the *NB* overlap with the text of the *Tractatus*, negotiations with the publisher holding the copyright for the *Tractatus* delayed publication until the new translation of the *Tractatus* appeared in 1961.

1.3.3 *The Blue and Brown Books*

The first volume that Rhees edited after the *RFM* was *Preliminary Studies for the Philosophical Investigations generally known as the Blue and Brown Books* (*BBB* 1958). Wittgenstein dictated what has been called 'The Blue Book' to students, as a supplement to his seminars in the 1933/34 academic session. During the following academic session (1934/35), he dictated what came to be called 'The Brown Book' to two of his students and friends. The Brown Book was a draft for what he envisaged would be his second book. Hence, the *BBB* originated—not from students' lecture notes, as is sometimes thought—but from sets of dictation in the proper sense of the term.

Even during Wittgenstein's lifetime, private copies of both sets of dictation were circulating. Immediately after Wittgenstein's death, some of these copies were offered to publishing houses. The literary executors wanted to prevent such pirate editions, so they published an announcement in *Mind* stating that they were the only ones authorized by Wittgenstein to publish his writings (Anscombe, Rhees and von Wright 1951, 584). In light of the continuing circulation of private copies, Rhees sought to publish an 'authorized' version of the dictation sets. In his editing process, he took account of Wittgenstein's corrections to Russell's version of the original dictation, which Russell had given to Rhees at the turn of 1953/54.

Rhees considered it his responsibility to guide the reception of Wittgenstein's works through his way of editing, putting Wittgenstein's writings in the right perspective and minimizing the risk of misunderstanding. He pondered how an envisaged edition of the dictated texts might be received and whether Wittgenstein himself would have published them:

> My only reason for hesitating about the printing of them is the fear that many will read them now instead of the Investigations. I do not think that this is any reason for not publishing them. (Probably Wittgenstein himself would not have wanted them published. But in this case that is not a conclusive reason against it either.) I wonder what we should call them. Neither you nor Elizabeth has said anything about this. I have no ideas myself. "Blue Books" and "Brown Book" are all right for the purpose of identification. But they would look a little silly as titles for published works. They were not names which Wittgenstein himself gave them, of course. (Rhees to von Wright, 22. July 1957)

As it turned out, the literary executors chose the title *Preliminary Studies for the Philosophical Investigations generally known as the Blue and Brown Books*, indicating that the edition should not be understood as on par with the *Tractatus* and *PI*, but as part of the work that eventually led to the *PI*. Accordingly, Rhees wrote in his preface that '[w]hat we are printing here are notes he gave to his pupils, and a draft for his own use; that is all' (BBB 1958, vi). Rhees went on to explain the main lines of reasoning in the dictated texts, thus further channeling the interpretation. However, when the translator of the German version later suggested including a preface that related the dictated texts to current debates in scholarship, Rhees vetoed the suggestion. He understood his introduction not as a scholarly contribution but rather as exposing main lines of thought in order to prevent misunderstanding. In fact, Rhees' subsequent editing projects would start from this exegetical understanding of his inherited task.

1.4   Rung Three: Rhees' Author-Centred Editing

The editions reckoned to be 'on the third rung' consist of publications edited from parts of Wittgenstein's Nachlass that were written before and after the *PI*. Together with the earlier editions, these third-rung volumes completed the publication of remarks which Wittgenstein wrote from 1929 (the year he returned to Cambridge) to 1951 (the year of his last writings). The literary executors' division of labour was further established at this rung: Rhees concentrated on editing Wittgenstein's writings from the time before the first version of *PI* (Urfassung; see footnote 14), while Anscombe and von Wright edited, mainly together, writings after the last version of *PI* (Spätfassung; see footnote 5). Work on these editions led the three to recognize in detail Wittgenstein's way of working and the resulting complexity of his Nachlass. Subsequent editing became an increasingly complex task: now the literary executors had to decide on editorial questions of merging, structuring, selecting, omitting and naming Wittgenstein's writings. Given that at this stage it was primarily Rhees who held a definite opinion on editing, the main concern while discussing this rung is to characterize his editorial approach.

1.4.1   *Philosophische Bemerkungen*

After the *BBB* was published, Rhees resumed work on the early parts of the Nachlass, beginning with the already mentioned Moore-Volume (Ts209) from 1929–1930 and the Big Typescript (Ts213) from 1933–1934. These writings stem from the time before Rhees attended Wittgenstein's lectures. Von Wright also resumed reading the two items, and, like Rhees, was fascinated to discover a 'middle Wittgenstein' that created a bridge between the *Tractatus* and the *PI*:

> I have in the last five weeks been doing concentrated reading of the two things by Wittgenstein, which we call the "Moore-Volume" and the "Big Typescript". The Moore-Volume I had, of course, read before (twice). But of the Big Typescript I had only read (12 years ago) the mathematical part. Reading the Big Typescript from beginning to end was a terrific experience. […]
>
> I am firmly of the opinion that it should in its entirety be published, and that in preparing it for publication and having it translated it must be given priority over the Moore-Volume.
>
> The editorial work which has to be done on the Big Typescript (and the Moore-Volume) is not a major concern. Perhaps Rhees prefers to do it all by himself. If, at the final stage, he wants our assistance, I am sure we could complete the job by joint efforts in one to three weeks. I have written to him and offered him my assistance, if he wants it. I hope he will not misunderstand me. Needless to say, I have not the slightest wish to interfere with his work and I trust it completely. (von Wright to Anscombe, 2. February 1963)

Rhees indeed took the job of editing the Moore-Volume and the Big Typescript, but in contrast to von Wright's prediction, he invested huge editorial efforts.

Rhees began with editing the Moore-Volume. It is the most finished and chronologically first typescript from the middle Wittgenstein period. It was used once by Bertrand Russell in connection with renewing Wittgenstein's research grant. Wittgenstein eventually left it with G.E. Moore (hence its name), and Moore turned it over to Rhees in 1951. This typescript forms the basis of *Philosophische Bemerkungen* (*PB* 1964, first English publication 1975). In his edition, Rhees followed Wittgenstein's changes in the sequence of the remarks and divided the text into sections and numbered the paragraphs. He also added a preface that Wittgenstein had written in November 1930 (in Ms 109). Between Wittgenstein's preface and text, Rhees included his own analytical table of contents, and he added appendices from Wittgenstein's later typescripts (Ts214a, 215a, 215b, probably from 1933). Thus, a unified product was shaped from a number of disparate sources.

While preparing the *PB* for publication, Rhees increasingly recognized that an understanding of Wittgenstein's writings from this period must take into account Wittgenstein's relation to the Vienna Circle. *PB* contains remarks from the ledgers (Bände I-IV) written during Wittgenstein's first year after his return to Cambridge in 1929, and it was that same year, during Christmas break, that he had met Moritz Schlick and Friedrich Waismann for discussions in Vienna. Moreover, while Rhees was working on his edition, Brian McGuinness discovered notes from those Vienna discussions in Waismann's Nachlass in Oxford (McGuiness' edition appeared as *Wittgenstein und der Wiener Kreis*, WWA 1967). Rhees and McGuinness then began an intense round of correspondence that led not only to synergy and a mutually reinforcing interest in discovering the Wittgenstein of the early 1930s, but also to including notes from Waismann's Nachlass as an appendix to *PB*.

1.4.2   *Philosophische Grammatik*

The natural candidate for the next edition was the document that the literary executors called the Big Typescript. With its 768 numbered pages, preceded by a 19-section table of contents with 140 chapters, the typescript appeared as if it could be printed right away. Indeed, as quoted above, von Wright first thought that only a little editing was needed. However, when Rhees started typing out Wittgenstein's manuscripts, he saw the complex interrelations between the items within Wittgenstein's Nachlass and became convinced that the Big Typescript was only a momentary crystallization in a continuously mutating working process. In his subsequent years of meticulous study, Rhees elaborated a picture of the corpus of Wittgenstein's manuscripts and typescripts from the early 1930s. It may be roughly summarized as follows (cf. Nedo 1993, 126): *PB* contained remarks from ledgers written during 1929–1930 (Ms 105–108, Bände I-IV). However, before the arrangement for the *PB*-typescript was made, another typescript (Ts

208, 1930) had been produced from the remarks in those ledgers. Using a copy of this typescript together with cuttings from two other typescripts (Ts 210, 1930 and Ts 211, 1931–1932), which had been distilled from yet other notebooks and ledgers (Ms 109–Ms 114, Bände V-X), Wittgenstein produced a collection of cuttings which he sorted and clamped together (Ts 212, 1932). When this collection of cuttings was retyped, the Big Typescript came into being (Ts 213, 1933). Given how Wittgenstein inserted new comments and notes for improvements in one of the three copies of the Big Typescript, Rhees considered that despite its book-like appearance, it was not a work for publication but rather an ordered collection for a further stage of elaboration. Rhees conjectured that there must be another volume that was the result of the reworking. Following Wittgenstein's annotations in the Big Typescript, Rhees discovered what he was looking for in the manuscript called Band X (Ms 114). He discussed this discovery in a letter to von Wright:

> What I told you of Bände X and XI in September was wildly inaccurate—as regards Band X especially. On looking through it, I had thought it was of much the same sort as the Bände I-VII; and this is true, on the whole, of the first 60 pages of it (although these are revisions and developments of what he had written earlier). Then comes a passage headed: "Umarbeitung", and under this heading: "Zweite Umarbeitung in großem Format".
> [...]
> The important point is: a) this is a Umarbeitung of the big typescript, not of the Philosophische Bemerkungen. Do not ask me how I was so stupid before. But I discovered this when I was trying to make a version of the big typescript, taking account of the corrections between the lines and on the opposite pages, and I was referring fairly often to Band X, which I took to be the manuscript Band. It became clear again and again that what was in Band X is a later version than the typed one. [...]
> b) the Band X Umarbeitung is not just a series of revisions. It is a continuous book: Even more than a revised statement of many or most of the passages, it is a new ordering of the material. It is coherent and forceful, and—for me as I typed it—extremely interesting.
> [...]
> If I can produce a book at all, I think it should be called „Philosophische Grammatik". This is what Band X is called [...] (Rhees to von Wright, 8. November 1965)

Having identified the manuscript that confirmed his hypothesis, Rhees knew which book he wanted to prepare for publication in order to present a position between the *PB* and *PI* in the development of Wittgenstein's philosophy. His goal was thus to carry out the corrections, alterations and annotations that Wittgenstein had written into the Big Typescript. He wanted to create a book that came closest to the one Wittgenstein himself would have produced if he had followed through with the corrections he made in the mid-1930s. Rhees was aware that carrying out this plan would mean an incredible amount of work, as he wrote to his friend Drury: 'What I hoped would be the chief work in this period—what I had hoped was a manuscript with corrections and variants which need to be edited—has now turned out to be not Siamese twins but Siamese quadruplets. And I wish I would see how to make it plain what this quartet is saying' (Rhees to Drury, 7. November 1965). Devoting himself completely to the task, Rhees resigned from his post at the University of Swansea. As a result, *Philosophical Grammar* (*PG*) appeared in 1969.

Today *PG* is perhaps best known for being a controversial edition made by one of Wittgenstein's literary executors. Anthony Kenny, who translated *PG* in 1972 and 1973 (English Edition: *Philosophical Grammar, PG* 1974), has appreciated the enormous complexity of Rhees' editing, but argued that *PG* is neither a systematic application of Wittgenstein's corrections nor that it would be possible at all to produce an un-ambiguous edition of the *corrected* Big Typescript (Kenny 1976, 41–53). Kenny had planned to include a translator's introduction in the English edition of *PG* that listed the editorial interventions. Rhees rejected such an introduction on the grounds that it would encourage pseudo-scholarship on Wittgenstein's manuscripts—something Wittgenstein would have loathed (cf. Rhees to Kenny, 27. February 1972). However, Kenny remained convinced that 'the most prudent editorial policy would have been to print the original Big Typescript as it stood rather than to seek a definite revision of it' (Kenny 1976, 52). As is obvious from the quotation above, Rhees would have liked this had it been possible for him. Seven years earlier he had even contemplated and rejected the option, as he wrote to von Wright:

> Perhaps you are inclined to ask: Why can you not just print the big typescript as it stands, ignoring all and every correction or revision.
>
>   Lord. If you really do want to ask this, I will try to answer in another letter. I really think this is impossible—and I mean that: I do not mean just inadvisable. (Rhees to von Wright, 8. November 1965)

Indeed, in answer to Kenny's criticism, Rhees wrote a letter explaining the reason for his editing. In it, he summarized his overall guiding editorial principle:

> In any editing I have done I have asked again and again what Wittgenstein would have wanted. This has guided me in what I have decided to leave out and what I have decided to include. (Rhees to Kenny, 2. March 1977)

Rhees' approach to editing Wittgenstein originated from an understanding of Wittgenstein and his philosophy. He had gained his special insight through knowing and discussing with Wittgenstein and from observing him working on his writings. Like Wittgenstein himself, Rhees cared most of all about paving the way for the right understanding of the remarks, while most of all fearing misunderstanding and abuse. In fact, Rhees was convinced that his own empathetic attitude was one of the reasons why Wittgenstein named him as his executor. This conviction is like a red thread running through all the editions Rhees created. Even so, when taken to the extreme, the attempt to be faithful to Wittgenstein's intentions and to prevent the abuse of his writings could be used to legitimize massive editorial intervention. A striking case is the chapter 'Philosophy' in the Big Typescript, the whole of which Rhees omitted from his edition of the *PG*. Such passages on Wittgenstein's method belong to the most popular remarks in the *PI* today. But this, it seems, was exactly what Rhees feared, as he explained to von Wright:

You will agree that you cannot tell anyone what philosophy is, if he has never been near enough the water to get his feet wet. And it is impossible to tell anyone what Wittgenstein's conception of philosophy is, if (he) has made no long or serious study of what Wittgenstein has written. It would have been impossible for Wittgenstein himself to do this. And the remarks in that section of the Typoscript [sic] 213 can have force or sense only against the <u>Hintergrund</u> of the philosophizing which Wittgenstein does, or has done. Wittgenstein used to say something in this sense to people who wanted to come to his lectures. It is why he used (for example) to speak of the work of philosophy as the work of changing one's way of looking at things, <u>durch lange Übung</u>. When I asked him first if I could come to his lectures, he asked if I had any idea of what went on in them. And when I said (or said something like) obviously I had only such ideas as came from discussion with those attending them, Wittgenstein said: "Suppose you asked someone 'can you play the violin?', and he said: 'I don't know, but I can try.'"

   Of course those remarks in Typoscript 213 will be published sometime, and people will quote them to show (sic) what Wittgenstein said doing philosophy was. And they will think this is all fairly easy to understand. We cannot prevent this. ---- You remember various remarks of his about trying to answer the question "What is mathematics?". (Rhees to von Wright, 22. January 1976)

Rhees held the opinion that those who actively followed Wittgenstein in his way of treating philosophical problems would recognize in any of his remarks what kind of activity philosophy was for him, but that for those who had not already entered into this way of philosophizing, there was no point in trying to describe it.

1.4.3   *Zettel, on Certainty* and *Remarks on Colour*

Rhees' development as an editor stood in some contrast to the development of the two other literary executors. Anscombe, for example, was not as fascinated by the middle Wittgenstein as Rhees and von Wright were, and she did not translate Rhees' editions of Wittgenstein's writings from that period. In the 1950s she taught on the *Tractatus* and the *PI* and wrote *Intention* and *An Introduction to Wittgenstein's Tractatus* (Anscombe 1957, 1959; see a list of Anscombe's lectures in: Gormally, Kietzmann and Torralba 2012). Thus, Anscombe was in lively philosophical discussion with the material she edited and translated. Contrasting Rhees' ambition to fulfil Wittgenstein's hypothetical intentions in intermediate stages of his development, Anscombe favoured staying with the published *Tractatus* and the quasi-authorized *PI* and to continue their philosophical discussion. Instead of completely devoting her professional life to the task of editing the papers of her teacher, she increasingly worked on her own writings and lectured internationally in the 1960s. She kept her sense of the spirit of Wittgenstein's philosophizing alive, not by incorporating it into her editorial work, but by pursuing her own thinking in a way that was inspired by him. However, together with von Wright, she also continued publishing texts from Wittgenstein's Nachlass, and by no means without editorial intervention.

   Zettel (Z 1967), as the name suggests, is made from yet another collection of Wittgenstein's cuttings. Most of its contents stem from documents written between 1945 and 1948. Von Wright conjectured that since the final version of *PI* (Spätfassung, see footnote 14) was printed from a typescript dating from 1945–1946 and since Part II of *PI* was made from a script typed in 1949, *Zettel* might fill a gap between the two parts. Wittgenstein had reworked the remarks in the collection of *Zettel* and had partly bundled them into groups. Yet the organization in the printed edition does not entirely follow Wittgenstein's own arrangement: what had been clipped together by Wittgenstein remained so, but the rest was posthumously woven into an arrangement by Anscombe's husband Peter Geach. Critics have pointed out that the edition does not distinguish clearly enough between the parts that follow Wittgenstein's arrangement and those arranged by Geach (Stern 1996, 461–462).

The editions *On Certainty* (*OC* 1969) and *Remarks on Colour* (*ROC* 1977, edited by Anscombe alone) may be discussed together because, in a certain sense, they belong together: both are made from manuscripts dating from the last 18 months of Wittgenstein's life. *OC* is a selection of remarks from five manuscripts, three of which are also the source for *ROC*. According to the editors, the different remarks were marked off by Wittgenstein as belonging to different topics. Although a later edition, namely *Last Writings on the Philosophy of Psychology, Volume 2*, seems to relativize this opinion, the main editorial issue in creating these two volumes was not selection, but rather giving them a name. Especially in the case of *OC*, the title might suggest a separate or even new thematic focus, a view which was controversially discussed, for example by Rhees. In a long letter written in March 1970, Rhees responded to a draft for a preface that opened up the possibility of understanding *OC* as a new work in Wittgenstein's oeuvre—one which had emerged after he made his last modifications to the *PI*. In the letter, Rhees showed how the remarks in *OC* were embedded into the whole of Wittgenstein's development; instead of beginning to work on a new topic, Wittgenstein returned to a line of thinking that had been there for a long time. Von Wright was so impressed by this letter that he asked Rhees to write a new preface to *OC* using the letter as a starting point. Rhees did so, but Siegfried Unseld, director of the German publisher of Wittgenstein's works, eventually refused to publish it. Unseld wanted *OC* to address a wide audience and regarded Rhees' introduction as too scholarly for this purpose. Taking into account Rhees' attitude towards what he somewhat contemptuously called 'scholarship' (described above while discussing *PG*), it is possible to see that Unseld's refusal to publish the new preface reflects Rhees' almost tragically isolated position: in his faithful loyalty to Wittgenstein's intentions, he was too unscholarly for the scholars and too scholarly for the general public.

1.5   Rung Four: Von Wright's Text-Genetic Editing

Although von Wright also disliked much of what was classified as Wittgensteinian scholarship, he was a natural academic and developed his own rather scholarly approach to editing Wittgenstein's papers. He was sympathetic to Rhees' concerns yet favoured quite a different editorial policy. Von Wright increasingly believed that the documents would speak for themselves when they were presented to the academic community, but that supplementing the documents with historical facts would help readers comprehend them correctly. Thus, in contrast to Rhees' approach of crafting a unified book based on an internal understanding, von Wright sought to preserve and present the historical documents just as they were, but to illuminate them by providing external information on their originary contexts.

Of course, von Wright's historical fascination was tremendously encouraged by Rhees' discoveries within the sub-corpus of the middle Wittgenstein, but he also made his own journeys into the Nachlass. In the early 1960s, von Wright searched the whole of Wittgenstein's Nachlass for coded remarks and endeavoured to decode them. A little later he re-scoured all the available material and selected remarks on topics of a general nature. This resulted in the edition called *Vermischte Bemerkungen* (*VB* 1977). *VB* was closely linked to von Wright's own philosophical development and personal acquaintance with Wittgenstein; it presented Wittgenstein as a man in touch with the currents of his time and as a critic of contemporary civilization. According to von Wright, it was important to recognize Wittgenstein as a person responding to a cultural context in order to understand his philosophy. Thus, although the remarks in *VB* do not belong to Wittgenstein's philosophical remarks in a strict sense, they provide a frame of cultural criticism for interpreting Wittgenstein's philosophizing. However, publishing a selection such as *VB* is rather untypical for von Wright's editorial work. His approach is most often characterized by little editorial intervention or interpretation.

During the first 15 years of the literary executors' custody of Wittgenstein's Nachlass, some manuscripts were lost or sold while others were discovered for the first time. On a visit to Austria in 1965, von Wright discovered an early version of the *Tractatus*. This find revived his desire to describe the origins of the *Tractatus*. He followed through by preparing his study *The Origins of the Tractatus* (von Wright 1982, 63–109) as an introduction to the facsimile edition of the newly found pre-version of the *Tractatus* (*Prototractatus*, *PT* 1971). Experiences such as this increased von Wright's awareness of both the historicity and vulnerability of the original documents, convincing him that the fate of the material should not depend only on the three literary executors. He then started negotiations which eventually led to a complete microfilm copy of the Nachlass and to the institutionalized preservation of the originals. This in turn gave rise to research into the Nachlass by scholars who stood outside the narrow circle of the literary executors and their collaborators.

1.5.1   The Cornell Microfilm

Von Wright's friend at Cornell University, Norman Malcolm, who had also been a student and friend of Wittgenstein, became intrigued by Wittgenstein's middle period while writing an encyclopedia article about him. In producing this article, Malcolm studied the relation between the so-called early and late Wittgenstein and was fascinated when von Wright told him about the manuscripts that document the transition. Malcolm suggested it would be worthwhile depositing copies of the corresponding ledgers (Bände) at the Cornell University Library. However, Rhees was against this proposition because he feared that the manuscripts would be copied and privately circulated, as had been the case with Malcolm's notes from Wittgenstein's lectures on the foundations of mathematics. In accordance with his editorial approach, Rhees grounded his refusal in what he thought Wittgenstein himself would have wanted:

> When I spoke to Wittgenstein about the task ten days before his death he was particularly anxious that care should be taken in what was published and how it was presented. This is vague, I know. But I am certain he would have said 'no' to 'Just circulate everything'. (Rhees to von Wright, 7. July 1965)

In 1965 von Wright agreed that it might be too early to create a complete copy of Wittgenstein's Nachlass, yet he was determined that efforts to preserve the original material would eventually be necessary. Thus, he and Malcolm worked on a scheme to accomplish this aim. Malcolm whetted Cornell University's interest in the project, and the university library made an offer to microfilm the entire Nachlass. Von Wright then forwarded the proposal to Rhees:

> On my way back from Pittsburgh I spent a week at Cornell. I discussed once again with Norman Malcolm the possibility of depositing copies of the Wittgenstein Nachlass in the Cornell Library. We also consulted an expert. I became convinced that the right thing to do is to have the entire Nachlass microfilmed. This microfilm would then be safely deposited in the Cornell Library and developed xerox-copy of it, exclusively of the passages in code, made available for research purposes.
> [...]
> This plan seems to me good. And I hope you will agree to it. It would solve, once and for all, the problem of taking copies of the originals. The existence of the microfilm, moreover, would be a safeguard of the preservation of the Nachlass in case of a disaster. (Rhees to von Wright, 28. April 1966)

With Rhees finally agreeing to the plan, all the parties signed a contract by the turn of 1966/67. Thus in 1967, the parts of the Nachlass that Anscombe and Rhees kept at their homes and the parts that Wittgenstein's family kept in Austria were filmed under the supervision of Malcolm and von Wright. This collection amounted to 117 bound volumes of photocopies. Libraries could purchase from Cornell University the microfilm or photocopy volumes made from it. In the official Cornell copy, the passages written in Wittgenstein's personal code were covered up. However, the literary executors also produced a second uncensored set, which was later used for publishing coded remarks without the executors' consent.

Although the microfilm was never considered to be a true edition, it made Wittgenstein's Nachlass almost entirely available to the public. Furthermore, as a result of negotiations between the three literary executors and Trinity College, it was resolved that the originals should eventually be deposited at the college, and that a consortium, consisting first of the literary executors and then of their chosen successors, should be consulted in questions of publishing. Wittgenstein's writings were thus preserved for future scholarship.

After the Cornell microfilm had been made, a catalogue of the material was produced at Cornell University. When von Wright received this catalogue, he discovered many mistakes. He therefore returned to Cornell to check all the copies. This resulted in the production of his own catalogue (Von Wright 1969, 483–503). Von Wright structured the corpus by using a numbering system that assigned an unambiguous reference to each item. Thus far in the 18 years of editing Wittgenstein's Nachlass, this had not happened. In particular, von Wright distinguished between three categories: he referred to manuscripts using numbers starting with 101; for typescripts, he used numbers starting with 201; and for dictations, he started with 301. The body of manuscripts was divided into (a) 'first drafts' and (b) 'more finished versions', the latter being further divided into two series of ledgers (Bände) and notebooks. This 'map', together with the Cornell microfilm, provided orientation in the whole corpus and laid the foundation for all subsequent studies and scholarly editions of the Nachlass.

1.5.2   The *Helsinki Edition*

The first steps towards a scholarly treatment of Wittgenstein's Nachlass were taken by von Wright himself. Using his more than 20 years of accrued knowledge about the Nachlass, plus the Cornell microfilm, he began what he henceforth called 'Nachlass-Research' (cf. Maury's studies on the sources of the remarks in: Maury 1981, 135–158, 1994, 349–378). Assisted by Heikki Nyman and André Maury, this work resulted in von Wright's article *The Origin and Composition of the Philosophical Investigations* (von Wright 1982, 111–136). Moreover, von Wright and his assistants produced a kind of critical edition of the *PI* which is sometimes called the *Helsinki Edition*. Von Wright himself referred to this as the *Nyman/von Wright-Edition*, thus acknowledging his assistant's contribution.

The *Helsinki Edition*, which amounts to a dozen volumes, presents (1) an early version of *PI* (Ts 225, 1938; Ts 220, 1937/38; Ts 221, 1938; Ms 141, 1935/36), (2) a worked over version of parts of it (Ts239, 1943), (3) a reconstructed middle version, (4) the late version (Ts 227, 1945/46) and (5) the last remaining pre-version of the typescript from which Part II had been printed in 1953 (Ms 144, 1949). All of the versions of *PI* in the *Helsinki Edition* are introduced by an editorial and source-genetic preface. The text itself mostly presents a single remark on each page. An apparatus of variants, deletions and so forth are added in footnotes, and a commentary is included on separate pages or even in a separate volume. In addition, cross-referencing tables point out the places where the various versions correspond. The *Helsinki Edition* has never been published, but several copies have been given to libraries and individual researchers in privately-bound volumes.

Eventually it has found its way into the public domain, insofar as it provides the basis for the critical-genetic edition of the *PI* (*PU* 2001, see round 4, below).

1.5.3   *Remarks on the Philosophy of Psychology, Last Writings on the Philosophy of Psychology*

Von Wright's assistant Nyman, in addition to being involved in creating the *Helsinki Edition*, also assisted in editing the volumes that might be seen as critical supplements to Part II of the *PI*. Wittgenstein wrote intensively on the philosophy of psychology after he had finished the remarks that became *PI* Part I. He filled at least eight manuscript volumes (Mss 130–138) and used them to dictate two type-scripts (Ts 229, Ts 232). The notebooks that he wrote during the last months of his life (from which *OC* and *ROC* had been edited) also contained remarks on this topic. Before 1980, only Part II of the *PI* and fragments in *Zettel* were published from this extensive corpus on the philosophy of psychology. Von Wright now pro-moted the publication of Wittgenstein's remaining writings on this topic, and his efforts resulted in four volumes:

Remarks on the Philosophy of Psychology, Volume I (*RPP* I 1980, edited by Anscombe and von Wright) presents the first of the typescripts on the philoso-phy of psychology (Ts229, 1947) and *Remarks on the Philosophy of Psychology Volume II* (1980, edited by von Wright and Nyman) the second (Ts232, 1948). The third volume, *Last Writings on the Philosophy of Psychology, Volume I* (*LW I* 1982, edited by von Wright and Nyman), covers the part of the mentioned man-uscripts that had not been dictated (Ms 137, 1948/49, Ms 138, 1949). Because more than half of the remarks in Part II of the *PI* are said to be taken from these manuscripts, this volume was given the subtitle *Preliminary Studies for Part II of Philosophical Investigations*. The fourth volume in this series is *Last Writings on the Philosophy of Psychology, Volume II* (*LW II* 1992, edited by von Wright and Nyman). The sources for this fourth volume are notebooks written during the last two years of Wittgenstein's life (Mss 169–171, 1949–50; Mss 173–174, 1950, Mss 176, 1951), parts of which had been published earlier in *ROC*.

Together, the four volumes display a new critical awareness that resulted from experiencing the editorial difficulties of publishing Wittgenstein's Nachlass. At the same time, they round off the series of printed works produced under the aus-pices of the literary executors. Anscombe, Rhees and von Wright had developed each their own attitude towards the task they had inherited from Wittgenstein. Anscombe chose to concentrate on the two main works and used them as the starting points for new philosophical discussions; Rhees used his understanding of Wittgenstein's philosophy to produce unified books that presented intermedi-ate stages in the development of that philosophy; von Wright ensured access to the whole corpus of historical documents and provided insight into their histori-cal contexts. These characteristic differences in the work of Wittgenstein's liter-ary executors are easily overlooked by readers when they are confronted with the 'smooth' appearance of Wittgenstein's printed works.

1.6 The Next Rounds of Editing

The first round of editing (Fig. 1.1, rungs 1–4) is characterized by the editors being students and friends of Wittgenstein. The unique personal relationships, not just to their teacher but to his philosophy, contributed to their respective understandings of what their duty was in caring for the publication of his writings. By contrast, the subsequent rounds of editing often consist of large international editorial projects involving many participants who did not know Wittgenstein personally. This new generation of scholars has had to comply with new editorial standards in academia: in particular, to present an unbiased projection of the original manuscripts or typescripts onto the printed page. To meet these demands, the scholars started including variants, footnotes, commentaries and appendices in the editions—precisely those elements the literary executors had deliberately avoided. The rise of computer technology also fueled these critical editing developments, thus affecting both the preparation and presentation of Wittgenstein's writings. The subsequent rounds of editing may therefore be characterized as the transference of Wittgenstein's Nachlass into the digital age of scholarship.

1.6.1 Round Two (Rung Five): *the Vienna Edition*

The first large editorial project in what can be called 'round two' was already underway when von Wright and Nyman prepared their last volumes. In 1974 the literary executors signed a contract founding the Wittgenstein Archives at the University of Tübingen. The aim of these archives was to produce a complete transcription of the Nachlass using the Cornell microfilm as the basis. Unfortunately, the team of researchers broke up because of internal disagreements, so the archives were closed in 1981. Rumours about the circumstances of these events spread to the wider academic community and the public press, thus damaging the scholarly reputation of the whole endeavour of editing Wittgenstein's Nachlass. Nevertheless, the project of transcribing the corpus could continue through other projects.

Ten years passed, however, before the first of the post-Tübingen projects announced the publication of new volumes. The *Vienna Edition* (*Wiener Ausgabe*, *WA*, see Table 1.2) was prepared under the directorship of Michael Nedo, who was also part of the group working in Tübingen. Nedo had moved to Cambridge and continued the work that would lead to the *WA*. In the introductory volume, he states that all the manuscripts and typescripts written between 1929 and 1933 (referred to as the middle period) are to be published in this series. In particular, the project's aim is to 'reproduce the manuscripts faithfully, comprehensively and in most readable form possible' (Nedo 1993, 95). Somewhere between 10 to 15 volumes, each covering 250 to 350 pages, are planned. So far, the *WA* has published Wittgenstein's first series of ledgers (Mss 105–114, Bände I-X, published as WA 1–5, 1994–1996) and the Big Typescript, including appendices (Ts 213, Ts

214–218, published as *WA* 11, 2000). The first five volumes (*WA 1–5*) are accompanied by a concordance (1997), a register (1998) and a synopsis (2000).

The *WA* presents Wittgenstein's writings with three different critical apparatuses: one at each margin and a third in the footnotes. Additionally, different underlining, insertions, variants and deletions are represented by different fonts and brackets. The great amounts of time and resources invested into finding this typographic form surely indicate the tremendous challenge faced by any project with editorial ambitions similar to that of the *WA*. The *WA* has presented volumes that satisfy the demands of a printed, critical and scholarly edition, but academic philosophers have noted that a more usable complete edition could have been produced using fewer resources and more conventional procedures (Hintikka 1991, 183–201; Kenny 2005, 341–355).

1.6.2   Round Three (Rung Six): *the Bergen Electronic Edition*

Yet another editorial project is rooted in the mid 1970s. In 1975 the philosophy departments of four Norwegian universities bought a photocopy set of the Cornell microfilm. By 1980 members of this group, which was then called the 'Norwegian Wittgenstein Project', wanted to use computer technology to make the Cornell photocopies more accessible (Huitfeldt and Rossvær 1988, 9). After negotiations with the literary executors and with the support of von Wright, this aim could be pursued; the Wittgenstein Archives at the University of Bergen (WAB) were established in 1990. By that time, the idea of using computer technology to make Wittgenstein's Nachlass available had become rather definite. A coding language was developed to produce a complete and machine-readable version (Huitfeldt 1994a, 275–294, 1994b, 37–43). After yet another ten years of transcribing and coding, *Wittgenstein's Nachlass: The Bergen Electronic Edition* (*BEE* 2000, see Table 1.2) was released on six CD-ROMs.

The *BEE* provides a full transcription in 'normalized' and 'diplomatic' formats: the normalized transcription renders Wittgenstein's emendations easy to read, while the diplomatic transcription carefully preserves the structure and appearance of Wittgenstein's original texts, for example by displaying deletions, variants and underlining. The *BEE* also contains facsimiles of 96 manuscripts, 53 typescripts and 8 dictations, plus functions for searching all the 157 documents according to names, dates or formulae. Through this rich array of functions, the *BEE* provides all means necessary for comparing printed editions and their sources. Thus, after the *BEE*'s publication, there have in principle been no more grounds for speculating about the possible repression or restriction of access to the Nachlass. In fact, one motivation for producing the *BEE* has been to bring clarity to such debates.

One might expect that editorial problems have finally come to an end with the publication of the *BEE*. Indeed, today the *BEE* has come to be seen as a standard source for Wittgenstein scholarship, not least because it provides a complete facsimile edition. It has also prepared the ground for further developing von Wright's reference system by creating new sigla, not only for each item, but for each remark. Nevertheless, with the *BEE*, a Pandora's box full of new editorial difficulties has opened. The way in which the *BEE*'s creators have coped with the technological requirements, such as by inventing a coding language for complex documents, has brought the project to the forefront of digital scholarly editions. Yet the *BEE* has also exposed the para-technological limitations of digital editions, namely, the problems scholars have with managing the software. Despite the *BEE* including an extensive user guide, few users have been able to fully exploit the search functions, and most have been dissatisfied when trying to copy or print the pages they found of special interest (Hrachovec 2005, 405–417).[7] Moreover, it has now become impossible to run the *BEE* with the latest operating systems. Thus, while the printed editions have presented readers with one set of challenges, now with digitization, new challenges related to technological developments and usability have emerged.

Since WAB released the *BEE*, it has treated these new challenges as opportunities for developing new forms of digital scholarly editions, including converting the *BEE* to web-standards and linking it with other online resources (Pichler 2010, 157–172). WAB thereby actively welcomes new opportunities for both online editions and philosophical archives in the transition from the digital age to the internet age (Erbacher 2011, 135–146).

1.6.3   Round Four (Rung Seven): the *Critical-Genetic Edition of PI*

Not all the editorial projects after round one have been sorties into new technological worlds. The latest round of editing Wittgenstein's main work has resulted in a more conventional publication. Von Wright always envisioned a complete printed edition of the Nachlass, the production of which he considered the literary executors' duty. Such a complete edition has not yet been realized, and it is questionable whether it is still desirable, given the many repetitions in Wittgenstein's Nachlass and the digital solutions available for handling them. However, using both von Wright's *Helsinki Edition* and the digital *BEE*, it has been possible to produce a critical-genetic edition of the *PI* (*PU* 2001, see Table 1.2) under the guidance of Joachim Schulte. In contrast to the *Helsinki Edition*, the critical-genetic edition includes the first version of the *PI* (Urfassung, Ms 142), which was discovered in 1993. Like the *Helsinki Edition*, it replaces the earlier Part II with its last existing pre-version (Ms 144, see rung 1). The text of the critical-genetic edition contains a typographical apparatus indicating underlining, deletion and variants. It shows the different ideas Wittgenstein had for the form of his book.

---

[7] For more reviews of the BEE see: http://wab.uib.no/wab_BEE.page.

1.7   Not Throwing Away the Ladder

The critical-genetic edition of the *PI* (*PU* 2001), together with the new reading version (*PU* 2003) and the revised translation (*PI* 2009), have brought 50 years of experience in editing Wittgenstein to fruition in book-form. Research on discrepancies between the published editions and their actual sources has created a heightened alertness to the implications of editorial interventions and promoted the demand for scholarly editions. It has also led to a critical understanding of the early editions and to an idea of what a complete printed edition would amount to. The *BEE* provides a complete digitized and searchable transcription with a corresponding complete facsimile collection. In addition, there are now also critical book editions of Wittgenstein's main works that form the basis for new reading versions. The editors of Wittgenstein's Nachlass have created a ladder consisting of seven rungs of editing, and all interested readers should be glad for it. Editors of future projects will add more rungs to the ladder, and it is likely that they will continue to discuss how Wittgenstein's later writings may be appropriately represented. Yet regardless of how different editors interpret 'appropriateness', Wittgenstein scholars can look forward to making new discoveries thanks to WAB having made large portions of Wittgenstein's Nachlass available on Internet. Also of great interest is whether, and if so how, future editions will assimilate the spirit of the critical-genetic edition of *PI* and how the results of that will appear.

This chapter has aimed to open yet another perspective on the history of editing Wittgenstein's Nachlass. Now that editorial projects have provided access to Wittgenstein's writings with as little filtering and interpretation as possible, Wittgenstein scholarship has reached a stage where it is easier to relaxedly recognize the earlier, more interpretive editing. It is hoped that the selected quotes from the literary executors' letters have shown that it is worth following the development of their unique ways of editing. With precisely this objective, a research project at the University of Bergen has begun to prepare a systematic and comprehensive presentation of the literary executors' archived correspondence.

Acknowledgements   The research undergirding this chapter has been funded by the Research Council of Norway, as part of the project 'Shaping a Domain of Knowledge by Editorial Processing: The Case of Wittgenstein's Work' (NFR 213080).

Many people have aided me in my research and writing. I am deeply grateful that Peg Smythies permitted me to quote from Rush Rhees' letters; sadly, she passed away while this chapter was in preparation. I wish to thank Anita and Benedict von Wright for permission to quote from Georg Henrik von Wright's letters, and Mary Geach for permission to quote from Elizabeth Anscombe's letters. The *Richard Burton Archives* at the University of Swansea granted permission to quote from the letters of Rhees that are in their possession. I am also deeply thankful to Brian McGuinness, the *von Wright and Wittgenstein Archives* (WWA), the *National Library of Finland* (NLF) and the *Richard Burton Archives* for giving me access to their holdings of quoted correspondence and other materials. For language corrections and improvements, I wish to thank Arlyne Moi and Mario von der Ruhr. An earlier version of this paper was presented to the Department of Philosophy at the University of Bergen; I thank all participants of that seminar for their valuable contributions.

List of Archival Sources

Anscombe to McGuinness, without date [presumably 1959], kept at McGuinness' private archives.

Anscombe to von Wright, 4. July 1954, NLF, COLL.714.11-12.

Anscombe to von Wright, 15. April 1991, NLF, COLL.714.11-12.

Rhees to Drury, 7. November 1965, edited in Rhees (2006, 257–260) and Rhees (2001, 153–156).

Rhees to Kenny, 27. February 1972, RBA, UNI/SU/PC/1/2/6/4.

Rhees to Kenny, 2. March 1977, WWA, WWA documents\Wittgenstein's Nachlass\Filing cabinet\Rush Rhees III (1975–1998); published in an edited form in Rhees (1996).

Rhees to von Wright, 2. March 1952, NLF, COLL.714-200-201.

Rhees to von Wright, 22. April 1953, NLF, COLL.714.200-201.

Rhees to von Wright, 22. July 1957, NLF, COLL.714.200-201.

Rhees to von Wright, 28. April 1966, NLF, COLL.714.200-201.

Rhees to von Wright, 7. July 1965, NLF, COLL.714.200-201.

Rhees to von Wright, 8. November 1965, NLF, COLL.714.200-201.

Rhees to von Wright, 10. August 1972, WWA, WWA documents\Wittgenstein's Nachlass\Filing cabinet\Rush Rhees II (1972–1974).

Rhees to von Wright, 7. May 1974, RBA, UNI/SU/PC/1/2/1/3.

Rhees to von Wright, 22. January 1976, WWA, WWA documents\Wittgenstein's Nachlass\Filing cabinet\Rush Rhees III (1975–1998).

von Wright to Anscombe, 7. May 1953, NLF, COLL.714.11-12.

von Wright to Anscombe, 6. June 1954, NLF, COLL.714.11-12.

von Wright to Anscombe, 6. November 1954, NLF, COLL.714.11-12.

von Wright to Anscombe, 19. November 1954, NLF, COLL.714.11-12.

von Wright to Anscombe, 2. January 1955, NLF, COLL.714.11-12.

von Wright to Anscombe, 19. April 1957, NLF, COLL.714.11-12.

von Wright to Anscombe, 30. April 1960, NLF, COLL.714.11-12.

von Wright to Anscombe, 2. February 1963, NLF, COLL.714.11-12.

References

Anscombe, G. E. M. 1953. Note on the English Version of Wittgenstein's Philosophische Untersuchungen. In *Mind* 62, 521–522.

Anscombe, G. E. M. 1957. *Intention*. Oxford: Blackwell.

Anscombe, G. E. M. 1959. *An Introduction to Wittgenstein's Tractatus*. London: Hutchinson.

Anscombe, G. E. M., Rhees, R., & von Wright, G. H. 1951. Note. In *Mind* 60, 584.

Black, Max. 1964. *A Companion to Wittgenstein's Tractatus*. Ithaca N.Y.: Cornell University Press.

Costello, Harry T. 1957. Notes on Logic. In *The Journal of Philosophy* 54, 230–245.

Erbacher, Christian. 2011. Unser Denken bleibt gefragt: Web 3.0 und Wittgensteins Nachlass. In *Wissenschaftstheorie, Sprachkritik und Wittgenstein*, eds. S. Windholz and W. Feigl, 135–146. Heusenstamm: Ontos.

Erbacher, Christian. 2015. Editorial Approaches to Wittgenstein's Nachlass: Towards a Historical Appreciation. In *Philosophical Investigations* 38(3): 165–198.

Gormally, Luka, Kietzmann Christian Kietzmann, and Torralba, José M. 2012. Bibliography of works by G.E.M. Anscombe, online: https://www.academia.edu/7618513/Gormally_L_Kietzmann_C_Torralba_J_M_Bibliography_of_Works_by_G_E_M_Anscombe_Seventh_version_June_2012. Accessed 13. October 2021; previous version published in: Torralba, José M. 2005. *Acción intencional y razonamiento práctico según G.E.M. Anscombe.* Eunsa, Pamplona, 233–241.

Hintikka, Jaakko. 1991. An Impatient Man and His Papers. In *Synthese* 87(2), 183–201.

Hrachovec, Herbert. 2005. Evaluating the Bergen Electronic Edition. In *Wittgenstein: The Philosopher and His Works*, eds. A. Pichler and S. Säätelä, 405–417. Heusenstamm: Ontos.

Huitfeldt, Claus. 1994a. Computerizing Wittgenstein. The Wittgenstein Archives at the University of Bergen. In *Wittgenstein and Norway*, eds. K. S. Johannessen, R. Larsen and K. O. Aamaas, 275–294. Oslo: Solum.

Huitfeldt, Claus. 1994b. Toward a Machine Readable Version of Wittgenstein's Nachlaß. Some Editorial Problems. In *Editio*, 6, *Philosophische Editionen*, ed. H. G. Senger, 37–43. Tübingen: Niemeyer.

Huitfeldt, Claus, and Viggo Rossvær. 1988. *The Norwegian Wittgenstein Project Report 1988.* Bergen: University of Bergen.

Kenny, Anthony. 1976. From the BIG typescript to the Philosophical Grammar. In *Essays on Wittgenstein in Honour of G.H. von Wright, Acta Philosophica Fennica* 28, ed. J. Hintikka, 41–53. Helsinki: University of Helsinki.

Kenny, Anthony. 2005. A Brief History of Wittgenstein Editing. In *Wittgenstein: The Philosopher and His Works*, eds. A. Pichler and S. Säätelä, 341–355. Heusenstamm: Ontos.

Klagge, James, & Nordmann, Alfred. 2003. *Ludwig Wittgenstein—Public and Private Occasions.* Maryland: Rowman & Littlefield.

Kreisel, Georg. 1958. Wittgenstein's Remarks on the Foundations of Mathematics. In *British Journal for the Philosophy of Science* 9(34), 135–158.

Maury, André. 1981. Sources of the Remarks in Wittgenstein's Zettel. In *Philosophical Investigations* 4, 57–74.

Maury, André. 1994. Sources of the Remarks in Wittgenstein's Philosophical Investigations. In *Synthese* 98, 349–378.

McGuinness, Brian. 2002. Bertrand Russell and the 'Notes on Logic'. In B. McGuinness, *Approaches to Wittgenstein: Collected Papers*, 243–258. London: Routledge.

Mühlhölzer, Felix. 2012. Teil III der Bemerkungen über die Grundlagen der Mathematik und die zugrundeliegenden Manuskripte 122 und 117—Ein Vergleich. In *Wittgenstein-Studien 3*, 19–44.

Nedo, Michael. 1993. *Einführung in die Wiener Ausgabe.* Wien: Springer.

Nedo, Michael. 2008. Anmerkungen zu Wittgensteins Bemerkungen über die Grundlagen der Mathematik. In *„Ein Netz von Normen"—Wittgenstein und die Mathematik*, ed. M. Kroß, 79–105. München: Parerga.

Pichler, Alois. 2010. Towards the New Bergen Electronic Edition. In *Wittgenstein after His Nachlass*, ed. N. Venturinha, 157–172. Houndmills, Basingstoke: Palgrave.

Pichler, Alois, Michael A. R. Biggs, and Sarah Szeltner. 2011. Bibliographie der deutsch- und englischsprachigen Wittgenstein-Ausgaben. In *Wittgenstein-Studien 2*, 249–286. Online available: http://www.ilwg.eu/files/Wittgenstein_Bibliographie.pdf. Accessed 13 April 2016.

Rhees, Rush. 1996. On Editing Wittgenstein. In *Philosophical Investigations* 19, ed. ed. D. Z. Phillips, 55–61.

Rhees, Rush. 2001. On Wittgenstein. In *Philosophical Investigations*, 24, ed. ed. D. Z. Phillips, 153–162.

Rhees, Rush. 2006. *Wittgenstein and the Possibility of Discourse*, 2nd Edition, ed. D. Z. Phillips. Oxford: Wiley-Blackwell.

Schulte, Joachim. 2005. What Is a Work by Wittgenstein? In *Wittgenstein: The Philosopher and His Works*, eds. A. Pichler and S. Säätelä, 397–404. Heusenstamm: Ontos.

Stenius, Erik. 1960. *Wittgenstein's Tractatus—A Critical Exposition of its Main Lines of Thought*. Ithaca N.Y.: Cornell University Press.

Stern, David. 1996. The Availability of Wittgenstein's Philosophy. In *The Cambridge Companion to Wittgenstein*, eds. H. Sluga and D. Stern, 442–476. Cambridge: CUP.

Von Wright, Georg H. 1969. The Wittgenstein Papers. In *The Philosophical Review* 78, 483–503, republished with revisions in von Wright (1982, 35–62).

Von Wright, Georg H. 1982. *Wittgenstein*. Minneapolis: University of Minnesota Press.

Von Wright, Georg H. 1992. The Troubled History of Part II of the Investigations. In *Grazer Philosophische Studien* 42, 181–192.

Von Wright, Georg H. 2001. *Mitt liv som jeg minns det*. Helsingfors: Söderstrom.

Wittgenstein, Ludwig. 1988. *Wittgenstein's Lectures on Philosophical Psychology 1946–1947*, ed. P. Geach. New York: Harvester.

Wittgenstein and His Literary Executors

2

Rush Rhees, Georg Henrik von Wright and Elizabeth Anscombe as Students, Colleagues and Friends of Ludwig Wittgenstein

2.1   Wittgenstein and Rhees 1 (1933–1939)

Born in Rochester, New York in 1905, Rhees was the oldest of the three literary executors and the one who knew Wittgenstein the longest. He arrived at Cambridge in 1933 and soon began attending Wittgenstein's lectures. However, by this time the 28-year-old Rhees was no longer an undergraduate and had already begun his philosophical life-journey.

At the age of 17, Rhees had begun studying philosophy at the University of Rochester. Though he had an outstanding position as the son of the president of that University, Rhees would not allow that his freedom of speech was restricted; quite the contrary. For example, Dr. George Mather Forbes — a distinguished professor of philosophy, head of the department of education and creator of the department of psychology at the University of Rochester — expelled Rhees from his ethics course because he would not comply with his teacher's doctrines. This revolt against institutional authority aroused the attention of the press and was even reported by *The New York Times* in a front-page story:

> Young Rhees said the professor's action was a "blessing". "I am a radical. Dr. Forbes is not. That is why I am barred from the course. [...] An anarchist does not believe in law. Nor do I. Therefore I say that law is directly opposed to any notion of ethics. Law is a system of compulsion and does away with any individual decision."[1]

---

[1] "Radicalism of Rochester President's Son Causes Professor to Bar Youth From Class", Special to The New York Times. 28. February 1924, 1. The preceding passage in the article reads: "'The most unsatisfactory notebook for the year's work I have ever had turned in to me.' Dr. Forbes told

---

This chapter is a revised version of Erbacher 2016.

© The Author(s), under exclusive license to Springer-Verlag GmbH, DE, part of Springer Nature 2023
C. Erbacher, *The Happy Afterlife of Ludwig W.*, Beiträge zur Praxeologie / Contributions to Praxeology, https://doi.org/10.1007/978-3-662-66155-0_2

Uncompromising advocacy for individual freedom had a tradition in the Rhees family. One of Rhees' ancestors, Morgan John Rhys, was a Welsh preacher who wrote pamphlets agitating for the ideas of the French Revolution.[2] In 1793, Rhys moved to Paris to experience the outcomes of the revolution firsthand, but he was prosecuted under the reign of terror. To save himself, he fled to America where he founded a colony for Welsh emigrants. In this mission, Morgan John Rhees (as he spelled his surname after emigration) was supported by Benjamin Rush, signatory of the Declaration of Independence. Expressing his gratitude to Rush, Morgan Rhees named his son after him. Ever since, the Christian name 'Rush' has been passed down from generation to generation. The Rush Rhees of our story not only continued the fight for freedom in the first Rush's name, he had also inherited the passion for defending his views with radical statements; and as with his distinguished ancestors, Rhees was prepared to act. Only 19 years old, Rhees left the land of his forefathers and went off to study philosophy in Europe.

"Wearing his shirt collar loose & open at the neck" (Von Hugel 1981, 275–276, quoted from Phillips 2006, 268), Rhees appeared like a young Percy Shelley to Professor Norman Kemp Smith when he arrived in Edinburgh in 1924. Kemp Smith, a Scotsman, had been professor of psychology and philosophy at the University of Princeton when he published an extensive *Commentary to Kant's 'Critique of Pure Reason'* (Kemp-Smith 1918). In 1924, Kemp Smith was professor of logic and metaphysics at the University of Edinburgh and would soon prepare his epoch-making translation of Kant's first *Critique* (Kant 1929). At the beginning of Rhees' years of study, Kemp-Smith understood that Rhees aspired to be a poet and mainly sought inspiration from philosophy (Phillips 2006, 268). However, he convinced the strong-headed youth that he could only achieve any of his high ambitions through disciplined work. Under the guidance of this thoughtful and strict teacher, Rhees, after four years, graduated from the University of Edinburgh with high honors. That same year, 1928, he was given a post as lecturer at the University of Manchester, where he distinguished himself through his "wholehearted commitment in teaching" (Phillips 2006, 268).[3]

When the post as lecturer at the University of Manchester expired after four years, Rhees took this as an opportunity to pursue philosophical research. In 1932 he moved to Innsbruck, Austria, in order to study the philosophy of Franz Brentano with Professor Alfred Kastil. Kastil, a former student of Brentano, had been appointed editor of Brentano's unpublished writings some 15 years earlier. While Rhees was in Innsbruck, Kastil edited the *Kategorienlehre* for Brentano's

---

his class of seventy-five students, referring to young Rhees's work. 'It attempted refutation of everything I had taught during the year'."

[2] Most of the biographical information in the following three paragraphs can be found in: Phillips 2006, 266–275.

[3] The qualification stems from a recommendation written by Rhees' superior, professor J. L. Stocks, at the University of Manchester.

complete works (Brentano 1968). This book contained Brentano's theory of the continuum. Rhees developed a keen interest in Brentano's treatment of continuity as a perceptual phenomenon and of the relation between continuous phenomena and their parts (cf. Körner and Chisholm 2010, ix–xx.). Kastil was impressed by Rhees' philosophical vigor and he believed that Rhees could elaborate on Brentano's theory:

> Brentano struggled with the difficulties of the continuum repeatedly throughout his life and developed a general theory of continuity, which sets forth the general laws for continua of various numbers of dimensions. In this connection he did not neglect the peculiarities which distinguish topic continua from chronic continua. But Brentano devoted special study to double continua, of which motion is the most important example. Here he developed the conceptions of teleiosis and of plerosis, the former of which applies to differences of velocity, the latter to the quantitative differences in the connections of boundaries. But even in regard to these relations of continuity Brentano's theory remains incomplete; indeed he indicated to me a few days before his death that his theory was in a process of alteration, without giving any further indication of the kind of improvements which he had in mind. It now appears very probable that Mr Rhees's acumen and unsparing diligence have succeded [sic] in finding the proper approach here. (Letter of recommendation, Easter 1935)

Since Brentano built on Aristotle's doctrine of relations, Kant-scholars accused him of scholasticism. In turn, it was Brentano's intention to target their jargon with his philosophy (Brentano 1968, XXVIII). Thus, key features of Brentano's work — namely, the thorough criticism of scholarly jargon and the firm conviction that psychology and philosophy ought to be conducted like the sciences — made him a congenial thinker to the movement of analytical philosophy in England. It is therefore no wonder that after working for one year on Brentano's theories of relations and continuity, Rhees was accepted as a doctoral student at Cambridge. In 1933, G. E. Moore became his supervisor.

Moore had been Wittgenstein's friend and one of his closest discussion partners since Wittgenstein's years of study at Cambridge before World War One; he had visited Wittgenstein in Norway in the spring of 1913, taking dictations from the student he believed to be a most significant philosopher. After Wittgenstein returned to Cambridge in 1929, the professor became an attendee of Wittgenstein's lectures. When Rhees arrived at Cambridge in 1933, Moore therefore recommended that he also attend Wittgenstein's lectures. By this time Wittgenstein had already worked through at least one major phase of his new philosophy: he had departed from the conception of philosophical analysis presented in the *Tractatus*, he had identified misleading ideas in his youth work and developed a method to clarify them, and he had just given a summarizing compilation of his new writings to a typist.[4] Around the time of Rhees' arrival at Cambridge, Wittgenstein was trying out new formats for presenting his views in a book. He was collaborating with Friedrich Waismann, a member of the Vienna Circle who wanted to give a

---

[4] Editions of a major step in this development have appeared as: Wittgenstein 1969b, 2000b.

systematic account of Wittgenstein's new philosophy, and he was dictating another draft to selected students (cf. Wittgenstein 1958; cf. Waismann 1976).

Amongst the Cambridge freshmen, Wittgenstein had become an almost mystical figure, famous, in any case, as an unconventional and eccentric teacher. Many students imitated his gestures and phrases when following him through Whewell's Court on their way to the lectures.[5] Rhees was put off by those acolytes (Monk 1991, 357), but for his supervisor's sake he approached Wittgenstein and received a probing reply:

> When I [Rhees] asked him [Wittgenstein] first if I could come to his lectures, he asked if I had any idea of what went on in them. And when I said (or said something like) obviously I had only such ideas as came from discussion with those attending them, Wittgenstein said: "Suppose you asked someone 'Can you play the violin?', and he said: 'I don't know, but I can try.'" (Rhees to von Wright, 22. January 1976)

On reflection, this puzzling response may be understood as a grammatical joke, showing the kind of philosophical investigation that took place in Wittgenstein's lectures.[6] However, Rhees was not taken with the philosophizing that he witnessed in Wittgenstein's class, as he told his Austrian mentor Kastil in a letter:

> I went to Wittgenstein a few times. He very much gives me the impression of being a straightforward and honest person; however, I don't think that I will go to him more often. I did not make this decision instantly, as Moore seems to be very appreciative of Wittgenstein. I, in turn, value Moore's judgment very highly, and I know that he would not have his opinion without a reason. Nonetheless, I think I will not go anymore. I find his style of lecturing confusing. He never prepares—as when he does, his lectures suffer. (I am convinced that he is no posturer in this, although he is probably mistaken.) He continuously speaks in similes (which are only partly actual examples), and says about himself that he always thinks in similes. If something does not become clear, he does not try to give an explanation in simple words but instead looks for a new simile. This method, though, is in accordance with his philosophical position, according to which the answers to the most important philosophical questions cannot be given through propositions or theories, but can only be "shown" by means of similes "or symbolic forms". Therefore, he says that he may be the right man for philosophy. (This is again, I believe, only naivety, not a sign of vanity.) But this is why his lectures do not ~~get~~ show a clear thread. Currently he lectures on the philosophy of language, particularly on the idea of meaning. He constantly emphasizes that the matter is exceptionally difficult. Sometimes he grabs his head, giving the explanation, "All this is tremendously difficult, we are in the middle of hell right now." And I asked myself if some of the attendees have any clear impression about philosophy, barring that the whole (quite undefined) matter is "tremendously difficult". This I regard as pedagogically bad. I hear that only after having heard him for a fairly long time one starts to recognize how much one gets from him. That I am willing to believe. But life is short; and the question is whether I would not profit even more if I used the time for something else (e.g. for the study of Marty's works). And at the moment,

---

[5] From notes of a personal conversation with Sir John Bradfield.

[6] I am especially indebted to James Conant for this suggestion.

it seems to me that this question has to be answered in the affirmative." (Rhees to Kastil, 5. November 1933)[7]

Wittgenstein himself was not satisfied with these lectures that were unusually crowded with 30–40 people (Wittgenstein 2003, 345). In fact, soon after Rhees had written the above letter, Wittgenstein announced that he couldn't continue to lecture and proposed that selected students should write down dictations that could then be distributed (Wittgenstein 2003, 345).

Though Rhees continued to attend Wittgenstein's lectures during the subsequent terms (Wittgenstein 2003, 346–347), he remained critical towards the philosophy he was confronted with at Cambridge. As a participant in lectures, he would not merely sit and listen, but pose challenging questions (Rhees 2006, XXV). Still in 1935, Rhees firmly hold on to the views he had acquired in Austria, as the following letter to Kastil shows:

My work here doesn't go particularly well. You have no idea which entanglement of fictions people here believe in; which different "meanings" of "is" and "exists". These are not regarded as homonymia pros hen (if people know, what that means?), but, apparently, as homonymia apo tuches. They indeed are supposed to be different forms of existence, but without having anything in common. And no matter to what extent one thinks to have uncovered such doctrines, new objections come from unexpected quarters—also based on different "meanings". In the course of one argument, I remarked that the apodictic "is impossible" includes an empiric "is not". Moore wanted to deny this and told me that Wittgenstein holds this opinion as well. He admits that if a round quadrangle is impossible, there is no round quadrangle. But, according to him, the latter must mean something different than the "there is no − −" as in "there is no green human being". The discussion about this point went on for quite a long time. Yet I still can't see what he suggests. His argument seems to mainly rest on the idea that I cannot learn through experience that no round quadrangle exists; therefore, the "is" or the "exists" must have a different meaning. If it is readily clear that we cannot learn it by experience? And if so, how does this give a different meaning to the "is"? Yes, Moore says, as it shows that the truth or the fact that is believed in is of a different kind.

Oh well; so, one should debunk the doctrine of "facts". I've partly already tried this. But when does one finish with the introduction to a theory of relations? (Rhees to Kastil, 5. January 1935)

One can imagine that Wittgenstein liked Rhees' obstinate attachment to his philosophical convictions. In turn, Rhees came to appreciate Wittgenstein's philosophizing despite his initial misgivings. Rhees' intelligent unruliness, his acquaintance with the University of Manchester — where Wittgenstein had once studied engineering — and his experiences in Wittgenstein's homeland Austria may have further contributed to a mutual sympathy. In any case, three years after their first encounter, Rhees and Wittgenstein had become discussion partners also outside class:

---

[7]Original in German, translation by Tina Schirmer and Christian Erbacher. A new edition of Moore's lecture notes of these lectures has appeared as: Wittgenstein 2016.

> At the end of the academic session, in June 1936, I had tea with him and he talked about
> the question of what he should do now. His fellowship was coming to an end, and the
> question was whether he should try to get a job of some sort or go somewhere by himself
> and spend his time working on his book. (Rhees 1984, 208–209)

As it turned out, Wittgenstein left Cambridge in order to return to Skjolden,
Norway, where he had made decisive breakthroughs for what became his Tractatus
logico-philosophicus. More than 20 years after this experience, he now envisaged going there again to work on his second philosophical book. He had written
a huge number of remarks during his fellowship at Cambridge. His latest strat-
egy for turning them into a book had been to dictate to two students and friends
throughout the academic year—four days a week for several hours at a time.[8]
Wittgenstein wanted to translate the results of this dictation into German whilst
staying at his cabin in Skjolden. Having been built especially for him before
the Great War, this small house was located in an isolated spot at bottom of the
Sognefjord.

Wittgenstein arrived at his cabin in August 1936 and began revising the volu-
minous dictation with the working title *Philosophische Untersuchungen—Versuch
einer Umarbeitung*. After working through 180 pages, he suddenly stopped,
drew a line and put down a devastating judgment: "This whole attempt at a revision from page 118 up to this point is <u>worthless</u>".[9] This uncompromising rejection turned out to be a decisive moment in twentieth century philosophy: in early
November Wittgenstein began writing a new manuscript entitled *Philosophische
Untersuchungen* (Wittgenstein 2000a, Ms 142). On the first page he declared this
new manuscript to be a bad Christmas present for his sister. Even so, what he produced was a beautiful, fair copy of 188 handwritten paragraphs. Today it is considered the very first version of what posthumously appeared as Wittgenstein's
Philosophical Investigations.[10]

For Rush Rhees, 1936 also proved to be a turning point because he gave up
his ambition to finish his dissertation. Moore, his supervisor, was very sorry to
learn of this; like Rhees' previous colleagues and superiors, Moore felt he had ben-
efited immensely from discussions with Rhees and regarded him as "exceptionally
well qualified to lecture" (Phillips 2006, 271). Abandoning the idea of submitting
a dissertation, however, did not mean Rhees would give up philosophical writing altogether. Rhees travelled to Austria in order to resume studies with Kastil,

---

[8] Later published in: *Preliminary Studies for the "Philosophical Investigations". Generally
Known as The Blue and Brown Books*; cf. Bouwsma 1961.

[9] Wittgenstein 2000a, Ms 115; the revision begins at page 118 (= Ms 115, 118[1]) and ends
on page 297 (= Ms 115, 297[5]). An edition of the manuscript is published in: *Preliminary
Studies for the "Philosophical Investigations". Generally Known as The Blue and Brown Books*.
Transcripts and facsimile of all items in Wittgenstein's Nachlass can be found in Wittgenstein
2000a.

[10] In German this very first version of the *Philosophical Investigations* is referred to as
"Urfassung" (foundational version), cf. Wittgenstein 2001.

who was by then professor emeritus and living in Vienna. Returning to England from this sojourn, Rhees substituted for his former professor at the University of Manchester in 1937, teaching a wide range of topics in philosophy. Wittgenstein travelled back and forth between Vienna, Cambridge and Norway during these years. In spring 1938, when Nazi-Germany annexed Austria, Wittgenstein decided to apply for British citizenship and stay in England. Soon afterwards, he resumed lecturing at Cambridge. Rhees—who lived in London since his temporary post at the University of Manchester had expired—was among the hand-picked invitees to Wittgenstein's classes on aesthetics and religious belief.[11] This refreshed their relationship and led to a phase of intensive cooperation.

Wittgenstein and Rhees met every afternoon for about three consecutive weeks in the autumn of 1938, mainly to discuss the problem of continuity (Rhees 1970, vii). Rhees was trying to write down his account of continuity in immediate experience. Like before, his treatment built on Brentano's theories of relations and the continuum.[12] But this was not what he discussed with Wittgenstein; he later remembered:

> I came to know Wittgenstein after I had known Kraus and studied Brentano, and I was interested to learn if I could whether Wittgenstein had read Brentano. I think it is certain that he had not. (…) And I cannot really find anything in Wittgenstein which reminds me of Brentano. (Rhees to McGuinness, 6. May 1963)

Wittgenstein's acquaintance with the problem of continuity had another background. Ten years earlier, in 1928, he had attended a lecture entitled "The structure of the Continuum" by the mathematician Luitzen Brouwer (Brouwer 1996, 1186–1197). It is said that the experience of Brouwer's lectures on the intuitionist solution to the foundational crisis of mathematics was a main reason for Wittgenstein to return to Cambridge and to take up his philosophical writing (cf. Stadler 1997, 449–450). In the notebooks Wittgenstein wrote upon his return, the problem of continuity appears, as well (cf. Wittgenstein 2000b, Mss 105–107).[13] Now, whereas Rhees deliberately excluded the mathematical concept of continuity in his study, Wittgenstein began discussing with Rhees precisely the use of continuity in mathematics and then went on to treat the use of continuity outside mathematics (Rhees 1970, 157). These discussions could take hours (Rhees 1970, vii). They found that dissecting continuity may have served certain purposes in mathematics, but that philosophical confusion was produced when one tried to transfer those mathematical terms to other contexts, for instance to the perception of continuous movement. Only then did the puzzle arise of how a continuity of movement could

---

[11] Notes from the lectures were later published as: Wittgenstein 1966; cf. Monk 1991, 402; from Wittgenstein to Rhees, 15. July 1938 in: Wittgenstein 2011.

[12] Rhees' extensive, but fragmentary treatise of 77 typewritten pages has been discovered recently. An edited excerpt is published in: Erbacher and Schirmer 2017.

[13] These notebooks contain Wittgenstein's so-called phenomenological phase. The problem of continuity appears, for example, in Ms 106, 38.

be built using individuated positions and points (Rhees 1970, 157). Thus, what was puzzling about the problem of continuity was not that continuity actually was discontinuous; rather, the puzzlement was created by transferring a mathematically useful conception to a non-mathematical context.

Rhees took notes from his discussions with Wittgenstein and published them later as "On Continuity: Wittgenstein's Ideas, 1938" (Rhees 1970, 104–157). At the same time, he tried to formulate his own account of continuity, and Wittgenstein encouraged him in this ambition:

> As you know, I wish you lots of luck with your writing. Just stick to it; and if possible, sacrifice coherence sometimes. I mean, if you feel you could just now say something, but it isn't exactly the thing which ought to come in this place—rather say it and jump about it a bit than stick to the 'single track' and not get on. That is, if you can do it. If you can't jump, just plod on. (Wittgenstein to Rhees, 9. September 1938)

Despite Wittgenstein's encouragement to submit this work as an application for a fellowship, Rhees would not send it off. Wittgenstein expressed his disagreement with this decision:

> I found your first chapter here and was disappointed that you had not sent it in. I think it was wrong not to do it and I think you ought *still* to do it if there is a chance that it might be overlooked that you're a bit late. I have only glanced at a few pages & can't do more at present, but I didn't at all have a bad impression! So why the hell you should wish to be your own examiner I can't see. (Wittgenstein to Rhees, 3. October 1938)

Rhees measured his philosophical writing according to the highest possible standards. His reluctance to submit a doctoral dissertation and his draft on continuity (as well as his reluctance to publish in later life) testifies to his belief that he seldom achieved the originality in his writing that he demanded from himself. His merciless self-criticism coupled with humility and an unwillingness to compromise with the customs of academic life certainly hindered Rhees from pursuing a smooth academic career; but who may have understood him better than Wittgenstein in this respect? Perhaps it was a shared attitude towards the requirements of decent writing in philosophy that made Rhees especially sensitive and attentive to Wittgenstein's concerns about publishing his work. In any case, Rhees became Wittgenstein's confidant in the question of publishing. This is understood, for instance, from a letter Wittgenstein wrote in the summer of 1938:

> this morning I had an idea which I can't very easily explain to you in writing. The gist of it is that I am thinking of publishing something before long after all so as to end the constant misunderstandings and misinterpretations. I very much want to talk the business over with you. (Wittgenstein to Rhees, 13. July 1938)

At this time, a couple of texts were circulating which Wittgenstein considered plagiarism and misrepresentations of his views. Some of his students had written about his new philosophy on several occasions. Richard Braithwaite had published his impression of Wittgenstein's philosophy, to which Wittgenstein responded with a disclaimer in Mind, stating that one part of Braithwaite's presentation was inaccurate and the other false (cf. Wittgenstein 1933, 335.). When Alice Ambrose wanted to publish an article on Wittgenstein's view on finitism in mathematics, Wittgenstein disapproved of the idea and tried to hinder the article's appearance in Mind (Monk 1991, 346). In early 1936, well after Wittgenstein had abandoned working with Waismann on a book intended to present his ideas, Waismann published an article and Wittgenstein accused him of appropriating ideas without acknowledging that he was the author of the views and similes put forward Wittgenstein to Waisman, 19. May 1936). As a consequence, Wittgenstein would not meet Waismann again, although the latter had also immigrated to England and settled in Cambridge by 1938 (Monk 1991, 335, 346).[14] These events incited Wittgenstein to publish his works. In addition, since he had resolved to live permanently in England, a publication might have been helpful, if not mandatory, for continuing his work at the university.[15] Thus, Wittgenstein envisioned publishing the typed and reworked version of the manuscript he had created in Skjolden. He wanted to know if Rhees would make an attempt to translate the book[16]:

> I think it was in June 1938 that Wittgenstein asked me if I would translate his book—certainly before the beginning of July. And he sent me a copy of his preface soon after this, asking me to translate it. Moore had already given me the typescript of the Untersuchungen which Wittgenstein had given him [...] (Rhees to von Wright, 13. May 1977)

Why Rhees was asked to do the translation may partly have to do with his familiarity with Wittgenstein's philosophizing and the fact that he had a good command of Austrian German. However, Theodore Redpath, another regular attendee of Wittgenstein's lectures at that time, was also asked to translate the preface. Redpath agreed and reported what an exhausting task working with Wittgenstein could be:

> We sat for several hours one day thinking out not only every sentence, but pretty well every word, and Wittgenstein got very worked up when he (or we) could not find words or phrases which entirely satisfied him. Time and again I found myself wishing to heaven that he would let me work on the German quite alone and present him with a version which he could then comment on and revise, but he pushed inexorably on, and though his interpositions were sometimes quite awry, as well as exasperating, one did learn something from the procedure, and it gave one an insight into Wittgenstein's fanatical care both for accuracy and for style. (Redpath 1990, 73)

---

[14] Wittgenstein would also try to make Norman Malcolm and others publish a correction of John Wisdom's presentation of his philosophy, cf. Malcolm 1958, 57–59.

[15] I am especially indebted to Peter Keicher for this suggestion.

[16] Wittgenstein 2000a, Ts 220; this typescript is referred to as "Frühfassung" (early version) of the *Philosophical Investigations* in: Wittgenstein 2001.

Rhees was probably one of the few people prepared for the struggle of crafting each and every formulation. In October 1938, Cambridge University Press agreed to publish the book in a bilingual edition under the title Philosophische Bemerkungen—Philosophical Remarks (Wittgenstein to Rhees, 6. October 1938; cf. Wittgenstein 2001, 20), and Rhees worked on his translation throughout the autumn and winter. He regularly met with Wittgenstein for discussions. In January 1939, Rhees' father died and Rhees travelled to the United States. Before departing, he left the translation with Wittgenstein (Wittgenstein 2000a, Ts 226). It was deemed unsatisfactory (Monk 1991, 414). But although Wittgenstein disapproved of the translation, he was always, in the same breath, keen to emphasize Rhees' qualities. To Moore he wrote: "please don't mention to anyone that I don't think highly of the translation. *Rhees* did his very best & the stuff is damn difficult to translate." (Wittgenstein to Moore, 1. February 1939). A few days later, Wittgenstein pointed out to John Maynard Keynes, to whom he had sent the German manuscript together with the translation: "Yes, the translation is pretty awful, & yet the *man who did it* is an excellent man." (Wittgenstein to Keynes, 8. February 1939). Wittgenstein's high esteem for Rhees was not altered by the disappointment over his translation, as is also evident from a recommendation that Wittgenstein wrote soon after:

> I have known Mr R Rhees for 4 years; he has attended my lectures on philosophy and we have had a great many of discussions both on philosophical and general subjects. I have been strongly impressed by the great seriousness and intelligence with which he tackles the problem. Mr Rhees is an exceptionally kind and helpful man and will spare no trouble to assist his students. His German is very good indeed. (Recommendation by Wittgenstein, quoted from: Phillips 2006, 271–272)

2.2   Wittgenstein and Von Wright 1 (1939)

Rhees' translation never appeared in print.[17] Wittgenstein began to revise it but soon gave up the idea of publishing the book at all. His dissatisfaction with the translation was most likely not the only reason (cf. Wittgenstein 2001, 19–21). In early 1939, Keynes informed Wittgenstein that he had been elected to succeed Moore as professor of philosophy (Keynes to Wittgenstein, 11. February 1939; Monk 1991, 415). Wittgenstein may then have seen a possibility to improve the book. After receiving word of his election, Wittgenstein resumed lecturing on the foundations of mathematics—the theme that was supposed to make up his book's second part. Again, Rhees was among the attendees of these lectures that were

---

[17]Though Rhees' translation (=Wittgenstein 2000b, Ts 226) never appeared in print, P. M. S. Hacker and J. Schulte have consulted it, together with Wittgenstein's comments on it, for their new translation of *Philosophical Investigations* (2009). I thank the anonymous reviewer for making me aware of this fact.

held twice a week in a friend's room at King's College (Wittgenstein 2003, 350).[18]
One day, two new faces appeared in class, as Redpath recalled:

> Knowing his aversion to such invasions, I wondered what would happen. If I remember
> rightly, Wittgenstein asked them what they were doing there and whether they intended
> to follow the course. They didn't really answer, at all events to his satisfaction. Indeed
> he hardly gave them time to, for he added, quite uncompromisingly: 'I don't want any
> tourists here, you know!' They were, however, allowed to stay for the rest of the lecture.
> (Redpath 1990, 86)

One of the intruders was Georg Henrik von Wright. He too described the
encounter:

> I went to his lecture in a room in King's College, introduced myself when he entered, and
> said that I had the chairman's permission to attend lectures in the faculty. Wittgenstein
> muttered something which I did not understand, and I seated myself among the audience.
> He started to lecture and I became at once fascinated. „The strongest impression any man
> ever made on me", I wrote in my diary that same day—and the statement remains true. At
> the end of the lecture, however, Wittgenstein expressed his great annoyance at the pres-
> ence of 'visitors' in his class. He seemed furious. Then he left the room without waiting
> for an apology or explanation. I was hurt and shocked. My first impulse was to give up
> efforts to approach this strange man. (von Wright 1990, 10–11.)

Von Wright, a 22-year-old doctoral student from Helsinki, was not accustomed to
such a brusque rejection. Indeed, his life up to this point seems to have been completely governed by polite conduct and gentle deportment. Nothing similar to the
ruptures and rebelliousness that characterize Rhees' early biography can be discovered in descriptions of von Wright's youth. However, like Rhees, von Wright
was wholeheartedly determined to make his way in philosophy.

Born in 1916, von Wright had grown up in a wealthy and well-educated family
that was part of Finland's Swedish speaking elite.[19] His father had graduated from
the Swedish commercial college and had gone on to study economics and philosophy at the University of Helsinki. Though he could have pursued an academic
career, he chose to become a businessman. Despite his success in business, the son
admired him not for being a smart manager but for being a generous gentleman, a
fine intellectual who met with the academics, writers and publishers who attended
Helsinki's cultural salons. Von Wright's education and physical care were left
to his mother. She too had graduated from the Swedish commercial college and
thereafter had continued her education in Germany. When von Wright was twelve

---

[18] Notes from the lectures were later published as: Wittgenstein 1976a. A new edition of
Wittgenstein's lectures from this period has appear as: Smythies 2017.

[19] Most of the biographical information in this section can be found in: von Wright 1990 and von
Wright 2001. For the sake of readability, additional footnotes to single sentences are only given
in cases of direct quotations or when a source different from "von Wright 1990" or "von Wright
2001" was used or when it seemed to be of special interest to the reader to refer to the specific
pages in "von Wright 1990" or "von Wright 2001".

years old, he and his mother went to a health-resort in Merano, Italy, which at the time was under the jurisdiction of Austria. Here, von Wright not only received private lessons in German but was also introduced to geometry by his mother — an experience von Wright regarded as his 'intellectual awakening': "It happened through my acquaintance with the elements of geometry in the spring 1929. This gave me a tremendous thrill—and sleepless nights of thinking about triangles and circles, cones and spheres, and the mysterious number π, whose value it was impossible to tell 'exactly'." (von Wright 1990, 4)

Only a few months later, around Christmas in 1929, the now thirteen-year-old von Wright asked his father what 'philosophy' was. In response, his father gave him a small selection of books. While reading them, he decided that philosophy would become his subject — and Georg Henrik von Wright would never question this decision again. His early mastery of German provided him with what would become his 'spiritual home': the literature of Schiller and Goethe, Nietzsche and Schopenhauer (von Wright 1990, 8).

Having made his vocational choice at this early stage in his life, von Wright began studying philosophy at the University of Helsinki immediately after finishing secondary school in 1934. A few years before, Eino Kaila (whose wife was a cousin of von Wright's mother) had been appointed professor of theoretical philosophy at the University of Helsinki. Von Wright admired him as a strong, charismatic person who was able to captivate large audiences. Kaila had earned his doctorate with a dissertation in experimental psychology and, as a professor, raised a whole generation of Finnish philosophers and psychologists in a new scientific spirit.[20] During the years that immediately preceded von Wright's matriculation, Kaila had been in contact with Rudolf Carnap and Moritz Schlick in Vienna. Since the Vienna Circle had gone public with its program in the late 1920s, Kaila paid research visits to Vienna and conducted psychological research in the city orphanage. Back in Helsinki, he was developing his own branch of logical empiricism. When von Wright began studying at university, Kaila was about to reach the peak of his academic creativity.

At the beginning of his studies, von Wright expressed to Kaila, perhaps naively, a preference for logic more than psychology (von Wright 2001, 54). As a consequence, Kaila introduced him to the writings of Carnap, and this was decisive for von Wright's career (von Wright 2001, 55–56). It only took one semester for von Wright to be convinced that logic would be his "gateway to serious philosophizing" (von Wright 1990, 5). At only twenty years old, he committed himself to the idea of becoming a professional in "Logistic Philosophy". This was also the title of an article the young von Wright published in the Swedish intellectual journal *Nya Argus* (von Wright 1938, 175–177). This article displays his gift of expressing philosophical ideas in an accurate, clear, and easily accessible language which is neither too technical nor too simplistic. Von Wright honed this skill of writing

---

[20] For this and the subsequent information on Kaila see von Wright's Introduction to: Kaila 1979.

lucidly for a broad audience by regularly contributing short essays to the student journal. Meanwhile, the article "Logistic Philosophy" shows that von Wright cleaved to the views of the positivistic movement. Wittgenstein's *Tractatus*, which Kaila had chosen as the topic for von Wright's final exam in philosophy, is also mentioned in this early piece and interpreted in a positivistic vein: von Wright celebrates the *Tractatus* as the first great work of logistic philosophy, the consequences of which were explicated by the Vienna Circle.

After graduating with a Master of Arts in Philosophy in 1937, von Wright wanted to proceed immediately to doctoral studies.[21] His suggestion to Kaila was to write a dissertation on "The Justification of Induction". Von Wright was aware of the problem's tradition in philosophy, especially of Aristotle's and Hume's expositions of the inconclusiveness of inductive inferences. The most important reason for making this suggestion, however, was that the problem of inductive reasoning was currently of prime interest for the type of logistic philosophy that aimed at clarifying the logic of the empirical sciences. Von Wright developed an understanding of the great role of inductive reasoning in the practice of research as well as in everyday life. Though Kaila had originally planned another topic for von Wright's dissertation — namely, a comparison of a Platonic and an Aristotelian philosophy of science — he approved of von Wright's suggestion.

Reading Hume and Bacon on the problem of induction shifted von Wright's focus towards philosophical works originally written in English. The works he had studied up to that point had been written almost exclusively in German. In fact, von Wright had not learned English before he began studying the classic works on the problem of induction (von Wright 2001, 71). Von Wright used the literature on his doctoral topic for learning English that became the new *lingua franca* of science since Nazi-Germany intellectually desiccated the German-speaking academia. First and foremost, von Wright studied treatises by Keynes, Braithwaite and Charlie D. Broad. Since all these authors taught at Cambridge at that time, and since the Vienna Circle was practically dissolved, it was only natural for von Wright to choose Cambridge as his destination for a period of study abroad which was a traditional element in Finnish doctoral studies.

Von Wright arrived at Cambridge in early March 1939.[22] Without having made any official pre-arrangements, he moved into a hotel and simply approached the scholars he knew from his readings. Upon paying his first visit to Braithwaite, he was surprised to hear that Wittgenstein currently taught at Cambridge. Without a second of doubt, von Wright wanted to attend his classes. When visiting Broad, who was the faculty chairman, he asked for permission to participate in courses in philosophy. Having Broad's permission in his pocket, von Wright went to Wittgenstein's class at King's College: here, as we saw, he was expelled, perhaps for the first and only time in his life. But contrary to his initial impulse of giving

---

[21] For information in this paragraph cf. von Wright 2001, 69–70.

[22] For information in this paragraph cf. von Wright 2001, 72–77.

up trying to approach Wittgenstein, von Wright had the courage to write a letter to
the man who had made such a strong impression on him through only one encounter. To his great surprise, he immediately received a friendly response with an invitation for tea for 4:45 pm on March 10th. This was still during von Wright's first
days in Cambridge.

The conversation von Wright and Wittgenstein enjoyed that afternoon was the
first step in their long friendship. What Wittgenstein found most interesting about
his young visitor was probably not his belief in logistic philosophy. Wittgenstein
knew this agenda from his discussions with Waismann, Schlick and Carnap. He
had never considered philosophy a science and was against deriving theories or
principles from the *Tractatus* or his new philosophy. In fact, just a few days before
Wittgenstein and von Wright met, Wittgenstein had made this clear at the Moral
Sciences Club (cf. Wittgenstein 2003, 334–335, 377–380). By contrast, what
Wittgenstein found of interest may have been that he met in von Wright a young
man who shared an upbringing rooted in the non-aristocratic and non-religious
cultural nobility of the central European world of the nineteenth century. In any
case, according to von Wright, he and Wittgenstein did not talk about philosophy
during their first meeting. They talked instead about architecture and Scandinavia,
the landscape Wittgenstein had come to adore since sojourning in Norway.[23]

It seems that a common ground for their conversation was not their philosophical views but a cultural resemblance. Indeed, there was a side to the young von
Wright that could not be descried from his professional interest in logistic philosophy. His intellectual passions were aroused by the nineteenth century art historian
and humanist Jakob Burckhardt, and he was greatly inspired by the philosopher of
history Oswald Spengler, whose books he first came across in his father's library.[24]
Spengler's morphology of world history put von Wright in a mood he described as
his 'early Spenglerism' that was in his own words:

> [...] to view history as a sort of *tableau vivant*, to be looked at in awe and contem-
> plated like a work of art. In the details of history one should try to discern the typical,
> the 'morphological similarities', the recurrent patterns. The great changes, the crises and
> revolutions of history, are like earthquakes and other catastrophes in nature. They cannot
> be judged under the moral categories of justice and rightness. But they may, like life as
> whole, be seen in the light of 'tragedy'. (von Wright 1990, 8)

Although 'rightness' was no category for contemplating history, 'greatness'
certainly was. 'Greatness' was the element von Wright integrated into his
Spenglerism from reading Jakob Burckhardt, in whose writing he found:

---

[23] Wittgenstein wrote to von Wright six months after their discussion: "I wish I were in that landscape of yours. It must be similar to the landscape in Norway, which I love." (From Wittgenstein
to von Wright, 13. September 1939).

[24] Von Wright read the German original of Spengler's *The Decline of the West* in the following
editions (Spengler 1923, 1922). The original copies from the library of von Wright's father can
be consulted at WWA.

greatness of achievement but also of personality (Goethe, Leonardo). Greatness is an unpredictable chance element in history; it is largely through greatness that the typical and recurrent gets its individuality. (von Wright 1990, 8)

Thus, in contrast to a pure cultural pessimism often associated with Spengler's subsequently proverbial book-title of The Decline of the West, von Wright's early Spenglerism involved a glowing appreciation of past cultures and great personalities. This sense of greatness and a romantic belief in man's cultural refinement through education were surely present in his first conversation with Wittgenstein, even though they did not explicitly talk about Spengler who Wittgenstein regarded as one of the authors that influenced him.[25]

Wittgenstein visited von Wright for discussing philosophy in the Easter vacation and invited him to attend his classes in Easter term.[26] He continued lecturing on the foundations of mathematics. During the lectures von Wright did not try to take notes, but wanted to concentrate on Wittgenstein's train of thought. Retrospectively, he confessed that he had understood next to nothing (von Wright 1990, 11). But already then, he was aware of witnessing a historical moment when Wittgenstein and the young Alan Turing fought what appeared to him dramatic intellectual duels (von Wright 2001, 77). Rhees and Norman Malcolm also attended these lectures, and both became good friends and colleagues of von Wright in later life. In 1939, however, von Wright did not associate with either of them (von Wright 1990, 11). After all, his main purpose for being at Cambridge was to work on his dissertation, and he pursued this goal with great determination.

The greater part of his stay at Cambridge von Wright spent either in the library or in discussions with Broad, who grew very fond of his student from Helsinki (von Wright 1990, 12). Broad would become von Wright's influential mentor and promoter. He invited von Wright to dine at the High Table of Trinity College where the bright young gentleman impressed all fellows he met (Broad to von Wright, 17. July 1939). This detail is remarkable for it gives an idea of von Wright's outstanding diplomatic talents: within a few weeks, he won favor with both the academic establishment at Cambridge and Wittgenstein, whose position can be regarded as diametrically opposed to that academic establishment. Indeed, Wittgenstein and Broad had for a long time been intellectual antipodes at Cambridge (cf. Broad 1959a, 304–6.).[27] Wittgenstein was appalled by the artificiality of the conversation at the High Table, where he was once reprimanded

---

[25] Cf. von Wright 2001, 127; Wittgenstein's note on Spengler's influence is to be found in: Wittgenstein 2000a, Ms 154, 15v. The remark stems from 1931 and is published in: Wittgenstein 1980c.

[26] For the information in this paragraph cf. von Wright 2001, 77; 1990, 11.

[27] Already in 1925 Broad wrote in the preface to his book "The Mind and its Place in Nature": "In the meanwhile I retire to my well-earned bath-chair, from which I shall watch with a fatherly eye the philosophic gambols of my younger friends as they dance to the highly syncopated pipings of Herr Wittgenstein's flute." Wittgenstein, in turn, mentioned Broad in his lectures of the academic year 1931–1932, cf. Wittgenstein 1982, 72–81.

for not wearing a tie (Malcolm 1958, 30). Broad, on the other hand, could not stand Wittgenstein's appearances at meetings of the Moral Sciences Club and had asked him to stop attending (Broad 1959a, 61; cf. Monk 2000, 201; cf. from Wittgenstein to Russell, 28. November 1935). This coincided with complaints from others that Wittgenstein tended to disturb and dominate the meetings. Accordingly, Wittgenstein had not been at the Moral Sciences Club between 1931 and 1938.[28] Though he resumed participating a few weeks before von Wright's arrival, there is no documentation that Wittgenstein was present when von Wright gave a talk on *The Justification of Induction* on 25th May 1939.[29]

Von Wright's talk at the Moral Sciences Club testifies to the influence that Wittgenstein had on him after only a few intense encounters. One can almost sense a departure from logical positivism when von Wright introduced the problem of induction as a "pseudo-problem" and then specified it as "a confusion of pictures which we associate with different terms" (von Wright, talk to the Moral Sciences Club 1939). While his notion of "pseudo-problem" belongs to the logistic diction, "confusion of pictures" sounds much more like the Wittgenstein of the 1930s. In his talk, von Wright presented the inductive problem as the "demand for a proof that inductive inference if not with certainty so at least with considerable degree of probability will be true" (von Wright, talk to the Moral Sciences Club 1939). Von Wright argued that the solution of this problem lay not in finding or construct-ing such a proof, but rather in avoiding the philosophical error that leads to the demand for proof in the first place. This too reminds us of Wittgenstein. So also does the very end of von Wright's talk, which is written in his hand at the end of his typescript:

> [...] the problem of finding a justification of induction is no problem at all in the proper sense of the word, that what matters is not that the justification of induction is lacking, but rather: that there is nothing to justify.
>   The inductive problem—like so many other problems in philosophy—is like a mist and to solve the problem is to make the mist disappear. What I have said is not meant to be a proof for this, I have merely tried to point out a way, which if followed ought to contribute to a clarification of the ideas which we are apt to connect with this particular problem. (von Wright, talk to the Moral Sciences Club 1939)

This is one of the rare cases in which von Wright can be said to have adopted a Wittgensteinian style. He later consciously resisted the temptation to imitate Wittgenstein's way of philosophizing, but this early talk shows that Wittgenstein immediately left a stamp on von Wright's thinking, and that von Wright was

---

[28] According to James Klagge in a note to the author, Wittgenstein was paying dues to the Morals Sciences Club again in Fall 1938.

[29] The minutes of the meeting with von Wright's talk are brief and do not indicate whether Wittgenstein was present. The minutes from the previous week's talk by Ayer show that Wittgenstein participated in that discussion. I am very thankful to James Klagge for this information.

capable of immediately recognizing and assimilating new thoughts of great significance. Of this intellectual impact, he later said:

> What Wittgenstein did was to completely 'shake me up'. The position in philosophy which I had come to hold during my studies with Kaila was being called into question, the basic problems of philosophy, which I had considered settled, revived. I felt that I had to start again from scratch in philosophy. (von Wright 1990, 11)

Von Wright's talk at the Moral Sciences Club in May 1939 was warmly applauded and probably was yet another high point of his five months at Cambridge (Redpath 1990, 87). As summer approached, Wittgenstein offered to finance an extension of von Wright's stay, which he would be able to afford in his future position as professor from autumn 1939 onwards (von Wright 2001, 77). Von Wright declined. As military airplanes began to appear over Cambridge, he feared the outbreak of war (von Wright 2001, 77–78). Von Wright discussed this issue with Wittgenstein. Although he was aware that Wittgenstein regarded Western civilization as a deteriorated culture, he was shocked when Wittgenstein indeed wished for its destruction. When von Wright asked him: "Do you really think that Europe needs another war?", Wittgenstein replied: "Not one, but two or three." (von Wright 1995, 5). This statement was outrageous, all the more since, as a young soldier, Wittgenstein had experienced the cruelties of World War One.[30]

Von Wright left England before the summer. From his family residence at the Finnish coast, he wrote to Wittgenstein about the significance of their acquaintance:

> I must add very sincerely that already what I got from your lectures and my discussions with you during my time in Cambridge has given me a certain 'tune' to follow into a realm of thoughts, on the border of which I am standing, trying to listen carefully in order to take the right course to the place, from where the tune is emanating. We do not know as yet wheather [sic] I shall arrive there or whether I only shall take the wrong course over and over again, but the fact that I hear the tune is enough to fill me with life-long happiness and thankfulness for that I have met you and been thought [sic] by you, even if for a very short time. (von Wright to Wittgenstein, 27. August 1939; cf. von Wright to Wittgenstein, 22. February 1940)

Wittgenstein, in his reply, expressed that the appreciation of both philosophical understanding and personal respect was mutual—and almost like a premonition, he wrote about the book manuscript that he had not sent to the printers at the beginning of that year:

> I should very much like to send you the M.S. of what would be the first volume of my book. I have an idea that it shall never be published in my lifetime & might perhaps be entirely lost. I should like to know that you had read it & had a copy of it. Write me if you like to have it; & if it can be sent I'll send it to you.

---

[30] I am thankful to Harald Johannessen for directing my attention to this aspect.

> I think it goes without saying that I shall always be exceedingly glad to hear from you.
> (Wittgenstein to von Wright, 13. September 1939)

2.3   Wittgenstein and Rhees 2 (1939–1946)

A few days after von Wright had written to Wittgenstein, World War Two broke out. Wittgenstein was greatly affected by this. In his reply to von Wright he revealed his state of mind and occupational doubts:

> I can't imagine how I shall be able to lecture. I feel as though, under the present shameful
> & depressing circumstances, I ought to do anything but discuss philosophical problems,
> with people who aren't really deeply interested in them anyway.
> [...] everything that I do seems to me futile & I don't know what sort of life I ought to
> lead. (Wittgenstein to von Wright, 13. September 1939)

Wittgenstein's contempt for modern and Western ways of living extended to the academic life that surrounded him. He had always been in doubt about his role as a university teacher, and he advised several students to leave academic philosophy for a more practical occupation. The war aggravated these concerns. Although Wittgenstein had just been appointed professor of philosophy at Cambridge, he wrote to Rhees the very same day he replied to von Wright's letter, stating that he considered leaving university again if the war should continue:

> [...] I am as unclear about what I ought to do as ever, except that I think, just now the
> right thing is to wait and see whether this war really develops into a war or not for this
> still seems to me very doubtful. In case it does I suppose one will get a job with the Red
> Cross pretty easily and not so many occupations will be 'reserved'. (Wittgenstein to
> Rhees, 13. September 1939)

The 35-year-old Rhees shared Wittgenstein's rejection of academic customs. He had, perhaps under Wittgenstein's influence, taken a job as a welder at a factory in Swansea.[31] Rhees soon contemplated quitting, but Wittgenstein advised him to stick to it:

> No job will ever absolutely & entirely fit you (just as ready made clothes don't ever fit
> certain people). What I mean is: please beware of drifting between jobs but thank the Lord
> that you've found one which however moderately, fits you somewhat. Forgive me for writ-
> ing to you in this way. (Wittgenstein to Rhees, 14. August 1940)

These words weighed heavily in Rhees' conscience. In a long letter written on New Year's Eve 1940, Rhees struggled to justify his decision to give up welding

---

[31] I am indebted to Brian McGuinness, who pointed out that Wittgenstein's influence may have led Rhees to take the welding job.

in order to take a teaching post at the University of Swansea. He finally explained this decision by appealing to yet another opinion of Wittgenstein:

> I would like to say that I didn't just disregard your advice. I was worried by your suggestions at the time when I finally did decide to come here; and I have seen a number of things which favour your view since then. My welding kept on being bad, and I thought (not so stupidly either) that it probably would never develop into anything decent. There was a lot more that was connected with this, but I'd better leave that out. I mention two considerations which played a considerable part. One was that such training as I had had was in the academic and pedagogical line. […] Another consideration, I confess, was a saying of yours which kept recurring to me. Your first opinion, when I suggested that I might go in for welding, was that it was foolish for me to try it. And one of your remarks about that sort of job generally was, 'It's too impersonal'. This kept going around in my head as I kept making a mess of things. (Rhees to Wittgenstein, 31. December 1940)

It is probably fair to say that Rhees' decision to give up welding was prudent. As in his earlier university posts, Rhees proved his outstanding capacity as a teacher in philosophy. Being highly respected by students and colleagues, he would, in later years, inspire the atmosphere at the department of philosophy in Swansea with his honest and deep thinking. Moreover, the post at the University of Swansea also introduced an element of stability in a life full of discontinuities.

Visiting Rhees in 1942 and 1943, Wittgenstein discovered Swansea to be a place of retreat and inspiration. Lecturing had become unbearable to him. In the autumn of 1941, he took a job as a porter at Guy's Hospital in London and scheduled his lectures for the weekends. After a year and a half, in spring of 1943, he moved to Newcastle where he assisted in a medical laboratory. During these years of war-work, Wittgenstein paid visits to Rhees in Swansea. They attended meetings of the Philosophical Society which Rhees had initiated and had many philosophical discussions, for example about Freud and psychoanalysis.[32] Just as Wittgenstein had come to like the Norwegian landscape and people, he now came to like Wales and the Welsh.

In his writing, Wittgenstein was still mainly occupied with his remarks on the foundations of mathematics. He heavily reworked them for the second part of his book and once again considered publishing it.[33] After discussions with Nikolai Bachtin (the older brother of Michail Bachtin), Wittgenstein thought that the *Tractatus* and his new book ought to be printed together in the same volume. Though Cambridge University Press had already received permission from Kegan Paul to reprint the *Tractatus*, the plan of publishing the book was once again abandoned, since Wittgenstein shifted the focus of his work during his next stay in Swansea: in 1944, Trinity College called Wittgenstein back to Cambridge, but he negotiated a sabbatical from teaching and decided to spend it with Rhees in

---

[32] Notes from their conversations are published in: Wittgenstein 1966. Memoir of a meeting at the Philosophical Society in: Rhees 1984, 201. A new edition of Rhees' philosophical discussions with Wittgenstein has appeared as: Wittgenstein et al. 2015.

[33] Selections of these writings were later published in: Wittgenstein 1976b.

Swansea. It was now that Wittgenstein entirely stopped working on the foundations of mathematics and turned towards investigating psychological concepts (cf.
Wittgenstein 2001, 23–24).

That Wittgenstein stopped elaborating his remarks on the foundations of mathematics seems to be a far more significant turn in his work than is usually recognized. For it was Wittgenstein's interest in the philosophy of mathematics that
brought him to philosophy in the first place: the idea of studying the philosophy of
mathematics incited him to visit Gottlob Frege in 1911, and Frege recommended
him to study with Bertrand Russell in Cambridge (cf. McGuinness 1988, chapter 4). In 1928, Brouwer's lectures on the foundational crisis of mathematics contributed to Wittgenstein's return to philosophy and, in 1929, his first fellowship at
Trinity College allowed him to carry out work on the foundations of mathematics.
Teaching at Cambridge, Wittgenstein devoted many of his lectures to the foundations of mathematics, and for several years his plan was that remarks on this topic
would constitute the second part of his book. Now, after so many years of creating, selecting and composing these remarks, he stopped working on them entirely,
without achieving a version he declared ready to be published. It seems that just
as the *Tractatus* took a new course after Wittgenstein's experiences in the Great
War, his work during World War Two was followed by a change in the course of
the *Philosophical Investigations*. While staying in Swansea between April and
September 1944, Wittgenstein wrote 114 new remarks (Wittgenstein 2000b, Ms
129). He read this new material to Rhees and discussed it with him (Rhees 2006,
257):

> He had read the last part of Part I aloud to me from Zettel clamped together, in September
> 1944. I cannot remember now just <u>how</u> much of the text now printed he read to me—
> partly because he discussed other parts—or rather: expounded to me the points he makes
> in them—when we walked or met indoors during earlier months. (Rhees to von Wright,
> 10. August 1972)
>   I remember in particular the finish of it, when he read the paragraph concluding "([sic]
> Man könnte auch von einer Tätigkeit der Butter reden, wenn sie im Preise steigt; und
> wenn dadurch keine Probleme erzeugt werden, so ist es harmlos." This was at the end of
> September, 1944. And I remember what a kick I got out of it. I thought his stuff was won-
> derful. (Rhees to von Wright, 27. February 1969)[34]

These remarks formulated during Wittgenstein's stay in Swansea in 1944 were
later typed (Wittgenstein 2000a, Ts 241) and incorporated into the already-
reworked typescript of the *Philosophical Investigations*.[35] This may have been
after Wittgenstein's return to Cambridge in autumn 1944. There, he wrote what

---

[34] The sentence quoted by Rhees became the last sentence of the last paragraph (§693) in the
Philosophical Investigations. In Anscombe's translation it reads: "(It would also be possible to
speak of an acitivity of butter when it rises in price, and if no problems are produced by this it is
harmless.)".

[35] Reconstructed Ts, referred to as "Zwischenfassung" (intermediate version) in: Wittgenstein
2001.

became the preface to the posthumous edition of the *Philosophical Investigations*. Having experienced Swansea as a stimulating place for philosophizing, it is no wonder that Wittgenstein later advised Rhees to stay there when now it was Rhees who wanted to leave. Being strongly attracted to anarchistic thought, Rhees considered joining a Trotskyist party. Wittgenstein objected: if one became a party member one could not question the party line, whereas in philosophy one had to be constantly prepared to change directions (Rhees 1984, 207–208). Wittgenstein obviously regarded Rhees as better suited for the latter and at the same time he urged him not to change his occupational direction again, but to accept the offer of a permanent post at the University of Swansea:

> I was glad to hear that they had the sense to offer you an appointment in Swansea. I wish to God you'ld take it!! I don't know, of course, what your special reasons are for wanting to leave Swansea, but please weigh them damn carefully. I should, for personal reasons, hate you to leave Swansea. Our talks & discussions have done me good. Don't stupidly throw away an opportunity of doing some good. Your derogatory remarks about your philosophical abilities & success are so much rubbish. You are all right. And I mean just that: nothing more & nothing less. – Philosophical influences much worse than yours & mine are spreading rapidly, & it's important that you should stay at your job. That your success won't be brilliant is certain; in fact it will be meagre, it's bound to be. Please, if you possibly can, resign yourself to it & stay on. – Don't misunderstand me. I'm not trying to appear wise. I'm just as silly as you are. But that doesn't make you any less silly.
>   So long!
>   Ludwig Wittgenstein
>   P.S. Read this letter again from the beginning. (Wittgenstein to Rhees, 21. May 1946)

Though this letter still echoes many of Wittgenstein's previous recommendations to Rhees to stick with what he began, its tone indicates that the relationship between the two men had changed after the months they spent together in Swansea. Wittgenstein no longer spoke as a tutor advising an undecided student; Rhees was a discussion partner on equal footing, and the two could speak frankly. Hence, after Wittgenstein resumed lecturing in Cambridge, their correspondence became a relaxed exchange between colleagues, two friends really, sharing their experiences in the same occupation of teaching philosophy. This comes across in a letter Wittgenstein wrote shortly after returning to Cambridge in 1945:

> I wish you one moderately intelligent & awake pupil to sweeten your labour! Please look after your health. You can't expect good work when your health isn't really good, & colds are nasty things. I've so far been in good health, & consequently my classes haven't gone too bad. (Or should I say "badly"?) Thouless is coming to them, & a woman, Mrs so & so who calls herself Miss Anscombe, who certainly is intelligent, though not of Kreisel's caliber. (Wittgenstein to Rhees, 28. November 1944)

2.4   Wittgenstein and Anscombe 1 (1942–1946)

Unlike Rhees and von Wright, Elizabeth Anscombe did not enter philosophy through the discipline's modern focus on the empirical sciences and their logic. Her thinking was embedded in and directed towards human action and its relations to reason and God. Anscombe, the daughter of a schoolmaster and a headmistress, fell for philosophy after reading a work called *Natural Theology* written by a nine-teenth century Jesuit:

> The book contained an argument for the existence of a First Cause, and as a preliminary to this it offered a proof of some 'principle of causality' according to which anything that comes about must have a cause. The proof had the fault of proceeding from a barely con-cealed assumption of its own conclusion. I thought that this was some sort of carelessness on the part of the author, and that it just needed tidying up. So I started writing improved versions of it; each one satisfied me for a time, but then reflection would show me that I had committed the same fault. I don't think I ever showed my efforts to anyone; I tore them up when I thought they were no good, and I went round asking people why, if some-thing happened, they would be sure it had a cause. No one had an answer to this. In two or three years of effort I produced five versions of a would-be proof, each one of which I then found guilty of the same error, though each time it was more cunningly concealed. In all this time I had no philosophical teaching about the matter; even my last attempt was made before I started reading Greats at Oxford. (Anscombe 1981a, vii)

In contrast to von Wright who, as a thirteen-year-old, had asked what philosophy was and then decided it should become his subject, Anscombe unintentionally slipped into philosophizing by stumbling upon a fallacy. Once her fascination for reasoning was awakened, it became her life's occupation.

In 1937, at the age of 18, Anscombe began studying classics and philosophy (*Literae Humaniores*) at St. Hugh's in Oxford, a college that enabled women from all backgrounds to gain a university education.[36] Shortly after matriculation, she converted to Roman Catholicism. This decision, she claimed, was based on her reading and reflection from twelve to fifteen years of age (Anscombe 1981a, vi). At the Corpus Christi procession the year after her conversion, she met another convert, Peter Geach, whom she married three years later. Given that both Anscombe and Geach were academic philosophers, it has been suggested that— besides for aesthetic reasons—Anscombe kept her maiden name in order to avoid ambiguity in their later publications (Teichmann 2001, 1).

Philosophy, faith and life — by some regarded as incompatible — informed and enlightened each other and merged into a unity in Anscombe's conduct. She was able to employ reason to answer a question that sprang from daily life while gaining orientation for her reasoning from Catholic doctrines and tenets. Hence, it could happen that she let teachings of the Catholic Church lead her in philosophy. This is beautifully illustrated by an event that probably took place in Blackwell's

---

[36] Much of the biographical information in this section can be found in: Teichmann 2008, 1–9.

bookshop when Anscombe was an undergraduate student at Oxford. Her daughter Mary Geach describes this event:

> She had come across a passage in Russell to the effect that an argument from the facts about the world to the existence of God could not be valid, as one could not deduce a necessary conclusion from a contingent premiss. She had not at the time been able to see what was wrong with the notion that necessities can only be deduced from necessities, but she had known that to deny the possibility of moving by reason from the facts about the world to a knowledge of the existence of God was to deny a doctrine defined as of faith by an ecumenical council.
>
> She went then to church and made an act of faith; I suppose it was the standard one 'My God I believe in thee and all thy Church doth teach, because thou hast said it and thy word is true'. She realized later that of course one can derive necessary conclusion form contingent premises. (cf. Geach 2008, xiii–xxvi, quote from: xvi)

It seems as though Russell's reaching a conclusion that contradicted her theological beliefs merely prompted her to try to see more clearly where the fault of the argument was. And there was no tension in this. In Anscombe's case, faith and rationality complemented each other. In particular, rather than providing a foundation for religion, Anscombe may have found that logical analysis helped to remove misunderstandings that hinder belief.

The ability of bringing together rationality and faith was evident already in Anscombe's first publication from 1939. In this pamphlet entitled *The Justice of the Present War Examined*, Anscombe derived from Catholic principles seven necessary and, in combination, sufficient conditions for a just war (reprinted in Anscombe 1981b, 72–81). She then carried out a sharp analysis of the conditions' fulfillment in the actual case of British policy in 1939 and came to the conclusion that the war of the then-present government was not a just war. This early piece of Anscombe's writing weaves a dense texture of religious belief, logical analysis and political criticism. These are seminal elements that would later differentiate into different lines of her writing. However, Anscombe always remained interested in arguments relevant for action, and in this she was not afraid of defending unpopular views. In the particular case of her undergraduate piece on the justice of war, criticism came not only from the public and academic philosophers but also from the Catholic Church. Anscombe and her co-author Norman Daniel gave their pamphlet an extra description as expressing a 'Catholic view' (Anscombe 1981b, vii). The Archbishop of Birmingham objected that they had no right to do so without an official *imprimatur*. Dutifully, Anscombe and Daniel withdrew the essay from bookshop-shops in Oxford and London (Anscombe 1981b, vii).

Obeying the teachings of the Catholic Church did not mean that Anscombe demanded such obedience from her partners in philosophical discussion. She loved working on arguments as such, and not only with regard to their potential implications for religious thought. She could focus entirely on an argument's structure and its significance for a discussion at hand. In doing so, she was at first not particularly interested in the contexts from which the arguments had historically originated. In this sense she may properly be called an analytical philosopher

from the start. Her interest in the philosophical gist of an argument became especially clear in her final exam at Oxford, when she counterbalanced a rather incomplete knowledge of history and literature with an outstanding performance in
philosophy. Indeed, it was due to her philosophical brilliance alone that she earned
exceptional honors in her exam.

After graduating from St. Hugh's College, Anscombe received a research studentship from Newnham, a women's College at Cambridge. From that time
onwards, she participated in almost all of Wittgenstein's lectures, which mainly
dealt with the philosophy of psychology (Wittgenstein 2003, 355–359). She
brought to them her original philosophical curiosity that could not be contented
by clever sophisms. Anscombe had enormous perseverance in working until her
original puzzlement was truly dissolved, something the 25-year-old experienced in
Wittgenstein's lectures:

> For years I would spend time in cafés, for example, staring at objects saying to myself: 'I
> see a packet. But what do I really see? How can I say that I see here anything more than
> a yellow expanse?' […] I always hated phenomenalism and felt trapped by it. I couldn't
> see my way out of it but I didn't believe it. It was no good pointing to difficulties about
> it, things which Russell found wrong with it, for example. The strength, the central nerve
> of it remained alive and raged achingly. It was only in Wittgenstein's classes in 1944 that
> I saw the nerve being extracted, the central thought 'I have got this, and I define yellow
> (say) as this' being effectively attacked. —At one point in these classes Wittgenstein was
> discussing the interpretation of the sign-post, and it burst upon me the way you go by it is
> the final interpretation. (Anscombe 1981a, xiii–ix)

It was the effort to get to the bottom of her philosophical perplexities that
made Wittgenstein's lectures so valuable for Anscombe. One might expect
that her rather ahistorical interest in philosophical arguments corresponded to
Wittgenstein's attitude, but that would be misleading: though Wittgenstein has
sometimes been imagined as a philosopher who neglected the tradition of thought
in the history of philosophy, Mary Geach makes clear that it was Wittgenstein who
stimulated Anscombe's interest in the great thinkers of the past:

> She recorded that before she knew him [Wittgenstein], the great philosophers of the past
> had appeared to her like beautiful statues: knowing him had brought them alive for her.
>
>   […]
>
> She said to me once that the contemporary philosophy teachers who called themselves
> philosophers were not philosophers: she would not call herself one. Who was, I asked, and
> she named Wittgenstein. She had learned, by walking and talking in the company of one
> of them, to move in the company of people who were, in this restricted sense, philoso-
> phers; not merely listening, but seriously entering into their concerns and criticizing their
> thoughts. This does not mean using a philosopher's work as a text about which to make
> erudite observations, nor did it mean taking him as a banner for her cause, nor employing
> his name as a label for a mindset which she might dislike: it meant interesting herself in
> the topics that the philosopher discusses, taking his thoughts apart, adopting some, finding
> deep problems through others, and rejecting what she found silly. For she was quite capa-
> ble of finding a great philosopher silly. (Geach 2011, xiii)

As for Wittgenstein, philosophy for Anscombe primarily meant the activity of discussing and arguing about a subject at hand. This implied the decency to respect good arguments regardless of who had uttered them or when. Ancient philosophers were thus to be respected for their good thoughts, and faulty arguments were to be rejected even if they were put forward by great thinkers. Though this way of philosophizing was probably lived and fostered by Wittgenstein, it demanded a high degree of independence from authorities. Anscombe demonstrated such independence early on, for example in 1948, when she presented a paper to the Socratic Club at Oxford, criticizing an argument in Clive Staples Lewis' book *Miracles* (cf. Lewis 1947). Lewis, the founder of the Club and already a prominent academic, was present at that event. Anscombe won what people remembered as a tense argument and Lewis changed the respective passage in a revised edition of his book.[37]

One may think that this was a bold attack by a young woman in an academic surrounding that von Wright had experienced to be completely dominated by men (von Wright 2001, 74). But as Mary Geach once put it: someone who was bold enough to confront Wittgenstein, could probably confront anyone.[38] Anscombe's faith may have emboldened her in bravely facing superiors and authorities, if indeed fear of God destroys all earthly fears, as her husband once wrote.[39] However, it is likely that in order to stave off gender prejudices, her arguments had to be more coherent and her attacks more precise than those of her male colleagues. Anscombe's intellectual assertiveness, on the other hand, may have just as well provoked comments on gender. Wittgenstein was not totally immune from this, as Anscombe's husband Peter Geach remembered:

> I heard him address Elizabeth several times as 'old man' on several occasions. It was not the only way in which he treated her as an honorary male. Each year at the beginning of his course of lectures Wittgenstein would have a great many listeners, largely female; this crowd would rapidly shrink to a hard core of regular attenders by the third or fourth lecture. This happened in particular during one year's attendance by Elizabeth; noticing this shrinkage, Wittgenstein looked round the room with gloomy satisfaction and remarked: 'Thank God we've got rid of the women!' (Geach 1988, xii)

---

[37] The revised edition appeared in 1960.

[38] Note from personal conversation.

[39] Cf. Geach 1969, 127: "worship of a supreme power […] is wholly different from, and does not carry with it, a cringing attitude towards earthly powers. An earthly potentate does not compete with god, not even unsuccessfully: he may threaten all manner of afflictions, but only from God's hands can any affliction actually come upon us. If we fully realize this, we shall have such fear upon God as destroys all earthly fears". The anonymous reviewer for JHAP made the following comment that is worth quoting here: "Interestingly Wittgenstein expressed the very same thought in a diary entry from January 28, 1937: 'I understood what it means that belief is bliss for a human being, that is, it frees him from the fear of others by placing him <u>immediately</u> under God.' (Wittgenstein 2003, 163).

This is probably best understood as a wry appreciation of Anscombe's abrasiveness and philosophical acumen. Wittgenstein regarded Anscombe as extraordinary talented, as is evident from a letter of recommendation that he wrote to Myra Curtis, principal of Newnham College, when Anscombe's studentship expired:

> She is, undoubtedly, the most talented female student I have had since 1930, when I began lecturing; and among my male students only 8 or 10 either equaled or surpassed her. She has an excellent grasp of philosophical problems, great seriousness, and ability for hard work". (Recommendation Wittgenstein to Curtis, 18. May 1945)

Thus, already in 1945, Wittgenstein considered Anscombe among his best 10 students he ever had. The emphasis of gender in his letter may be accounted for by the fact that Newham was a women's college. However, even with such a recommendation from a thinker like Wittgenstein, it was difficult to gain a foothold in the academia of that time. During the hard transition period after her studentship, "Wittgenstein showed himself a true friend" (Geach 1988, xi), as Peter Geach recollected:

> We were very poor. He tried to persuade Newnham to do something for Elizabeth's career; indeed though he regularly did not wear a tie, he wore one for an interview with the Principal of the College—quite in vain. Later on he paid the fee for Elizabeth to go to a private maternity home for the birth of our second child, John Richard, in December 1946. He refused to regard this as anything but a gift: a characteristic expression of a generosity to which other friends have borne witness. (Geach 1988, xi)

In 1946 Anscombe obtained a research fellowship from Somerville College, Oxford. While living in Oxford, she travelled regularly to Cambridge to visit Wittgenstein for discussions. In addition to attending his lectures, she participated in his tutorials on the philosophy of religion (Wittgenstein 2003, 358; cf. Monk 1991, 497–498). An expression by her husband seems to capture her determination: "Elizabeth did not let her pregnancy interfere with attendance at Moral Sciences Club meetings and at Wittgenstein's lectures" (Geach 1988, xi).

2.5   Wittgenstein and Von Wright 2 (1947–1948)

In Wittgenstein's last lecture at Cambridge in spring term 1947, Anscombe met a guest from Finland: Professor von Wright.[40] Von Wright had pursued his academic career under the hard circumstances of war. He had published the article "On Probability" in *Mind* in 1940, one year before defending his doctoral dissertation (von Wright 1940). Shortly afterwards he was given a lectureship at the University of Helsinki. As long as censorship during the war permitted, von Wright had regularly corresponded with Broad, who had praised von Wright's dissertation in three

---

[40] Notes from the lectures were later published in: Wittgenstein 1988.

long contributions to *Mind* as the best treatment known to him of the problem of induction (Broad 1959b, 1). By 1947 von Wright was professor in Helsinki and at times even held a second professorship at the Academy of Åbo. When Broad invited von Wright to lecture in Cambridge after the war, von Wright also received invitations to lecture in London and Oxford. Before departing for England, he informed Wittgenstein about his return to Cambridge and invited him to his lectures. Wittgenstein replied:

> I'm glad that you are going to lecture here, & I know that by attending your lectures I could learn a very great deal. In spite of this I will not come to them – for the sole reason that, in order to live & to work, I have to allow no import of foreign goods (i.e., philosophical ones) into my mind. For the same reason I haven't read your book, though I am convinced of its excellence. If you think that I'm getting old – you're right. So long! & good luck! (Wittgenstein to von Wright, 21. February 1947)

As promised, Wittgenstein did not attend von Wright's lectures; but von Wright did attend Wittgenstein's class, which marked the endpoint of Wittgenstein's lecture series on the philosophy of psychology and, indeed, of his career as a university professor. During the sessions von Wright met Anscombe, Geach, and Malcolm, all of whom became friends during and after the lectures.

The adult von Wright sitting in Wittgenstein's class in 1947 was very different from the doctoral student who had sat there eight years earlier. Not only had he become a successful and sought-after professor; he had married and started a family.[41] Along with the changes in his professional and personal status, his philosophical standpoints had changed significantly. In the year of his dissertation, von Wright had written the book *Den logiska Empirismen* (von Wright 1943), which was to him a farewell to logical positivism. This sentiment was sustained in the talk that von Wright gave to the Moral Sciences Club upon his return to Cambridge. Contrasting his previous philosophical belief in logistic philosophy, he turned in his talk to the activity that he now called "analytical philosophy" and sketched the kinds of problems it may tackle. One sentence—though it is crossed out in the manuscript—is illustrative of his critical reflection on his previous faith in logical positivism:

> As a matter of fact there has on a comparatively large scale been advocated in modern philosophy a conventionalist view that appears to have made philosophy almost to an art of sophistry. [I am thinking on the main trend of thought known as logical positivism or logical empiricism as advocated in particular by Professor Carnap] (von Wright, talk to Moral Sciences Club 1947, 10)

The programmatic talk von Wright gave in 1947 stands in stark contrast to what he had said as a doctoral student at the same place almost exactly eight years earlier. Reading his manuscript, one gets the impression that throughout the entire

---

[41] For information in this paragraph cf. von Wright 2001, 79–113.

talk, his matured intellect commented on his own statements from 1939. Though von Wright's professional philosophizing was still scientific in spirit, his intellectual passions were nourished by his acquaintance with the distinguished Brazilian diplomat Mario De Millo, in whose cultural world Nietzsche was central and logical empiricism did not even exist. De Millo had directed von Wright's attention to the book *Paideia*, the third volume of which had just appeared (Jaeger 1934–1947). Von Wright was immediately fascinated by this humanistic historiography of higher education in Plato's time. *Paideia* inspired von Wright to write essays in a new vein, following more freely his attraction to the work and style of a public intellectual (von Wright 1947). This change was probably also noticed by Wittgenstein, with whom von Wright repeatedly discussed during his stay in Cambridge (von Wright 1990, 14). Wittgenstein lent him the typescript of the then-current version of the *Philosophical Investigations*, and von Wright read it on his way to lectures in Oxford. This gave him insights into Wittgenstein's unpublished work. Nevertheless, even more than the writings, the philosophical conversations with Wittgenstein impressed von Wright:

> I saw a great deal of Wittgenstein and the impression he made on me was even deeper than that of eight years earlier. Each conversation with Wittgenstein was like living through the day of judgment. It was terrible. Everything had constantly to be dug up anew, questioned and subjected to the tests of truthfulness. This concerned not only philosophy but the whole of life. (von Wright 1990, 14)

The torment reverberating through this published passage is also apparent in the sincere letter von Wright wrote to Wittgenstein after his return to Finland. Von Wright began the letter by stressing the great philosophical benefit he had gained from their renewed discussions:

> Never before, to my memory, going abroad [sic] meant so much to my education.
> I learnt an enormous mass [of] philosophy. Why and how it came to be so, you know as well as I do. What will be the consequences of it, is not as yet to be foreseen, – I can only hope they will be of more good than harm, in the long run. I know that a hard struggle is needed before the imported goods will become my own. Certain things will be ejaculated, other things assimilated. If, at the end, no visible traces of your influence remain in my thought, which is extremely unlikely, so shall I at least always have to acknowledge that I learnt from you, how difficult philosophy must be, if it is to be more than a collection of materials for academic controversy and learned conversation. (von Wright to Wittgenstein, 31. July 1947)

A second tone, as it were, grounds the significance of that encounter in a more existential dimension:

> Still more, perhaps, did the stay in Cambridge mean to my human being, so to say. It was as though something, which had begun to grow in me in the last years, suddenly had ripened. Things which I hardly thought of before, became of vital importance, new values and ideals appeared and greatly revised my outlook on life. (von Wright to Wittgenstein, 31. July 1947)

A third tone, however, turns the chord into a minor key, as the greatness von Wright experienced in Wittgenstein also gave rise to doubt and fear:

> The question may again be raised, whether for good or bad. I have an awful feeling, I might as well have said conviction, that nothing I consciously undertake for the sake of my soul can make me substantially different from what I am, a pharisee in minutest details, because I shall always lack courage to let myself down in the abys of despair which I know I had to pass in order to be saved. (von Wright to Wittgenstein, 31. July 1947)

These words, which were written immediately after his second stay at Cambridge, show that von Wright felt that any serious engagement with the great philosopher may come at high personal cost. He must have regarded it a privilege to go for walks and have philosophical talks with Wittgenstein, yet being under the spell of such a powerful mind may have threatened von Wright's philosophical identity. This does not need to be a matter of rivalry with his much admired companion; it could rather be that von Wright was concerned about whether he would be able to free his mind again after having tuned into Wittgenstein's way of thinking. Von Wright wrote about this concern to his friend Göran Schildt:

> When I came to Cambridge before the war, and to my surprise found out that Wittgenstein was there it was self-evident that I would approach him and come to receive his teaching. In two respects this was of the greatest significance for me: partly because Wittgenstein pulled me out of a dangerous philosophical jargon which I had acquired under the impression of the general development of logical empiricism in the 30s; partly, which I understood only much later, I acquired a new philosophical jargon, which for many years totally chained my thinking. (Fortunately almost all my publications have been in a very narrow field in which I more or less have been able to be myself.) Only during the two last years I experienced that I have reached a certain independence, found the beginning of a style of my own.
> Then came the renewed and much deeper contact with Wittgenstein which among other things has given me a sense of significant parts of his unpublished works. This time it could not be a question of uncritical reception; it was rather a struggle of life and death. I don't say death lightly here, for god only knows, whether after this I will ever be able to think a thought of my own. (von Wright to Schildt, 15. June 1947)

Despite the intensity of this inner conflict, von Wright once again made an extraordinarily good impression on everyone during his time in Cambridge. If a personal struggle was noticeable at all in the conduct of the consummately composed gentleman, it may have even added to the decency of his demeanor. Wittgenstein, in any case, obviously did not believe von Wright's philosophical sovereignty was in danger: during one of their walks through Trinity's Fellows Gardens, he revealed his plans to resign from his chair and that he would like von Wright to become his successor. Von Wright remembered that moment as equally flattering and intimidating (von Wright 2001, 129; 1990, 14). It was not unimportant that as von Wright contemplated this proposition, he received encouragement from several friends. Broad supported the idea that his admired colleague and beloved friend would apply for the professorship. Anscombe concurred, as she made clear in a letter to von Wright after his return to Finland:

> You will I expect by now have heard of Wittgenstein's resignation from the professorship at Cambridge. As I expect you know, he has not done it for the reasons which he used to have for wondering whether he should not—the general beastliness of the situation at Cambridge and his feeling of incongruity about his being in that job—but because he can't get on with his book. In a few weeks he is going to live near Dublin, so I suppose none of us will see him for some time. He is in a rather depressed state at present, but is not, he tells me, having any twinges of doubt about his resignation, and I think that if when he gets away he is able to work he is going to find it a great relief.
>
> Meanwhile one feels very gloomy about things at Cambridge. I suppose that sooner or later they will be advertising the professorship. Is there any remote chance of your applying for it? It isn't of any significance that you are the only person I can think of in that job without acute depression—but I've no doubt that others whose opinion does count will have the same idea. But I have a fear from certain things that you said about your job at Helsingfors that loyalty may keep you there apart from anything else. (Anscombe to von Wright, 13. October 1947)

By the time von Wright read this, he was undecided whether he really ought to apply for the professorship. He was unsure whether at the age of 31, he was suited for this most outstanding position of professor of philosophy at Cambridge. In addition, he hesitated to force his family to resettle in England. Wittgenstein expressed his sympathy for these doubts and would have been neither surprised nor disappointed if von Wright had decided to stay in Finland (Wittgenstein to von Wright, 22. December 1947). The decisive consideration in favor of applying was seemingly a political one: von Wright feared that Finland might be incorporated into the Soviet Union. If this happened, he would be isolated from his cherished colleagues to the west and prevented from philosophical exchanges with them (von Wright 2001, 132; from Wittgenstein to Malcolm, 30. April 1948). Thus, after intense deliberation, von Wright applied for the professorship in January 1948. While Broad informed him of the formal requirements for applying for the post, von Wright asked Wittgenstein for a letter of recommendation. Wittgenstein agreed, but not without a word of warning:

> Dear von Wright,
>
> Miss Anscombe wrote to me a few weeks ago that you had put in for the professorship. I shall write the recommendation in a few days & send it to the Registry as you suggest. May your decision be the right one! I have no doubt that you will be a better professor than any of the other candidates for the chair. But Cambridge is a dangerous place. Will you become superficial? smooth? If you don't, you will have to suffer terribly. – The passage in your letter which makes me feel particularly uneasy is the one about your feeling enthusiasm at the thought of teaching in Cambridge. It seems to me: if you go to Cambridge you must go as a sober man. – May my fears have no foundation, & may you not be tempted beyond your powers! (Wittgenstein to von Wright, 23. February 1948)

In contrast to Wittgenstein, Anscombe had no doubts about von Wright's prospects as professor. In a long letter, she expressed her delight about von Wright's application and addressed many themes besides the new position, such as the *Tractatus*,

Parmenides, Leibniz and the current situation of English academia. Anscombe may have wished for a friend in such an influential position.[42] First and foremost, however, her letter shows that friendship and mutual professional respect had begun to grow between herself and von Wright. Of course, their relationship was rooted in their acquaintance with Wittgenstein and his philosophy, but other strands grew out from this. Despite many shared philosophical interests, however, their mutual literary recommendations remind one of how different they must have been. In a letter to von Wright, she commented on the already-mentioned three volumes of Werner Jaeger's *Paideia*, which von Wright had obviously recommended to her:

> Werner Jaeger, I have got to confess, does not appeal to me; it may be because I have not read a great deal of his book; I think it probable that one should read a great continuous chunk of it in order to get anything out of it; but I am afraid that I have got impatient with the atmosphere of general adulation. (Anscombe to von Wright, Mai 1948)

Anscombe added her literary recommendation of her own in a post-script:

> Have you ever read a short (unfinished) story of Franz Kafka's called "The Burrow"? I did not understand it for a long time, but now I do and I think it incomparably the most significant thing of his, &[43] one of the most significant things I have ever read. I'd like to know what you think of it.

Compare these works by Jaeger and Kafka and the contrast could hardly be more striking! Adding Wittgenstein's reading suggestions completes a peculiar literary triangle: after Anscombe once lent Wittgenstein a work by Kafka, Wittgenstein is reported to have said that Kafka "gives himself a great deal of trouble not writing about his trouble" (Monk 1991, 498). According to biographer Ray Monk, Wittgenstein recommended that Anscombe instead read Otto Weininger's *The Four Last Things* and *Sex and Character* (Monk 1991, 498). Despite the contrast between Wittgenstein's and Anscombe's reading lists, it is doubtful whether Wittgenstein shared von Wright's enthusiasm about Jaeger's philological edifice. Wittgenstein encouraged him to read Wilhelm Busch.[44] These differences in literary taste may provide some hint of the characteristic dissimilarities that persisted amongst these three thinkers in spite of all their respectful friendship and philosophical resemblance.

There is a second post-script in Anscombe's letter to von Wright:

---

[42] I am especially thankful to Harald Johannessen for this suggestion.

[43] Anscombe often uses an abbreviation for "and" which is here transcribed as "&".

[44] For an account of Wittgenstein and von Wright's exchange on Wilhelm Busch cf.: Erbacher and Österman, 2014.

I delay a day or two even in posting this—and now I hear from Cambridge that you are elected (from my husband, who asks me to send you his good wishes & congratulation.)—I am extremely glad. (Anscombe to von Wright, Mai 1948)

On 15th May 1948, von Wright received the official telegram offering him the professorship. Two days later von Wright wrote to Broad:

I have to-day cabled to the Vice-Chancellor that I accept the invitation to the professorship. I feel very much surprised, overwhelmed and honoured. I shall do my best to become a good professor, and I hope I shall not fail in my efforts. (von Wright to Broad, 17. May 17, 1948)

Gilbert Ryle, professor at Oxford and one of the electors, telegraphed to von Wright: "You will be respected for your work and welcomed for yourself" (von Wright 2001, 133) — a message that certainly encouraged von Wright to meet his new and daunting task. After all, von Wright was only 32 years old when he filled Wittgenstein's shoes as professor of philosophy at Cambridge.

2.6   Wittgenstein and Anscombe 2 (1948–1951)

By the time von Wright arrived at Cambridge to assume his professorial duties, Wittgenstein had already moved to Ireland in order to finish his book. After his last lecture, he visited Rhees in Swansea and he had his latest remarks on the philosophy of psychology typed. Wittgenstein took the resulting typescript to Dublin in December 1947 (Wittgenstein 2000a, Ts 229; later published in: Wittgenstein 1980a). He stayed at a farm in the south of Dublin owned by a colleague of his friend Maurice Drury who had recently been appointed psychiatrist at St. Patrick's Hospital. At first Wittgenstein's work went well. Around Easter 1948, however, illness and depression stopped the auspicious flow. Once more Wittgenstein began doubting whether he would ever finish his book. Towards the end of April, he secluded himself further by moving into a small cabin on the west coast of Ireland. There his work improved, slowly at first, but with increasing productivity as summer approached. Except for a visit from his friend Ben Richards and daily meetings with his "assistant" Tommy, who had to burn pages of rejected remarks, Wittgenstein spent the summer living and working in isolation (Monk 1991, 525–526). In the autumn of 1948, Wittgenstein went to Vienna to visit his sister Hermine who was seriously ill. On his way back to Ireland he stopped in Cambridge where he had his recently revised remarks typed (Wittgenstein 2000a, Ts 232; later published in Wittgenstein 1980b). While staying in Cambridge, he discussed the *Philosophical Investigations* with Anscombe and lent her a typescript of the work (Wittgenstein 2000a, Ts 227a; referred to as "Spätfassung" (late version): in: Wittgenstein 2001).

Wittgenstein had initially planned to spend the winter of 1948/49 in his cabin at the Irish coast, but instead decided to remain in Dublin and moved into the

Ross Hotel. It was there that he experienced a rush of creativity, as he wrote to Malcolm:

> When I came here I found to my surprise that I could work again; and as I am anxious to make hay during the very short period when the sun shines in my brain I've decided not to go to Rosro this winter but to stay here where I've got a warm and quiet room. (Wittgenstein to Malcolm, 6. November 1948)

In a period of intense work lasting from October to December 1948, Wittgenstein completed a series of manuscripts on the philosophy of psychology (Ms 137, Wittgenstein 2000a). During the first half of December, Anscombe came to visit. They discussed the new work and Wittgenstein indicated to her that it should be incorporated into his book.[45] Around the same time, he wrote to Moore with a view to make sure that his manuscripts should be given to his executors (Wittgenstein to Moore, 16. December 1948). Shortly after Anscombe's departure, in the second half of December, Rhees visited Wittgenstein at the Ross Hotel. The two discussed Wittgenstein's new remarks and Rhees, like Anscombe, was told that they should be incorporated into his book.[46] On New Year's Eve, one day before Rhees left Dublin, Wittgenstein informed Moore:

> My executors are Rhees and Burnaby of Trinity. (Wittgenstein to Moore, 31. December 1948)[47]

Wittgenstein stayed in Ross Hotel for the first half of 1949, with the exception of a visit to Vienna in April (cf. Wittgenstein 2012, 396–407). He was ill for many weeks during spring, but eventually able to travel to Cambridge in late June. Here he had typed his new remarks. The resulting typescript would later be used for printing Part II of Rhees and Anscombe's posthumous edition of the *Philosophical Investigations*.[48] During the typing process, Wittgenstein and Anscombe had lunch together several times, as she later told von Wright:

> I remember his reading it a bit and exclaiming at some point 'Gescheit!' (Anscombe to von Wright, 15. April 1991)[49]

---

[45] This information was the reason to include "PART II" in Anscombe and Rhees' edition of the *Philosophical Investigations* (1953). The relevant quotes can be found in chapter 1.

[46] See footnote 48.

[47] Rev. John Burnaby was an ordained priest, fellow of Trinity College, Junior Bursar and, in 1948, Dean of Chapel and University lecturer in Divinity. Later he became Regius Professor of Divinity; according to a note in a personal conversation with Michael Nedo, Burnaby declined the proposal to become Wittgenstein's executor.

[48] Ts now lost; last existing pre-version: Wittgenstein 2000a, Ms 144; published in: Wittgenstein 2001.

[49] 'Gscheit!' is an idiomatic expression in Austrian dialect; it is difficult to translate, but helpful approximations may be "bright!","smart!", "shrewd!", but also "well done!".

While staying in Cambridge, Wittgenstein was the guest of von Wright who rented a large house on Lady Margaret Road. Here they sometimes enjoyed tea in the garden. Half jokingly, Wittgenstein even offered to design a house that von Wright was planning to build—a proposal that, to von Wright's relief, went unfulfilled. About their discussions during that period, von Wright later gave a report:

> When Wittgenstein was with us, he and I had daily talks, sometimes on things he was working on then, sometimes on the logical topics which were mine at the time, but most often on literature and music, on religion, and on what could perhaps best be termed the philosophy of history and civilization. Wittgenstein sometimes read to me from his favourite authors, for example, from Grimm's Maerchen or Gottfried Keller's *Zuericher Novellen*. The recollection of his voice and facial expression when, seated in a chair in his sickroom, he read aloud Goethe's *Hermann und Dorothea* is for me unforgettable. (von Wright 1990, 15)
>   His reading was full of expression and precision, without any theatricality. (von Wright 2001, 129, translated by Christian Erbacher)

Von Wright felt that his mutual sympathy with Wittgenstein was rooted in these shared non-philosophical interests, in their shared taste in art and their common background of central European culture (von Wright 2001, 74). Discussions between Anscombe and Wittgenstein, by contrast, seem to have been more directly focused on philosophy. Once she noted to von Wright that she considered it "a very striking fact about Wittgenstein's thought that he reverts to problems of Greek philosophy" (Anscombe to von Wright, Mai 1948). She continued:

> one of the things for which I am grateful to him is that he has caused me to read Plato and Parmenides with more understanding. (Anscombe to von Wright, Mai 1948)

In fact, Anscombe was working on an essay in which she used the means she had learned from Wittgenstein to treat a philosophical problem the first expression of which she had found in Parmenides: the question of whether we must regard the concept of the past as a delusion, since there is no state of affairs to which statements about the past can point. In this formulation, the problem of our knowledge of past time is the question how statements about the past can have meaning. In her essay entitled *The Reality of the Past* (Anscombe 1950, 113), Anscombe presented the inclination to construct a theory of knowledge about past events as a foundation for how statements about the past can be true. This led her to take into consideration possible theories of memory and consciousness. By introducing intriguing scenarios of how we actually do and possibly can meaningfully speak about the past, she delicately and carefully sorted out misleading analogies in our striving for such general theoretical accounts. Working through the problem piecemeal, Anscombe identified the source of her philosophical perplexity:

> The idea of the past as something *there*, to which true statements about the past correspond as a description corresponds to the object that we can compare with it, is what produces the puzzlement of which this paper is a discussion; for now when I wish, as it were, to locate this object I cannot do so. (Anscombe 1950, 113)

Anscombe would not come up with a coherent theory that would justify our way of speaking about the past, yet her scenarios from everyday life showed that we do understand the examples of talking about the past. How then can statements about the past have meaning? Echoing von Wright's conclusion in his early talk to the Moral Sciences Club in spring 1939, Anscombe tunes into a philosophical dissolution by refusing to provide a theory and, instead, treating the demand for a theory: "The purpose of answering the question 'How does the past tense have meaning?' by giving a description of use is to make one think that this search for a justification is a mistake" (Anscombe 1950, 118).

Anscombe was very clear about the fact that she owed to Wittgenstein the course of her discussion in *The Reality of the Past*. She ends her essay thus:

> And so far I can judge, only the account of meaning given by Wittgenstein enables one without begging the question to introduce mention of actual past events into one's account of knowing the past that one *has* witnessed. This is made possible precisely by that feature of his method which is most difficult to accept: namely, that he attacks the effort at justification. (Anscombe 1950, 118)

Anscombe had been working on *The Reality of the Past* since 1948,[50] and it was published in a volume of essays by several of Wittgenstein's students in 1950. Thus, it is likely that Anscombe has shown it to Wittgenstein before publication. If so, it is telling since *The Reality of the Past* can really be read as an application of Wittgenstein's thought and method. Anscombe was aware of this and made it patently clear in a footnote:

> Everywhere in this paper I have imitated his ideas and methods of discussion. The best I have written is a weak copy of some features of the original, and its value depends only on my capacity to understand and use Dr Wittgenstein's work. (Anscombe 1950, 50)

This footnote is interesting in light of how furious Wittgenstein was with earlier attempts to paraphrase his ideas: against this background, it is informative that he did not intervene in Anscombe's article.[51] Indeed, Anscombe's essay seems to differ in one crucial aspect from other author's publications that Wittgenstein had condemned: whereas earlier writers may have claimed to present original thinking while imitating Wittgenstein, Anscombe admitted imitation while presenting original thinking.[52] *The Reality of the Past* does not mimic Wittgenstein's style

---

[50] Anscombe mentioned this in her letter to von Wright, Mai 1948.

[51] I am especially indebted to James Conant for making me see the relevance of Anscombe's essay *Reality of the Past* in the context of the question how it came that Anscombe was asked to translate the *Philosophical Investigations*.

[52] I owe to the anonymous reviewer for JHAP the following suggestion that is worth quoting here: "Another case backs up this general line of thinking. For John Wisdom published a paper entitled 'Philosophical Perplexity' in the 1936/7 *Proceedings of the Aristotelian Society*, and Wittgenstein did not complain. In it Wisdom wrote an acknowledgement very similar to Anscombe's (in his first footnote): "Wittgenstein has not read this over-compressed paper and I warn people against supposing it a closer imitation of Wittgenstein than it is. On the other hand

nor does it lightheartedly repeat his slogans. Anscombe makes effective use of Wittgenstein's method in order to clarify her genuine philosophical puzzlement. Unlike Wittgenstein, she follows a clear argumentative structure that proceeds from one step to the next in order to untie the intellectual knot. Like Wittgenstein, however, she uses a language that is simple, strong and so dense that it requires slow reading. If Wittgenstein saw the article, he certainly noticed these stylistic qualities and this might have further contributed to the idea that Anscombe could be the right person for translating the *Philosophical Investigations*. He knew her capability to render his words into English from earlier experiments, as this recollection of Anscombe shows:

> In 1946 I decided to learn German, and started with Hugo. I told Wittgenstein, and he said 'Oh, I am very glad, for if you learn German, then I can give you my book to read'. This had been my hope, and it spurred me on. We read the introduction to Frege's Grundlagen together. He professed amazed admiration at my laying hold of the construction of the sentences. He said, what no doubt was true, that it must have been the fruit of a training in Latin. But I was struck by the incongruousness of his admiring the exercise of so elementary a skill, which I thought a very slight display of intelligence, when one could get into fearful trouble in his lectures for not grasping something which I was sure it needed great powers and hard thought to grasp. We eventually read the early part of the Investigations; I remember he reacted with real pleasure when I told him that I had read to §35 and had found it intoxicating; which was the case. As we read it we discussed translating it—he would explain the import of words, and I would suggest an English rendering, about which he would be very enthusiastic. (I don't know if I remembered any of these when I came to translate the book for its publication in 1953.)[53]

At the latest in early 1950, Anscombe had "committed herself to translating the *Investigations* and wanted to equip herself for the task with a good knowledge of Viennese German." (Geach 1988, xiii) For this purpose, Wittgenstein arranged for

---

I can hardly exaggerate the debt I owe to him and how much of the good in this work is his-not only in the treatment of this philosophical difficulty and that but in the matter of how to do philosophy. As far as possible I have put a W against examples I owe to him. It must not be assumed that they are used in a way he would approve." It seems to me that both Wisdom's and Anscombe's acknowledgements make two points that were jointly necessary for Wittgenstein not to get angry: (i) they make a full-throated acknowledgement that many of the ideas in the work are taken directly from or derived from Wittgenstein; and (ii) they equally acknowledge that in the transfer process they may have distorted them from Wittgenstein's original intention. Wittgenstein's annoyance with Waismann seems to have derived from the lack of (i) in his paper; and his annoyance with Braithwaite seems to have derived from lack of (ii)." Cf. Wisdom 1937.

[53] Transcript from Ancombe's notebook. I thank Prof. Luke Gormally for sending this transcript to me and Dr. Mary Geach for permitting to quote it. Prof. Gormally added the following note: "Hugo refers to a series of elementary language learning texts, including German."

her to spend several months in Vienna in spring 1950.[54] At least during a part of this visit she stayed in the house of Wittgenstein's friend Ludwig Hänsel.[55]

Wittgenstein too was in Vienna in early 1950, principally to visit his sister Hermine for the last time. He had then returned from visiting Malcolm in Ithaca, New York. Already during this journey, he had appeared weakened himself, and after returning to England in November 1949, he had been diagnosed with cancer. In Vienna in early 1950, Anscombe and Wittgenstein met for discussions two to three times a week (cf. Wittgenstein to von Wright, 12. February 1950). Once they attended a meeting of the philosophical circle around Viktor Kraft, a member of the former Vienna Circle who was just finishing a summarizing book on this philosophical movement (Kraft 1950). Being a student of Kraft, Paul Feyerabend was also present at that meeting. As a result of the discussion, Feyerabend wished to write a doctoral dissertation under Wittgenstein's supervision—a wish that the course of Wittgenstein's life left unfulfilled.

By April 1950, Wittgenstein and Anscombe had returned to England and Wittgenstein moved into Anscombe's house in Oxford. They most likely discussed the translation of his book. Given his keen interest in earlier translations of his work, it is hard to imagine that he would have lived in the same house with his translator and not paid due attention to the process underway. In fact, Jenny Teichman, a friend of Anscombe's family, wrote that the translation "was carried out under his guidance" (Teichmann 2001, 2). According to Peter Geach, the translation of all remarks in the then-current version of the *Philosophical Investigations* was finished while Wittgenstein was still alive (Geach 1988, xiii).

During the summer of 1950, Wittgenstein waited for his friend Ben Richards to finish an exam so that they could travel together to Skjolden. Wittgenstein used the time to write about questions of knowledge and certainty, themes he had discussed with Malcolm in the United States. These new remarks, however, were not meant to go into his book (Wittgenstein 2000a, Mss 169–176; later partly published in: Wittgenstein 1969a, 1977, 1982, 1992). His work on the *Philosophical Investigations* had, it seems, come to an end. In the autumn of 1950, Wittgenstein and Richards finally took their journey to Skjolden, to the spot at the end of the Sognefjord where the philosopher had experienced an intellectual rush as a youth and achieved another breakthrough in his later work as a man in his prime. Now he was inspired once again. Despite illness, Wittgenstein even planned to return to Skjolden to resume his philosophical work. This he wrote in a letter to von Wright:

---

[54] Notes from personal conversation with Ingrid Hänsel and with Dr. Mary Geach. According to both, Anscombe was sent to Vienna by Wittgenstein. Later, Prof. Luke Gormally specified in a note to the author that Wittgenstein "arranged for her to spend nine months in Vienna in 1950 so that she could perfect her knowledge of Austrian German."

[55] Notes from personal conversation with Ingrid Hänsel. According to I. Hänsel, Anscombe lived at the house of Wittgenstein's friend Ludwig Hänsel. Cf.: Somavilla, Ilse et al. 1994.

If all goes well I shall sail on Dec. 30th and go to Skjolden again. […] I don't think I'll be able to stay in my hut because the physical work I've got to do there is too heavy for me, but an old friend told me that she'd let me stay at her farmhouse. Of course I don't know whether I'm able any more to do decent work, but at least I'm giving myself a real chance. If I can't work there I can't work anywhere. (Wittgenstein to von Wright, 7. December 1950)

Despite this flare of hope, Wittgenstein's health now deteriorated rapidly and he was unfit for the ship's departure. Anscombe informed von Wright on New Year's Day 1951:

He is still in England, as he wasn't able to make arrangements in Norway. Also he has been rather ill, but apparently it is—or ought to be—a temporary thing and to pass off in another week or two. He already seems much better after having been pretty wretched and having a good deal of pain ever since his return in November. Of course he has not been able to do any work and he told me that he had not even felt any frustration at this, but was vegetating. He spent Christmas here at the Bevans' house and has returned to Oxford today—or so I believe; this was his plan last night. (Anscombe to von Wright, 1. January 1951)

Wittgenstein suffered severe attacks of pain in the subsequent weeks (Anscombe to Wittgenstein's sister 8. June 1951). Returning to Oxford from yet another treatment session in Cambridge on 29th January 1951, he gathered witnesses to sign his will by which he entrusted Rhees, Anscombe and von Wright with the task to decide what to publish from his writings:

I GIVE to MR. R. Rhees Miss Anscombe and Professor G.H.v.Wright of Trinity College Cambridge All the copyright in all my unpublished writings and also the manuscripts and typescripts thereof to dispose of as they think best but subject to any claim by anybody else to the custody of the manuscripts and typescripts
    I intend and desire that Mr. Rhees Miss Anscombe and Professor von Wright shall publish as many of my unpublished writings as they think fit but I do not wish them to incur expenses in publication which they do not expect to recoup out of royalties or other profits (Wittgenstein's will, 29. January 1951)

In February 1951, treatments were stopped and Wittgenstein moved into the house of his medical doctor Edward V. Bevan in Cambridge. Von Wright visited him there several times, and Wittgenstein once came to see von Wright in his college office. They talked about Sergej Aksakov's 'Family Chronicle' but not about questions related to editing his papers. In fact, Wittgenstein did not tell von Wright that he was to inherit this task (von Wright 2001, 158). With Rhees, on the other hand, he directly addressed the issue. As late as ten days before his death, Wittgenstein spoke with Rhees about preparing the manuscripts for publication. According to Rhees, Wittgenstein "was particularly anxious that care should be taken in what was published and how it was presented" (Rhees to von Wright, 7. July 1965). However, when Anscombe asked Wittgenstein how they ought to deal with variant versions in his manuscripts, Wittgenstein is said to have answered that he could not help them any longer (Nedo 1993, 75). He left these decisions to the literary heirs he had chosen. In one of their last conversations about the matter and a few days before his death, Wittgenstein said to Rhees: "I trust you absolutely, and I trust Miss Anscombe absolutely" (Rhees to Kenny, 22. March 1977).

2.7   Concluding Remarks on the Chosen Heirs (1951)[56]

Wittgenstein died in April 1951. The fact that he passed the copyright for his unpublished writings on to Rhees, Anscombe and von Wright may seem like the final acknowledgement that he would not live to see his book printed. This thought, however, was already familiar to him. Finishing the *Tractatus* during World War One, he had been compelled to consider what should happen to his work if he died. This is why the very first sentence in the first of his preserved philosophical notebooks states that "After my death to be sent to Mrs. Poldy Wittgenstein XVII. Neuwaldeggerstr. 38—to be sent to Hon. B. Russell Trinity College Cambridge." (Wittgenstein 2000a, Ms 101, iii, entry from August 9, 1914).[57] In June 1917, at the age of 28, Wittgenstein wrote what may be considered his first more extensive will.[58] This concern for the posthumous fate of his writings was not exclusively caused by the life-threatening conditions of war. Since resuming philosophical writing in 1929, shortly after his return to Cambridge, he told Frank R. Leavis that "When I am engaged on a piece of work I'm always afraid I shall die before I've finished it. So I make a fair copy of the day's work, and give it to Frank Ramsey for safe-keeping" (Rhees 1984, 61).

This practice was later repeated in different forms and found its final expression in the will Wittgenstein signed in 1951, naming Rhees, Anscombe and von Wright as his literary executors. Thus it may be safely assumed that Wittgenstein did not make this choice in haste. Indeed, the presentation in this essay has aimed at showing how personal and philosophical friendships grew over many years and eventually led Wittgenstein to choose his three literary executors. At this point it may be worthwhile explicating some further suggestions for why he chose them, though much of this must naturally remain speculation.

The entire foregoing story indicates that Wittgenstein was convinced of Rhees', Anscombe's and von Wright's philosophical acumen and integrity. He had advised some of his most trusted and loyal friends to leave philosophy and pursue other more suitable occupations. This was not the case with Rhees, Anscombe or von Wright. Wittgenstein actually helped to establish their academic positions by

---

[56] I thank the anonymous reviewer from JHAP for suggesting this concluding section.

[57] The German original reads: "Nach meinem Tod zu senden an Frau Poldy Wittgenstein Wittgenstein, Leopoldine XVII. Neuwaldeggerstr. 38 Zu senden an Hon. B. Russell Russell, Bertrand Trinity College Cambridge England"; translated by Christian Erbacher.

[58] The critical edition of the *Tractatus* informs about a letter (dated June 7, 1917) that contains instructions for what should be done with Wittgenstein's manuscripts after his death; this letter may be regarded as the first will Wittgenstein wrote. Cf.: Wittgenstein 1989, XIV.

writing recommendations for each of them. Two of these recommendations still exist and have been quoted above; the third one concerning von Wright has not yet been found, but there is a letter by Wittgenstein which confirms that he indeed wrote such a letter (also quoted above); Wittgenstein concludes it by saying "If I wanted to play providence I'd write you a lukewarm recommendation; but I won't. I'll write you as good a one as you can possibly wish for. For what can I know about the future?" (Wittgenstein to von Wright, 2. February 1948).

Besides trusting their overall philosophical talent, Wittgenstein extensively discussed his work with Rhees, Anscombe and von Wright; hence he was aware of their understanding of his philosophy. This is also true for von Wright, even if he felt his friendship with Wittgenstein was based on similarities in taste and culture rather than on philosophical resemblance. This, however, points to another important aspect: none of the three were inclined or tempted to imitate Wittgenstein by using his methods or expressions in their own names. Judging from Wittgenstein's loathing of plagiarism, he certainly valued this intellectual independence.

A similar account may to some extent be given for other trusted friends whose philosophical talent Wittgenstein appreciated. But in contrast to them, Rhees, Anscombe and von Wright may have possessed further qualities especially relevant for the practical task of publishing his papers. Two aspects immediately come to mind: first, all three had a very good command of German—the language Wittgenstein almost exclusively wrote. Rhees spent long periods in Austria when studying with Kastil, Anscombe became acquainted with Austrian German when preparing herself to translate the *Philosophical Investigations* and von Wright was educated in a mainly German-speaking academic environment. Second, all three lived in Great Britain at the time of Wittgenstein's death: Rhees was a lecturer in Swansea, Anscombe was a research fellow at Oxford and von Wright had succeeded him as professor of philosophy at Cambridge. In addition to these qualities that apply to all three, other more specific qualities may have further distinguished them from other candidates. A consideration of these specific qualities may best be made in a way that follows the order in which the literary executors appear in Wittgenstein's will. This order may also reflect the temporal order of Wittgenstein's decisions to include each of them.

Rhees was the first to be chosen for the task: in a letter to Moore he was named executor as early as 1948. Since Rhees was visiting Wittgenstein when this letter was written, it may be assumed that he had been asked and had agreed. At that time, Wittgenstein had known Rhees for 15 years. Rhees had started attending Wittgenstein's lectures albeit with some hesitation, but became a regular attendee in the subsequent years. Through discussions outside class and on repeated visits, he gained insight into the development of Wittgenstein's book, witnessed his way of working and was aware of his considerations as he composed his remarks with a view towards publication. Rhees was sympathetic to Wittgenstein's second thoughts about authorship and customs of academia. Thus, Rhees shared Wittgenstein's views in many crucial respects, and Wittgenstein could be certain that Rhees would be loyal to these views. This combination of philosophical understanding and unconditional loyalty may have contributed to Wittgenstein choosing him as an executor, not only in 1948, but also in the final will from 1951:

> I appoint my friend MR. R. RHEES of 96 Bryn Road Swansea to be the EXECUTOR of this my will *and I hope that he will accept £ 50 for his personal Expenses in discharging this Trust* (Wittgenstein's will § 2)

In 1948, Wittgenstein envisaged both Rhees and Rev. John Burnaby to be his executors. When Burnaby declined, it might have been possible to leave the task to Rhees alone. In a sense this is what happened, as Rhees became the sole executor of Wittgenstein's will in 1951. However, the fact that Wittgenstein thought about entrusting the task to two men may indicate that he considered it too much of a burden for only one person. Thus, the idea of appointing a consortium of literary executors may have occurred after Burnaby declined. Since Wittgenstein had early on planned a bilingual edition of his book, Anscombe was a natural candidate. Rhees' unsuccessful attempt to translate the early version of the *Philosophical Investigations* in 1938 ruled him out as a translator. Anscombe, on the other hand, had been chosen and instructed by Wittgenstein to translate the most finished version of his book at least one year before his death. However, if Wittgenstein had wanted her to deal exclusively with the translation and not with judgments about what to publish, he would have had many opportunities to express this wish. But there is nothing to indicate that he wanted to restrict Anscombe's role to translating his writings. He may have thought that she would have a special sensibility for a different aspect of his philosophy than would Rhees. The same may be true for von Wright.[59] At any rate, Anscombe's recollections of her visit to Dublin in 1948 show that Wittgenstein informed not only Rhees but also Anscombe about his plans for how to improve his book. As this was precisely the time when he decided that Rhees ought to become his executor, he may already then have thought of integrating Anscombe into the task of publishing his writings.

Wittgenstein informed Rhees and Anscombe about the task he wanted them to do. In this respect, there is a clear difference between their appointment as literary executors and that of von Wright, who may have been the last to be included in the consortium.[60] It is striking that Wittgenstein did not even tell von Wright about his will. Why not? Did he not consider it necessary? Did he fear that von Wright would not accept? Or did he want to keep the option open of removing him from the list? The answers to these questions will probably never be known. However,

---

[59] Anthony Kenny has suggested that each of the literary executors covered one aspect of Wittgenstein's philosophy: von Wright the logical, Anscombe the philosophy of mind and Rhees the mystical. Quoted from notes of a personal conversation; see also: "The life and work of Georg Henrik von Wright", public discussion with Sir Anthony Kenny, accessible at: www.helsinki.fi/wwa/Video.html. In this connection, it is worth noting that von Wright was early on aware of the cultural context and literary quality of Wittgenstein's writings, cf. von Wright 1955.

[60] That von Wright was included last in the list of literary executors was also assumed by M. Nedo in a personal conversation.

it is thought-provoking in this context that Rhees remembered Wittgenstein saying he would absolutely trust Rhees and Anscombe, bearing in mind that this statement was made when Wittgenstein had already signed the version of his will that included von Wright as the third literary executor. The statement cannot possibly mean that Wittgenstein did not trust von Wright in general. This would not only be absurd given their relationship; had he not trusted von Wright, there would have been no reason to include him in the first place. It seems obvious that von Wright was just as loyal and trustworthy as the other two. Nevertheless, one may be inclined to understand the statement as a hint concerning the future decisions about which parts of his writings ought to be published. Indeed, Rhees seems to have understood the statement in this sense:

> And he might have said of someone that he 'did not altogether trust him', or perhaps of someone that he did not trust him at all: meaning, of course, that he trusted, or did not trust the person's judgment in deciding what should be published. For it was plain that he expected or took it as obvious that there would have to be selection, and so there would have to be decisions. (Rhees to Kenny, 22. March 1977)

The fact that von Wright did not participate in preparing the typescript for Anscombe and Rhees' edition of the *Philosophical Investigations* may be regarded as support for such an interpretation (cf. Erbacher and Krebs 2015). On the other hand, again, Wittgenstein did not, in his will, distinguish between the future roles of his literary executors. All three are included in the "they" of "what they think fit". The only documentation hinting that Wittgenstein might have been making a distinction between the three literary heirs is Rhees' double position as executor of the will and literary executor, as well as the order in which the literary executors are named. This order can be explained neither by alphabet nor by age or gender. However, this seems too weak to justify the strong interpretation of Wittgenstein's statement according to which he would not have trusted von Wright's judgment in making selections for publication. Von Wright may have considered it inappropriate to intervene in the editing of the *Philosophical Investigations* since—contrary to Rhees and Anscombe—he had not been expressly asked to do so, and neither may Rhees and Anscombe have asked him to participate in it. However, his exclusion may also be explained by the fact that he retired from his professorship and moved to Finland while the editing took place (von Wright 2001, 152–157). Furthermore, there could be many reasons for not mentioning von Wright in Wittgenstein's statement about trustworthiness. It simply may have been inappropriate to mention to Rhees that von Wright was meant to become one of the literary executors before having informed von Wright himself. But then we are left again with the question that triggered this line of thought: why did Wittgenstein not inform von Wright?

A positive reason why Wittgenstein included von Wright as a literary executor may be seen when considering once more the letter from 1948 that names Rhees and Burnaby as his executors. Placing "Burnaby of Trinity" at Rhees' side indicates that Wittgenstein wanted to ensure a strong connection to Trinity College.

Despite all his reservations about academic customs at Cambridge, Trinity College had provided an academic home for Wittgenstein for many years—for his discussions, lectures and writing. As his successor as professor of philosophy, von Wright certainly provided this connection to Trinity College. Further, as the first months of the posthumous editing show, it was advantageous that von Wright had an academically authoritative position: he played a central role in organizing the publication, in clarifying questions of copyright with publishers and college representatives and in acquiring funding that would facilitate working on the manuscripts (Erbacher and Krebs 2015). This function of von Wright may also give an idea of the special abilities he brought to the team: von Wright was an efficient manager who achieved the academic goals he set for himself and he was able to take fastidious care of all the practical necessities a decent publication would require. In addition, von Wright was a natural gentleman and diplomat. It may have occurred to Wittgenstein that von Wright could act as a mediator in cases of conflict between the other two rather uncompromising characters—one a devout Catholic, the other a strong-headed anarchist. Thus, naming von Wright as one of his literary executors significantly reduced the risk of disagreement within the group while increasing the likelihood that the endeavor of publishing his book would soon be successfully concluded.

Rhees, Anscombe and von Wright appear as a carefully chosen and balanced triumvirate of literary executors. Considering their personal integrity, philosophical ability and pragmatic capacities, it is comprehensible that Wittgenstein chose precisely these three for publishing his writings. Furthermore, he obviously felt that he could entrust them with this burden, and he knew from Rhees and Anscombe that they would accept. When appointing them, he may have thought first and foremost of publishing the *Philosophical Investigations*. This was the book that he had prepared for publication to the greatest extent. The literary executors knew this and were sure that publishing the *Philosophical Investigations* was their first task (Erbacher and Krebs 2015). However, in his will Wittgenstein referred to the entirety of his writings, and for Rhees at least, it was obvious that they should continue publishing selected material after the *Philosophical Investigations*.[61] Wittgenstein may have foreseen that they would spare no trouble in fulfilling this wish. Perhaps this is why he, in his will, reminded them not to "incur expenses in publication which they do not expect to recoup".[62] However, at that point of time, no one envisaged that Wittgenstein's last will would give rise to an editorial story that, as of today, has been expanding for 65 years.

Acknowledgements I am grateful to Peg Smythies for permitting me to quote from Rush Rhees' letters; sadly, she passed away while this essay was in preparation. Prof. Volker Munz

---

[61] An overview of subsequent phases in the history of editing Wittgenstein are presented in chapter 1.

[62] Wittgenstein's will; this statement reminds also of Wittgenstein's unwillingness to pay for the paper and the printing of the *Tractatus* in 1919, cf. McGuinness 1988, 287.

renewed her permission. The copyright for the letters and notes by G. E. M. Anscombe belongs to Mrs M. C. Gormally (Dr Mary Geach) who has given permission for publication. Anita and Benedict von Wright granted permission to quote from Georg Henrik von Wright's letters. The *Richard Burton Archives* at the University of Swansea (RBA) granted permission to quote from the letters of Rush Rhees and Alfred Kastil that are in their possession. Permission to quote from Rhees' letter to Alfred Kastil was granted from the *Franz Brentano Archiv Graz* and Prof. Volker Munz who represents the copyright-holder of Rhees' letters in this case. Permission to quote from Wittgenstein's will was granted by The Master and Fellows of Trinity College Cambridge. I am thankful to the *Wittgenstein Archives at the University of Bergen* (WAB), *The von Wright and Wittgenstein Archives at the University of Helsinki* (WWA), the *National Library of Finland* (NLF), The *Richard Burton Archives* at the University of Swansea and the *Franz Brentano Archiv Graz* for providing access to resources and to their holdings of quoted correspondence and other materials.

This work was funded by the Research Council of Norway as part of the project "Shaping a Domain of Knowledge by Editorial Processing: The Case of Wittgenstein's Work" (NFR 213080) and by the Deutsche Forschungsgemeinschaft (DFG) as part of the Collaborative Research Centre "Media of Cooperation" (SFB 1187).

Many people have aided me in my research and writing underpinning this essay. More than anyone else, Ralph Jewell inspired me to write this story. Earlier versions of the present text were presented to the Department of Philosophy at the University of Bergen and to the Department of Philosophy at the University of Helsinki. Participants of these presentations generously contributed their views and knowledge. Bernt Österman shared his valuable insights during many additional discussions. James Conant, Cora Diamond, Luke Gormally, Ingrid Hänsel, Claus Huitfeldt, Anthony Kenny, Brian McGuinness, Anselm Müller, Michael Nedo, Alois Pichler, Mario von der Ruhr and Anita and Benedict von Wright very kindly supported this work through interviews and conversations that improved the essay considerably. For language corrections I wish to thank Harald Johannessen, James Klagge, David LaRocca, Sonja Lewandowski, Arlyne Moi, Tina Schirmer and Konstantin Seitz. James Klagge further contributed by commenting on historical facts.

List of Letters and Archival Sources

For the sake of brevity, the following abbreviations are used:
NLF = National Library of Finland
RBA = Richard Burton Archives at the University of Swansea
WWA = Von Wright and Wittgenstein Archives at the University of Helsinki
Wittgenstein to Waisman, 19. May 19, 1936, quoted in: Pichler, Alois. 2004. *Wittgensteins Philosophische Untersuchungen. Vom Buch zum Album.* Amsterdam: Rodopi, 135.
Anscombe to von Wright, 13. October 1947, NLF, COLL. 714.11-12.
Anscombe to von Wright, Mai 1948, NLF, COLL. 714.11-12.
Anscombe to von Wright, 1. January 1951, NLF, COLL. 714.11-12.
Anscombe to von Wright, 15. April 1991, NLF, COLL. 714.11-12.
Anscombe to Wittgenstein's sister 8. June 1951, quoted from an offer for sale by Kotte Autographs GmbH, Germany.
Broad to von Wright, 17. July 1939, NLF, COLL. 714.28-32.

Keynes to Wittgenstein, 11. February 1939, Wittgenstein 2012, letter 243.

Rhees to Kastil, 5. November 1933, Franz Brentano Archive at the University of Graz, inventory number 000616-000622.

Rhees to Kastil, 5. January 1935, Franz Brentano Archive Graz, inventory number 000643-000645; original in German, translation by Tina Schirmer and Christian Erbacher.

Rhees to Kenny, 22. March 1977, copy at WWA. An edited version of this letter has been published in: Rhees, Rush. 1996. "On Editing Wittgenstein", edit by D. Z. Phillips, Philosophical Investigations, 19(1): 55–61.

Rhees to McGuinness, 6. May 1963, RBA, UNI/SU/PC/1/1/3/5.

Rhees to von Wright, 7. July 1965, WWA.

Rhees to von Wright, 27. February 1969, WWA.

Rhees to von Wright, 10. August 1972, WWA.

Rhees to von Wright, 22. January 1976, WWA.

Rhees to von Wright, 13. May 1977, RBA, UNI/SU/PC/1/2/1/3.

Rhees to Wittgenstein, 31. December 1940, Wittgenstein 2012, letter 288.

von Wright to Broad, 17. May 1948, NLF, COLL. 714.28-32.

von Wright to Schildt, 15. June 1947, in: von Wright, Georg Henrik. 2008. En livslång vänskap: brevväxlingen mellan Göran Schildt och Georg Henrik von Wright 1937–2001. Edited by E. Kruskopf. Christine och Göran Schildts stiftelse. Translation of the letter by Bernt Österman.

von Wright to Wittgenstein, 27. August 1939, Wittgenstein 2012, letter 259.

von Wright to Wittgenstein, 22. February 1940, Wittgenstein 2012, letter 269.

von Wright to Wittgenstein, 31. July 1947, Wittgenstein 2012, letter 370.

Wittgenstein to Keynes, 8. February 1939, Wittgenstein 2012, letter 242.

Wittgenstein to Malcolm, 30. April 1948, Wittgenstein 2012, letter 385.

Wittgenstein to Malcolm, 6. November 1948, Wittgenstein 2012, letter 393.

Wittgenstein to Moore, 1. February 1939, Wittgenstein 2012, letter 240.

Wittgenstein to Moore, 16. December 1948, Wittgenstein 2012, letter 394.

Wittgenstein to Moore, 31. December 1948, Wittgenstein 2012, letter 395.

Wittgenstein to Rhees, 13. July 1938, Wittgenstein 2012, letter 227.

Wittgenstein to Rhees, 3. October 1938, Wittgenstein 2012, letter 233.

Wittgenstein to Rhees, 6. October 6, 1938, Wittgenstein 2012, letter 234.

Wittgenstein to Rhees, 9. September 1938, Wittgenstein 2012, letter 230.

Wittgenstein to Rhees, 13. September 1939, Wittgenstein 2012, letter 261.

Wittgenstein to Rhees, 14. August 1940, Wittgenstein 2012, letter 281.

Wittgenstein to Rhees, 28. November 1944, Wittgenstein 2012, letter 321.

Wittgenstein to Rhees, 21. May 1946, Wittgenstein 2012, letter 352.

Wittgenstein to Russell, 28. November 1935, Wittgenstein 2012, letter 199.

Wittgenstein to von Wright, 13. September 1939, Wittgenstein 2012, letter 263.

Wittgenstein to von Wright, 21. February 1947, Wittgenstein 2012, letter 361.

Wittgenstein to von Wright, 22. December 1947, Wittgenstein 2012, letter 378.

Wittgenstein to von Wright, 2. February 1948, Wittgenstein 2012, letter 381.

Wittgenstein to von Wright, 23. February 1948, Wittgenstein 2012, letter 381.

Wittgenstein to von Wright, 12. February 1950, Wittgenstein 2012, letter 419.

Wittgenstein to von Wright, 7. December 1950, Wittgenstein 2012, letter 430.

Letter of recommendation, Easter 1935, Richard Burton Archives, UNI/SU/PC/1/1/2/3. Cf. Erbacher, C. & Schirmer, T. Forthcoming. "On Continuity: Rush Rhees on Outer and Inner surfaces of Bodies", Philosophical Investigations, 39.

von Wright, talk to Moral Sciences Club 1947, typescript for the talk kept at WWA.

von Wright, talk to the Moral Sciences Club 1939, quoted from the typescript for the talk kept at WWA.

Recommendation Wittgenstein to Curtis, 18. May 1945, Wittgenstein 2012, letter 324.

Wittgenstein's will § 2, copy at WWA. The sentence in italics represents an addition in Wittgenstein's hand, here transcribed by Christian Erbacher.

Wittgenstein's will, 29. January 1951, copy at WWA.

References

Anscombe, Elizabeth. 1950. "The Reality of the Past", Philosophical Analysis: A Collection of Essays. Edited by M. Black. Ithaca: Cornell University Press.

Anscombe, Elisabeth. 1981a. *Metaphysics and the Philosophy of Mind. The Collected Philosophical Papers of G. E. M. Anscombe. Vol. II*. Oxford: Blackwell and Minneapolis: University of Minnesota Press.

Anscombe, Elizabeth. 1981b. *Ethics, Religion and Politics. The Collected Philosophical Papers of G. E. M. Anscombe. Vol. III*. Oxford: Blackwell and Minneapolis: University of Minnesota Press.

Bouwsma, Oets K. 1961. The Blue Book. In *The Journal of Philosophy* 58(6): 141–162.

Brentano, Franz. 1968. *Kategorienlehre*. Edited by A. Kastil. Hamburg: Meiner.

Broad, Charlie D. 1959a. Review of 'Ludwig Wittgenstein—A Memoir. In *Universities Quarterly* (=Higher Education Quarterly) 13(3): 304–306.

Broad, Charlie D. 1959b. *Intellectual Autobiography. The Philosophy of C.D. Broad. Library of Living Philosophers Vol. 10*. Edited by L. E. Hahn and P. A. Schilpp. New York: Tudor.

Brouwer, Luitzen. 1996. The structure of the Continuum. In *From Kant to Hilbert. A source book in the foundations of mathematics*. Edited by W. Ewald. Oxford: Clarendon Press.

Erbacher, Christian. 2016. Wittgenstein and his literary executors. Rush Rhees, Georg Henrik von Wright and Elizabeth Anscombe as students, colleagues and friends of Ludwig Wittgenstein. In *Journal for the History of Analytical Philosophy* 4(3): 1–39.

Erbacher, Christian and Krebs, Sophia Victoria. 2015. The First Nine Months of Editing Wittgenstein: Letters from G. E. M. Anscombe and R. Rhees to G. H. v. Wright. In *Nordic Wittgenstein Review* 4(1): 195–231.

Erbacher, Christian, and Österman, B. 2014. A Passport Photo for Two. On an Allusion in the pictures of Wittgenstein and von Wright in Cambridge. In *Nordic Wittgenstein Review* 3(1): 139–149.

Erbacher, Christian, and Schirmer, T. 2017. On Continuity: Rush Rhees on Outer and Inner surfaces of Bodies. In *Philosophical Investigations* 40(1): 3–30.

Geach, Mary. 2008. Introduction. In *Faith In A Hard Ground: Essays On Religion, Philosophy and Ethics*. Edited Mary Geach and Luke Gormally, xiii–xxvi. St. Andrews: St. Andrews Studies in Philosophy and Public Affairs.

Geach, Mary. 2011. Introduction. In *From Plato to Wittgenstein*. Edited by M. Geach and L. Gormally, xiii–xx St. Andrews: St. Andrews Studies in Philosophy and Public Affairs.

Geach, Peter. 1969. The moral Law and the Law of God. In *God and the Soul*. London: Routledge & Kegan.

Geach, Peter. 1988. "Editor's Preface" In *Wittgenstein's Lectures on Philosophical Psychology 1946–1947*, ed. Peter T. Geach, xii–xv. Chicago: Chicago University Press.

Jaeger, Werner. 1934–1947. *Padeia. Die Formung des griechischen Menschen*. Berlin: De Gruyter.

Kaila, Eino. 1979. *Reality and Experience—Four Philosophical Essays*. Edited by R. S. Cohen. With an Introduction by G. H. von Wright. Dodrecht: Reidl.

Kant, Immanuel. 1929. *Immanuel Kant's Critique of Pure Reason*. Translated by Norman Kemp-Smith. London: Macmillan.

Kemp-Smith, Norman. 1918. *A Commentary to Kant's 'Critique of Pure Reason'*. London: Macmillan.

Körner, Stephan and Chisholm, Roderick M. 2010. Editors' Introduction to the English Edition. In *Philosophical Investigations on Space, Time and the Continuum*, Franz Brentano. New York: Routledge.

Kraft, Victor. 1950. *Der Wiener Kreis. Der Ursprung des Neopositivismus. Ein Kapitel der jüngsten Philosophiegeschichte*. Wien: Springer.

Lewis, Clive Staples. 1947. *Miracles*. London and Glasgow: Collins/Fontana. (Revised edition appeared in 1960).

Malcolm, Norman. 1958. *Ludwig Wittgenstein—A memoir*. London: Oxford University Press.

McGuinness, Brian. 1988. *Wittgenstein A Life. Young Ludwig*. London: Duckworth.

Monk, Ray. 1991. *Ludwig Wittgenstein—The Duty of Genius*. London: Vintage.

Monk, Ray. 2000. *Bertrand Russell. The Ghost of Madness*. London: Jonathan Cape.

Nedo, Michael. 1993. *Einführung in die Wiener Ausgabe*. Wien: Springer.

Phillips, Dewi Z. 2006. Rush Rhees: a biographical sketch. In *Wittgenstein and the Possibility of Discourse*. Edited by D. Z. Phillips. 2nd edition. Malden: Blakcwell.

Pichler, Alois. 2004. *Wittgensteins Philosophische Untersuchungen. Vom Buch zum Album*. Amsterdam: Rodopi.

Redpath, Theodore. 1990. *Ludwig Wittgenstein—A Student's Memoir*. London: Duckworth.

Rhees, Rush. 1970. *Discussions of Wittgenstein*. London: Routledge.

Rhees, Rush (ed.). 1984. *Recollections of Wittgenstein*. Oxford: Oxford University Press.

Rhees, Rush. 1996. On Editing Wittgenstein. In *Philosophical Investigations* 19(1): 55–61, ed. D. Z. Phillips.

Rhees, Rush. 2006. *Wittgenstein and the Possibility of Discourse*. Edited by D.Z. Phillips. 2nd edition. Malden: Blackwell.

Smythies, Yorick. 2017. *Wittgenstein's Whewell Court lectures: Cambridge 1938–1941, From the Notes by Yorick Smythies*. Edited by Volker Munz and Bernhard Ritter. Oxford: Wiley-Blackwell.

Somavilla, Ilse et al. 1994. *Ludwig Hänsel—Ludwig Wittgenstein. Eine Freundschaft. Briefe. Aufsätze. Kommentare*. Innsbruck: Haymon.

Spengler, Oswald. 1922. *Der Untergang des Abendlandes*. Vol. 2. München: C. H. Beck.

Spengler, Oswald. 1923. *Der Untergang des Abendlandes*. Vol. 1. München: C. H. Beck.

Stadler, Friedrich. 1997. *Studien zum Wiener Kreis. Ursprung, Entwicklung und Wirkung des Logischen Empirismus im Kontext*. Frankfurt/Main: Suhrkamp.

Teichmann, Jenny. 2001. (Getrude) Elizabeth Margaret Anscombe (1919–2001). Oxford Dictionary of National Biography. http://www.oxforddnb.com/. Accessed 10. December 2013.

Teichmann, Roger. 2008. *The Philosophy of Elizabeth Anscombe*. Oxford: Oxford University Press.

Von Hugel, Friedrich. 1981. *The Letters of Baron Friedrich von Hugel and Professor Norman Kemp-Smith*. Edited by L. F. Barmann, New York: Fordham University Press.

Von Wright, Georg Henrik. 1938. Logistik filosofi. In *Nya Argus* 13: 175–177.

Von Wright, Georg Henrik. 1940. On Probability. In *Mind* 49: 265–283.
Von Wright, Georg Henrik. 1943. *Den logiska empirismen. En huvudriktning i modern filosofi.* Helsingfors: Söderströms.
Von Wright, Georg Henrik. 1947. Paideia. In *Nya Argus* 40: 229–231.
Von Wright, Georg Henrik. 1990. Intellectual Autobiography. In *The Philosophy of Georg Henrik Von Wright, Library of Living Philosophers* Volume 19, ed. L. E. Hahn and P. A. Schilpp. Chicago: Open Court.
Von Wright, Georg Henrik. 1995. Wittgenstein and Twentieth Century. In *Wittgenstein: Mind and Language*, ed. E. Egidi, 1–19. Dodrecht: Kluwer.
Von Wright, Georg Henrik. 2001. *Mitt Liv som jeg minns det.* Helsingfors: Söderström.
Von Wright, Georg Henrik. 2008. *En livslång vänskap: brevväxlingen mellan Göran Schildt och Georg Henrik von Wright 1937–2001.* Edited by E. Kurskopf. Christine och Göran Schildts stiftelse.
Waismann, Friedrich. 1976. *Logik, Sprache, Philosophie.* Stuttgart: Reclam.
Wisdom, John. 1937. Philosophical Perplexity. In *Proceedings of the Aristotelian Society* 37: 71–88.
Wittgenstein, Ludwig, Rhees, Rush, Citron, Gabriel (ed.). 2015. Wittgenstein's Philosophical Conversations with Rush Rhees (1939–50): From the Notes of Rush Rhees. In *Mind* 124(493): 1–71.
Wittgenstein, Ludwig. 1933. Letter to the Editor. In *Mind* 42: 415–416.
Wittgenstein, Ludwig. 1953. *Philosophical Investigations.* Edited by G. E. M. Anscombe and R. Rhees, Oxford: Basil Blackwell.
Wittgenstein, Ludwig. 1958. *Preliminary Studies for the "Philosophical Investigations". Generally Known as The Blue and Brown Books.* Edited by R. Rhees. Oxford: Basil Blackwell.
Wittgenstein, Ludwig. 1966. *Lectures and Conversations.* Edited by C. Barrett. Oxford: Basil Blackwell.
Wittgenstein, Ludwig. 1969a. *On Certainty / Über Gewißheit.* Edited by G. E. M. Anscombe and G. H. von Wright. Oxford: Basil Blackwell.
Wittgenstein, Ludwig. 1969b. *Philosophische Grammatik.* Edited by Rush Rhees. Oxford: Basil Blackwell.
Wittgenstein, Ludwig. 1976a. *Wittgenstein's Lectures on the Foundations of Mathematics: Cambridge, 1939.* Edited by C. Diamond. Ithaca: Cornell University Press.
Wittgenstein, Ludwig. 1976b. *Remarks on the Foundations of Mathematics.* Edited by G. H. von Wright, R. Rhees und G. E. M. Anscombe. Third edition, revised and reset, parts IV, V, VI, VII. Oxford: Basil Blackwell.
Wittgenstein, Ludwig. 1977. *Remarks on Colour / Bemerkungen über die Farben.* Edited by G. E. M. Anscombe. Oxford: Basil Blackwell.
Wittgenstein, Ludwig. 1980a. *Remarks on the Philosophy of Psychology / Bemerkungen über die Philosophie der Psychologie*, Vol. 1. Edited by G. E. M. Anscombe und G. H. von Wright. Oxford: Basil Blackwell.
Wittgenstein, Ludwig. 1980b. *Remarks on the Philosophy of Psychology / Bemerkungen über die Philosophie der Psychologie*, Vol. 2. Edited by G. H. von Wright und H. Nyman. Oxford: Basil Blackwell.
Wittgenstein, Ludwig. 1980c. *Culture and Value.* Edited by G. H. v. Wright. Oxford: Basil Blackwell.
Wittgenstein, Ludwig. 1982. *Wittgenstein's Lectures: Cambridge, 1930–1932.* Edited by D. Lee. Oxford: Basil Blackwell.
Wittgenstein, Ludwig. 1988. *Wittgenstein's Lectures on Philosophical Psychology 1946–1947.* Edited by P. T. Geach. Chicago: Chicago University Press.
Wittgenstein, Ludwig. 1989. *Logisch-philosophische Abhandlung / Tractatus logico-philosophicus. Critical edition.* Edited by B. McGuinness and J. Schulte. Frankfurt: Suhrkamp.

Wittgenstein, Ludwig. 1992. *Last Writings on the Philosophy of Psychology / Letzte Schriften über die Philosophie der Psychologie*. Vol. 2. Edited by G. H. von Wright und Heikki Nyman. Oxford: Basil Blackwell.

Wittgenstein, Ludwig. 2000a. *'The Big Typescript'*. Wien: Springer.

Wittgenstein, Ludwig. 2000b. *Wittgenstein's Nachlass. The Bergen Electronic Edition*. Edited by the Wittgenstein Archives at the University of Bergen. Oxford: Oxford University Press.

Wittgenstein, Ludwig. 2001. *Philosophische Untersuchungen. Kritisch-genetische Edition*. Edited by J. Schulte in cooperation with Heikki Nyman, Eike von Savigny und G. H. von Wright. Frankfurt a. M.: Suhrkamp.

Wittgenstein, Ludwig. 2003. *Ludwig Wittgenstein—Public and Private Occasions*. Edited by J. C. Klagge and A. Nordmann. Maryland: Rowman & Littlefield.

Wittgenstein, Ludwig. 2009. *Philosophical Investigations*. 4th edition. Edited by P. M. S. Hacker and J. Schulte. Translated by E. Anscombe, P. M. S. Hacker and J. Schulte. Oxford, New York: Wiley-Blackwell.

Wittgenstein, Ludwig. 2011 *Gesamtbriefwechsel - Innsbrucker elektronische Ausgabe*. 2nd release. Edited by A. Coda, G. Citron, B. Halder, A. Janik, U. Lobis, K. Mayr, B. McGuinness, M. Schorner, M. Seekircher and J. Wang for the Forschungsinstitut Brenner-Archiv. Innsbruck: Forschungsinstitut Brenner-Archiv.

Wittgenstein, Ludwig. 2012. *Wittgenstein in Cambridge—Letters and Documents 1911–1951*. Edited by Brian F. McGuinness. Malden: Wiley-Blackwell.

Wittgenstein, Ludwig. 2016. *Lectures, Cambridge 1930–1933. From the Notes of G. E. Moore*. Edited by D. Stern, B. Rogers and G. Citron. Cambridge: Cambridge University Press.

"Ludwig Wittgenstein"

A BBC radio talk by Elizabeth Anscombe in May 1953

3.1   Introduction

In October 1944, after a prolonged leave of absence during the Second World War, Wittgenstein resumed lecturing at Cambridge University. Among the attendees of his lectures that dealt with the philosophy of psychology was Elizabeth Anscombe, who had come to Cambridge with a studentship from Newnham College (Wittgenstein 2003, 355–356). She had already shown her extraordinary capacity for philosophical questions while studying at St. Hugh's College in Oxford, but it was only in Wittgenstein's classes that she experienced an extraction of the "central nerve" of her philosophical perplexities (Anscombe 1981, xiii–xiv). In turn, Wittgenstein soon recognized Anscombe as being one of the ten best students he ever had (cf. Wittgenstein 2012, No. 324). Before another year had passed, Anscombe started to learn German:

> I told Wittgenstein, and he said 'Oh, I am very glad, for if you learn German, then I can give you my book to read'. This had been my hope, and it spurred me on. We read the introduction to Frege's Grundlagen together. He professed amazed admiration at my laying hold of the construction of the sentences. He said, what no doubt was true, that it must have been the fruit of a training in Latin. But I was struck by the incongruousness of his admiring the exercise of so elementary a skill, which I thought a very slight display of intelligence, when one could get into fearful trouble in his lectures for not grasping something which I was sure it needed great powers and hard thought to grasp. We eventually read the early part of the Investigations; I remember he reacted with real pleasure when I told him that I had read to §35 and had found it intoxicating; which was the case. As we read it we discussed translating it—he would explain the import of words, and I would suggest an English rendering, about which he would be very enthusiastic. (Anscombe 1946, transcription by L. Gormally, quoted from chapter 2)

This chapter is a revised version of Erbacher et al. 2019.

© The Author(s), under exclusive license to Springer-Verlag GmbH, DE, part of
Springer Nature 2023
C. Erbacher, *The Happy Afterlife of Ludwig W.*, Beiträge zur Praxeologie /
Contributions to Praxeology, https://doi.org/10.1007/978-3-662-66155-0_3

Wittgenstein had tried to find a translator for his work before the war. But none of the candidates had delivered a satisfying result. The joyful experience of toying with the translation together with Anscombe may have incited him, in their subsequent meetings, to ask her to do it. By early 1950 at the latest, when Wittgenstein had been diagnosed with cancer upon his return from the USA, Anscombe had committed herself to translating Wittgenstein's book. To prepare for the task, she spent several months in Vienna studying Viennese German (Wittgenstein 1988, xiii). Wittgenstein, who had arranged for her to stay at the house of his good friend Ludwig Hänsel, was present for part of the time (note from L. Gormally, see chapter 2). By April 1950, both Wittgenstein and Anscombe had returned from Vienna, and Wittgenstein moved into Anscombe's slim Oxford townhouse. Here they resumed translating the then-current version of the *Philosophical Investigations*. According to Anscombe's husband Peter Geach, the translation of all remarks was finished while Wittgenstein was still alive (Wittgenstein 1988, xiii). What is more, Jenny Teichman, a friend of Anscombe's family, noted that the translation was carried out under Wittgenstein's guidance (Teichman 2001, 2). Indeed, given Wittgenstein's great interest in earlier attempts to translate his work, it is hard to imagine that he would not be involved in some way in Anscombe's work. What is most likely is that they cooperated in a way that would allow Anscombe to sharpen her apprehension of Wittgenstein's writing and how to render it into English. She certainly could build on these experiences after Wittgenstein's death, when she translated the remarks she and Rhees included as "Part II" of the *Philosophical Investigations*, and when she prepared the whole translation for print. In any case, Anscombe did not stop searching for mistakes and ways to improve the text until the book went to press in 1953, and she continued even after that, as she wrote to von Wright:

> I hope you like the book.- I've been reading out translation mistakes for the American edition, but the axe has fallen now and they will accept no new corrections; though I still have one or two to make. Ryle has agreed to publish a list of my corrections in the July Mind. (Letter Anscombe to von Wright, 17 May 1953)

The result of Anscombe's tireless efforts is well known: a translation that Anthony Kenny eloquently described:

> The Anscombe translation is fluent and readable and has been universally accepted as if it contained the *ipsissima verba* of Wittgenstein: I can think of no other English translation of a philosopher—not Jowett's Plato, nor Kemp Smith's Kant—that has achieved such canonical status in the world. (Kenny 2005, 342)

In the moment of adding the last strokes to this monumental achievement of translating the *Philosophical Investigations*, Anscombe did a recording for the BBC Third Programme. In two continuous broadcasts, she gave a talk on Wittgenstein (recorded probably on 2 May 1953, broadcasted on 9 July 1953, 8.05 pm) and read out the passage on "reading" from her translation of the *Philosophical Investigations* (recorded on 2 May 1953, broadcasted on 11 July 1953, 9.35 pm).

Presented below is a transcript of the manuscript used for the first recording, that is, Anscombe's talk on Wittgenstein in connection with the publication of the *Philosophical Investigations*. The document testifies to Anscombe's awareness of Wittgenstein and his work at a time when her memories of him were still fresh and she was fully immersed in the translation project. This makes the BBC radio talk a valuable source for learning about Anscombe's understanding of Wittgenstein's philosophy and about the standards according to which she measured her translation. She says, for instance, that translating Wittgenstein is particularly difficult, because his style is at the same time literary and colloquial and that this combination does not work in English. This apprehension fits well with what she wrote to Brian McGuinness, referring to Frank Ramsey's translation of the *Tractatus*:

> Wittgenstein's German is always very expressive; sometimes very plain, even colloquial, and straight, always terse, sometimes splendid and rather poetic; it has great rhythm. Now Ogden has something of this in him. Only in him it splits up into two things, one meretricious and the other not. It's meretricious when there is an air of profundity through obscurity and almost pseudo Biblical or pseudo poetic language. But when his methods of translation don't lead to this, and don't contain errors, they sometimes have beauty and force. They are never heavy or academic. (Letter from Anscombe to McGuinness, n. d.)

Where Ramsey succeeded in translating Wittgenstein, Anscombe admired his "free but excellent renderings" (Anscombe 1959, 17), and this may be a heuristic she adhered to in translating the *Philosophical Investigations*.

The BBC radio broadcast was an occasion to announce Wittgenstein's work to the broader philosophically interested public. Hence, it is most interesting to see how Anscombe described it in an accessible language and how she placed the *Philosophical Investigations* in the philosophical landscape of the time. Being broadcast in the heyday of the "Ordinary Language Philosophy" at Oxford, Anscombe was keen to distinguish Wittgenstein's philosophy from this philosophical movement. She thus argued against a tendency in the then upcoming historiography of the analytical tradition that presented Wittgenstein primarily as Bertrand Russell's student who had elaborated his teacher's logical atomism and then paved the way for the logical positivism of the Vienna Circle (cf. Conant 2015). According to this view, Ordinary Language Philosophy was said to bring to full fruition what Wittgenstein had only hinted at (cf. Urmson 1956). By contrast, Anscombe insisted that this would be a gross misunderstanding of Wittgenstein's work; it had to be read against another background: first, the *Tractatus* would remain incomprehensible if the influence of Gottlob Frege's work was neglected; and second, the *Philosophical Investigations* had to be read against the background of this Frege-oriented understanding of the *Tractatus*. In her talk for the BBC, Anscombe took the opportunity to champion both this line of philosophical heredity (i. e. Frege–*Tractatus*–*Philosophical Investigations*) as well as the unique freshness of method and style in the writings that Wittgenstein had left behind.

3.2   Ludwig Wittgenstein—Talk by G. E. M. Anscombe

Wittgenstein came to Cambridge, I think in the year 1911, at the age of twenty-two, in order to study under Bertrand Russell. He had been to school in Austria and had studied engineering for some years in Manchester. After a few months it was arranged, by the help of Russell and of the logician Johnson, that he should not have to read the Tripos but should be accepted as a PhD student straight away. As he had no degree and no previous study of philosophy to recommend him, this is some indication of the impression he made on his teachers.

For the next 7 years he was engaged in writing the 'Logisch-Philosophische Abhandlung', most generally known under the title given to its English translation: Tractatus Logico-Philosophicus. The book itself is short: this is because it is extremely compressed. A very great mass of writing lay behind it. (This Wittgenstein had burned in 1950 in view of his approaching death; it comprised several boxes full of MS volumes.) Someone who admired his 'Philosophical Investigations' once asked him why he called it not good. He turned the pages over with an expression of distaste, and then said "It limps." And then "If this were philosophy, you could learn it by heart!" This singular ideal he did achieve in his first book.

Philosophical influences on him were few but powerful. As a boy of 16 he read Schopenhauer's 'World as idea and will', and thought it tremendous: as far as the 'world as idea' was concerned, he thought what Schopenhauer said true, only needing a few adjustments. Later he characterised S. as a thinker capable [of] a certain limited depth and no more. The great influence on him was Frege, for whom he always had the most intense admiration both as a writer and as a thinker, and to whom he presents certain marked similarities. To Bertrand Russell he owed a very great deal, mostly to Russell in discussion in the period 1911–14. He often spoke of how wonderful Russell was to discuss with in that period. The best introduction I know of to Wittgenstein's Tractatus [–] if you sift out Russell's phenomenalism [–] is to be found in Russell's Lectures on Logical Atomism, delivered in 1918, in which Russell says: "They are very largely concerned with explaining certain ideas which I learned from my friend and former pupil Ludwig Wittgenstein." This was of course written before the Tractatus appeared: the lectures are a reflection of the discussions which they had together before the first world war.

Otherwise in philosophy, one can only speak of likings not of influences. Wittgenstein had a liking for Plato, a great love of St. Augustine (in the Confessions only) and a fondness for William James (in the Principles of Psychology); also a certain limited liking for Aquinas: that is limited to some of the questions that Aquinas asked. I should add to this list Lichtenberg, of whom Goethe said "Where Lichtenberg makes a joke, there you will find a problem." There are passages in Lichtenberg that are extraordinarily like Wittgenstein: "Yes, I might have written it myself," he said once on being shown an unfamiliar paragraph of Lichtenberg:

The thing that makes the study of any profound philosophy so very difficult is that in everyday life we take lots of things to be so natural and easy, that we think things just couldn't be otherwise. And yet we ought to know that one needs to realise the enormous importance of such apparent trifles before one can explain the difficulty that is spoken of really is one. When I say: This stone is hard and so first attach the concept stone which belongs to a plurality of things, to this individual, and then speak of hardness [,] and then combine the being hard with the stone—this is such a miraculous operation that we may ask whether so much goes into the preparation of some books. "But aren't these subtleties? does one have to know this?"—As far as the first question goes, they are not subtleties, for it is just in these simple cases that we must get to understand the operations of the mind. If we try to begin with complex ones, all our labour is lost. Finding these easy things difficult betrays no small advance in philosophy. But as far as the other question goes, I answer: No, one doesn't have to know it, but one doesn't have to be a philosopher either.

There is a set of German writers—I don't think I can speak of a tradition—whose style has a special daylight character: tough, lucid, crisp, lively and serious: Lessing, Lichtenberg, Frege, all display to a less or greater degree the character I have in mind; and Wittgenstein preeminently.

Of all other philosophers, besides the ones I have mentioned, Wittgenstein was on the whole ignorant. He would sometimes read a page, and find himself unable to go on. If he mentioned any philosopher, it was to quote and comment on some quite concrete remark; he never made general remarks on philosophers' views. (This has had an odd effect on some of those who directly or indirectly, have been influenced by him. It is fairly common now to read criticisms at large of celebrated philosophers backed by a rather slight consideration of their writing.)

The Tractatus is of the greatest possible importance for understanding the 'Philosophical Investigations'. W. came to realise this and wanted the two books bound up together, which will, I hope, be done in a purely German edition. It is important because Wittgenstein clearly remained in love with the thoughts of the Tractatus, though he attacks and most powerfully undermines them. The Tractatus haunts the Investigations.

It is quite commonly said that Wittgenstein taught, not a doctrine, but a method of doing philosophy. This is unluckily in an important sense not true. If someone teaches a method, it ought to be possible for someone else both to learn and to teach it: it ought to be quite clear what the procedure is, what moves you make at what points, and so on. Now it is possible perhaps to list a number of tricks which Wittgenstein used and, therefore, taught. E.g., that of asking "As opposed to what?" or "and what would it be like if it were not so?" when a proposition is advanced. Or that of asking "What is the picture that is being used here?". Or that of taking a solution in a peculiarly literal, empirical sense. Or that of inventing different cases which shew quite clearly that the implication of a term or the meaning of a statement is not determined in advance in some way in which one thought it was. Or that of asking 'To whom is this said, and in what circumstances?' or 'What kind of proposition is this?'. Or that of assuming a criterion of identity of a kind suggested by a philosophic thesis and deducing absurd consequences. Or that of asking what would shew that a word had a certain sense if you had to learn the language it belonged to without interpreters. I could go on. But none of these moves, nor all of them taken together, guarantee that anybody will find a solution to any problem at all. There is no method taught by which you know when such and such a move will be fruitful, carry you deeper, cause you really to touch the nerve of the problem under consideration. These tricks can be played with complete superficiality. Nothing takes the place of having ideas, of being capable of observation and insight; and Wittgenstein did not I think teach a method of attaining these. When he makes one of these moves it has great point; but he does not teach you when it will have point to make a given move.

He had a great and a bad influence on current philosophy. He knew this: "But," he said, "I don't think its my fault." It is possible to point to certain definite phenomena as examples of his bad influence. A certain amount of current philosophical discussion concerns itself with linguistic usage. This is a direct result of Wittgenstein's teaching that in a great many cases, in which we speak of 'meaning', though not in all, it can be defined thus: the meaning of a word is its use in the language. But use is not usage; he did not wish to base anything on idiom. "I distinguish," he wrote "between the essential and the inessential features of an expression. The essential features are the ones that would make us translate some otherwise unfamiliar form of expression into this, our customary form." What is or is not correct English usage is of no conceivable philosophic interest; nor does it matter if I choose to use words in an extraordinary manner, so long as it [is] clear what I am saying. So far, I think you can say that 'it's not his fault'. On the other hand the objection "but the word is not used like that"[;] "but we don't say that"; "but that is not how this statement is used", which has acquired such dogmatic force in philosophical discussion, is more directly his responsibility. It ought, however, never to be used unless it is clearly shewn how, for the particular problem in hand, some particular feature of a use is essential to a meaning. Otherwise it is the expression of a philosophical dogma of which some are addicts, while others cannot see the point at all. (And they are right.) Wittgenstein was not an addict of this dogma: but it may not always be clear that he was not. He is always saying 'look at the use!' But it is in fact a difficult thing to do; and it is very easy to think that one is doing it by attending to unimportant features: a procedure which he once compared to describing a naval lieutenant in terms of the stripes on [his uniform.]

Here I can mention the misinterpretation of Wittgenstein's work which I can most easily foresee, and which I believe will be the dominant one. It will be thus: Wittgenstein formulates (with great subtlety) a theory of meaning as use: and what else he says is a deduction from, or a working out of, this theory. Those who are not caught up by the theory, but who hear of it, will probably notice it as a puzzling thing that work of which this is the sum should have so excited and fascinated people.—It will be a complete misunderstanding. In what Wittgenstein has to say about use he manufactures one tool which he employs in philosophical investigation. No part of his work presupposes another as a theoretical foundation: he does not treat his problems from the point of view of a system which he is engaged in constructing. This fact may be obscured by the fact that some parts of the book do presuppose others in the sense that you will perhaps not understand the methods of argument employed without having read certain passages.

In the style used by people talking [and] writing philosophy his influence has been very marked and often very disagreeable. He was unacademic both in manner and in matter; some people found this novel and stimulating and tried in one way or another to imitate it, sometimes with embarrassing results: a would be humanism of style & examples.

Further, it is true—though not at all informative—to say that Wittgenstein's way of dealing with philosophical problems ends, if it is successful, in their dissolution rather than in the presentation of a theory. When you consider this; and consider also how it was carried out: in an unsystematic way, accompanied by wit and imagination; always making the impression of very fresh and very hard thinking; supported by striking examples and analogies; full of an obvious passion for the subject, of a kind not often to be met with—when you consider all this, it becomes easy to understand how it often went to the heads of his listeners. Then they would try to deal with problems in the same way, to achieve the same effect: and as the effect was the dissolution of the problems, they would make that their aim. Thus it has come about that a great deal of the philosophy written at the present day consists in a debunking and shelving of problems without serious investigation: the lengthiness of what is written or said consisting of tedious linguistic description or the like.

One of the best known writings which shew his influence is Professor Ryle's Concept of Mind. One of Professor Ryle's purposes in this book is to depreciate the role of formulated thought in the life of human beings. The kind of examples of intelligence that must suit his purpose are such things as the tumbling of clowns, playing football, tying your bootlaces, which are certainly intelligent and purposive, but the execution of which perhaps does not require the presence of what are ordinarily called mental acts. Throughout the book Professor Ryle is at ease when he is describing the actions which are the expression of mental acts, and evasive when he is in danger of pinning himself down to considering a mental act divorced from action; he tends to content himself with denying that we need to have any hidden process described to us, and with affirming that we all know quite well from childhood in what situations we describe people as, e.g. imagining. The contrast with Wittgenstein [is] strong; for Wittgenstein is not at all interested in things like tying shoelaces or playing football, but entirely absorbed by such questions as what it is to grasp a rule, to mean or understand an order, to recognize the same, to take a word in a sense, to suddenly see how to continue a series, to have been going to say something, to mean a man by his name, and so on. Professor Ryle, writing on volition, hardly does more than ridicule the idea of a "mental" or as he also calls it a "ghostly" "thrust". He does not confront himself with the problem; which Wittgenstein states thus: "When I raise my arm, my arm goes up. What is left when I subtract the fact that my arm goes up from the fact that I raise my arm?"

"I spend more time than you perhaps could ever understand, thinking about questions of style," Wittgenstein once said to someone. The state of the MSS and

TSS that he left behind him are a witness to this. He wrote an enormous amount; he threw away a good deal, and what is left is a formidable quantity of MSS written from 1929 onwards. He would often write first in small notebooks, then transfer siftings from these to larger ones, then further-polished-siftings to still larger ones. Then he would dictate to a typist. Then [he] would cut up the typescript and throw a lot away, and try different arrangements of the rest: for he always wrote in the form of isolated paragraphs capable of rearrangement. A great part of the material of the Philosophical Investigations exists in two other quite different arrangements, each brought to a final form and ready for the printer, and each elaborately cross referenced; for he hoped at one time to supply his 'Remarks' as he called them, with cross references to every other one with which he saw a fruitful connexion. His MSS. sometimes contain remarks written over and over again in various forms. They always contain a huge number of variant readings, with variant punctuations; and if you read carefully through each possibility, you notice how sharply aware Wittgenstein was of small rhetorical differences.

The final product of all this work has very remarkable literary qualities; once it is published, I think there will be no more wonderment why Wittgenstein—who spoke English well—wrote in German. It was horribly difficult to translate. I doubt whether much of a reflection of its style would be possible in English at all; at any rate it was not possible for me to achieve it. In general, German has possibilities of a homeliness—the very epithet sounds horrid in connexion with English—that is not in the [slightest] in conflict with the highest literary style. For an example, you only need to look at Gretchen's lines in Faust when she comes in after Faust and the Devil have been in her room. Wittgenstein's German is at once highly literary and highly colloquial. Good English, in modern times, goes in good clothes; to introduce colloquialism, or slang, is deliberately to adopt a low style. Any English style that I can imagine would be a misrepresentation of this German. All I could do, therefore, was to produce as careful a crib as possible. I bent over backwards to write in a spare and compressed English, since the German is spare and compressed; and in part I the translation turned out several lines a page shorter than the original. (This was right, because English is a shorter language than German.) But in part II I found, when it was set up, that the German was seldom longer and was sometimes shorter. This is one small index of the new degree of compactness to which Wittgenstein rose in his last period; for compression, together with rich and sharp expressiveness; for wealth of incontestable observations and hard investigation; this transcends everything he ever wrote.

The constant characteristics of Wittgenstein's writing are close reasoning and strong imagination. But the book has also the character of great variety of tone: this is a rare character, and particularly rare in philosophical writing. (The only other examples I can think of are some of Plato's dialogues). You get long passages of very sober, straightforward enquiry and argument; then a burst of breathless dialogue (always, of course, between himself and himself); sudden turn of humour, passages full of passionate feeling; pronouncements reached after perplexed enquiry, which have the air of being written with that feeling: And that settles everything; pieces of delicate, accurate characterisation of some particular temptation; remarks that are like a grasp or cry of realisation. And you get certain themes, certain moods recurring and recurring with different variations. I have long been tempted to compare this book with a musical composition; but hesitated to do so, until I found it elicited this reaction independently from someone who read it de novo.

One of the things which will interest me very much will be German reactions to the book as a literary achievement.

Editorial Note

The manuscript kept at the BBC Archives is written in Anscombe's own handwriting, with the exception of technical instructions on the front page that are written with a typewriter, and a note for the radio programme inserted in different handwriting on page 2. Apart from the title that stems from the typewritten front page and that is transcribed below in capital letters, only Anscombe's handwritten talk is represented. The manuscript contains deletions, corrections and insertions so that it seems that Anscombe revised wording in the process of drafting. Though these revisions are sometimes illuminating, the edition does not represent them for the sake of readability. Thus, what is presented below is a normalized transcript, in which Anscombe's deletions, corrections and insertions have been omitted. The result is a fair copy, most likely resembling the text that Anscombe read for the broadcast. Line breaks and page breaks of the manuscript have not been preserved. Occasional additions or suppositions by the editors are placed in rectangular brackets.

Acknowledgements   Anscombe's manuscript has been reproduced and edited with permission from Mrs M. C. Gormally (Dr Mary Geach) and the BBC. The document was found and analyzed during a Research Fellowship at the Research Centre for Analytic German Idealism at the University of Leipzig (FAGI). The editorial work has been funded by the Collaborative Research Centre "Media of Cooperation" at the University of Siegen (SFB 1187). For most helpful support in deciphering Anscombe's handwriting I am very grateful to Luke Gormally. For help in editing, I am most grateful to Julia Jung and Anne dos Santos Reis.

References

Anscombe, G. E. M. 1953. Letter to von Wright, 17 May 1953. National Library of Finland, NLF COLL. 714.11–12; quoted with permission from Mrs M. C. Gormally (Dr Mary Geach).

Anscombe, G. E. M. n. d. Letter to McGuinness. McGuinness's private archives, now kept at the Brenner Archives at the University of Innsbruck; quoted with permission from Mrs M. C. Gormally (Dr Mary Geach) and Brian McGuinness.

Anscombe, G. E. M. 1959. *An Introduction to Wittgenstein's Tractatus*. London: Hutchinson.

Anscombe, G. E. M. 1981. *Metaphysics and the Philosophy of Mind—Collected Philosophical Papers of G. E. M. Anscombe*, Vol. II. Oxford: Blackwell.

Conant, James. 2015. "The Emergence of the Concept of the Analytic Tradition as a Form of Philosophical Self-Consciousness". In *Beyond the Analytic-Continental Divide Pluralist Philosophy in the Twenty-First Century*, eds. J. A. Bell, A. Cutrofello, and P. M. Livingston. New York: Routledge, 17–58.

Erbacher, Christian, dos Santos Reis, Anne, and Jung, Julia. 2019. "Ludwig Wittgenstein"—A BBC radio talk by Elizabeth Anscombe in May 1953, edited by Christian Erbacher, Anne dos Santos Reis and Julia Jung. In *Nordic Wittgenstein Review* 8(1-2): 225–240.

Kenny, Anthony. 2005. "A Brief History of Wittgenstein Editing". In *Wittgenstein: The Philosopher and His Works*, eds. A. Pichler and S. Säätelä. Wittgenstein Archives at the University of Bergen (WAB), 341–355.

Teichman, Jenny. 2001. (Gertrude) Elizabeth Margaret Anscombe (1919–2001). *Oxford Dictionary of National Biography*. https://doi.org/10.1093/ref:odnb/75032. Accessed 20 May 2019.

Urmson, James O. 1956. *Philosophical Analysis: Its Development between the Two World Wars*. Oxford: Oxford University Press.

Wittgenstein, Ludwig. 1988. *Wittgenstein's Lectures on Philosophical Psychology 1946–1947*. Ed. Peter T. Geach. Chicago: University of Chicago Press.

Wittgenstein, Ludwig. 2003. *Ludwig Wittgenstein: Public and Private Occasions*. Eds. J. C. Klagge and A. Nordmann. Lanham. MD: Rowman & Littlefield.

Wittgenstein, Ludwig. 2012. *Wittgenstein in Cambridge: Letters and Documents 1911–1951*, Ed. B. F. McGuinness. Malden. MA: Wiley-Blackwell.

"Good" Philosophical Reasons for "Bad" Editorial Philology?

4

On Rhees and Wittgenstein's *Philosophical Grammar*

4.1   I Did not Even Try to <u>Have</u> an Editorial Policy…

> …unless this be one: In any editing I have done I have asked myself again and again what Wittgenstein would have wanted. (Rhees to Kenny, 2. March 1977)

4.1.1   Editions as Readings

Ludwig Wittgenstein published only one philosophical book during his lifetime: the *Tractatus logico-philosophicus* (Wittgenstein 1921; 1922). Between 1929 and 1951 he worked on a second book that he eventually wanted to call "Philosophical Investigations". After about 16 years of writing, he hinted in a draft for a preface that his work would soon end: "I should have liked to produce a good book. This has not come about, but the time is past in which I could improve it" (Wittgenstein 1958, xe; Ts 227a,4[4]: http://www.wittgensteinsource.org/BFE/Ts-227a,4_f).[1] Despite these words, Wittgenstein continued his investigations for several more years—particularly into the use of psychological concepts. In the end, however, he

---

[1] References to manuscripts and typescripts in Wittgenstein's *Nachlass* follow the catalogue numbers that were first introduced by von Wright (1969). Wittgenstein's papers are published in *Wittgenstein's Nachlass – The Bergen Electronic Edition* (BEE). Single remarks typescripts are quoted with sigla that were agreed on at the Wittgenstein Archives at the University Bergen during the DISCOVERY-Project. These consist of 1) the indication of the manuscript or typescript according to von Wright's cataloguing, 2) the page number and possibly whether it is a recto- ("r") or verso-page ("v"), and 3) the order of priority of the remarks on this page in square brackets (cf. Pichler 2010). Single sigla are followed by the URL that leads to the stable reference of the given manuscript page on www.wittgensteinsource.org.

This chapter is a revised version of Erbacher 2019.

© The Author(s), under exclusive license to Springer-Verlag GmbH, DE, part of Springer Nature 2023
C. Erbacher, *The Happy Afterlife of Ludwig W.*, Beiträge zur Praxeologie / Contributions to Praxeology, https://doi.org/10.1007/978-3-662-66155-0_4

did not deliver a manuscript to a publisher. Instead he entrusted three of his former students and close friends with the task of publishing what they thought fit from his altogether 18,000 pages of philosophical writings.[2] When the three accepted this task, the history of editing Wittgenstein's works began, and it has been going on now for more than 60 years (see Chap. 1).

In trying to fulfil Wittgenstein's last wish, Rush Rhees, Elizabeth Anscombe and Georg Henrik von Wright created the editions that have entered the philosophical canon as Wittgenstein's works. The three literary heirs had almost no experience or training in scholarly editing. They therefore did not apply principles of editorial philology when preparing books from Wittgenstein's papers. Instead they followed their own philosophical understanding and judgement as Wittgenstein's students, as readers of his writings and as philosophers in their own right. The editorial work of Rhees, Anscombe and von Wright may thus be called the "philosophical phase" in the history of editing Wittgenstein's writings.

A milestone in this first phase of editing Wittgenstein was the production of a microfilm in 1967–68. Through this microfilm, which had been produced at von Wright's instigation, Wittgenstein's manuscripts and typescripts became available to scholars almost in their entirety (see Chap. 5). On this basis, researchers began to compare the then-published editions with the microfilmed sources. The outcome of these comparisons suggested that Wittgenstein's literary heirs had intervened more strongly in the selection and composition than their austere prefaces and epilogues indicated (Stern 1996). This insight, in connection with the fact that some passages were covered up even in microfilm, incited scholars from the mid-1970s onwards to question the authenticity and editorial integrity of the editions that were available at that time. As a result, and in conjunction with advances in editorial philology in German speaking academia, they began calling for a complete and critical edition of Wittgenstein's writings. This led to a second, "critical" phase in the history of editing Wittgenstein's *Nachlass*.

The second phase is characterized by editors who did not know Wittgenstein personally and who wanted to produce editions strictly according to philological principles. This text-critical examination branched out into three kinds of editions: first, critical editions of the two texts generally regarded as Wittgenstein's main works (Wittgenstein 1989, 2001); second, the *Vienna Edition* (Wittgenstein 1994a, 1994b, 1995a, 1995b, 1996, 2000a), which is a critical edition of Wittgenstein's writings up to the mid-1930s; and third, the *Bergen Electronic Edition* (BEE)

---

[2] The relevant passage in Wittgenstein's will reads: "I GIVE to MR. R. Rhees Miss Anscombe and Professor G.

H. v. Wright of Trinity College Cambridge All the copyright in all my unpublished writings and also the manuscripts and typescripts thereof to dispose of as they think best but subject to any claim by anybody else to the custody of the manuscripts and typescripts I intend and desire that Mr. Rhees Miss Anscombe and Professor von Wright shall publish as many of my unpublished writings as they think fit but I do not wish them to incur expenses in publication which they do not expect to recoup out of royalties or other profits", (Wittgenstein's will, §3, quoted from chapter 2).

(Wittgenstein 2000b), which provides the complete writings of Wittgenstein in diplomatic and normalized transcriptions as well as in facsimile. The changes in digital formats and the rapid development of digital technology necessitate continuous updating of the BEE. The Wittgenstein Archives at the University of Bergen has now launched the BEE on Internet and equipped it with various software (See wab.uib.no, wittgensteinsource.org, wittfind.csi.uni-muenchen.de). These latest technological developments ultimately empower readers to explore, structure and display Wittgenstein's writings according to their own individual needs and wishes (Pichler and Bruvik 2014). But such options—initially the privilege of selected editors—are also an imposition on readers, for they are now confronted with questions of composition and internal relations in Wittgenstein's papers. Hitherto, only editors had to answer these questions when preparing their volumes. In the face of the ultimate empowerment of readers, insight into this preliminary work of the first editors would be a welcomed help for readers to orient themselves in the "jungle" (Venturinha 2010, 1) of Wittgenstein's writings. This new interest in the early research on Wittgenstein's *Nachlass* is characteristic for a third phase in the history of editing Wittgenstein's writings, one which we may call "post-critical". It is on this threshold that we now stand.

In the third phase, the history of editing Wittgenstein acquires a new function: today's ultimately empowered readers can treat the editorial decisions that were criticized in the second phase as invitations to reconstruct the reasons and motives for the different ways of editing that were used in the first phase. The various editions no longer need to be judged merely as candidates for canonizing, but can be accepted as results that the editors created in their capacity as outstanding readers of the sources. To understand editions of Wittgenstein's writings as 'paradigmatic materializations of readings' can help new readers inquire into the origins of those editions in an unprejudiced way, and to openly appreciate the editorial work that went into them, above and beyond the perspectives of critical editorial philology (Erbacher 2016; for a first-person third-phase account see Stern 2017). In the case of Wittgenstein's writings, third-phase histories of editing can represent the work of the original literary heirs as philosophically relevant and editorially sensible, although the editions may differ from what the majority of today's editorial philologists may regard as editorially sensible. The decisions that have been identified as philological shortcomings in the second phase can provide starting points for the constructive contextualization of editorial practices. By using archival and biographical information, the work of the literary heirs can be understood as a series of human stories of philosophical inheritance.

Thus, the third phase in the history of editing Wittgenstein's writings is a multi-layered hermeneutical endeavour to understand anew Wittgenstein's writings under the conditions of the first editors' understanding, and thereby understand the meaning of editing in the context of philosophizing. Some topoi for coming to terms with this complex challenge are given in a striking case story: Anthony Kenny's criticism of Rhees' edition *Philosophical Grammar* (Wittgenstein 1969), in particular, his criticism of Rhees' decision to exclude a chapter called "Philosophy".

4.1.2   The Case

Kenny's essay "From the Big Typescript to the *Philosophical Grammar*" (Kenny 1977) exemplifies the conflict between the philosophical orientation of the first-phase editors of Wittgenstein's writings and the philological concerns of the second-phase editors. Kenny translated the *Philosophical Grammar* from German into English in the first half of the 1970s. Three years after the publication of the English edition (Wittgenstein 1974), he published the essay in which he fundamentally criticized Rhees' editorial work. According to Kenny, Rhees' *Philosophical Grammar* does not adequately represent Wittgenstein's so called Big Typescript (Ts 213; Wittgenstein 2000b). Two assumptions—that the Big Typescript is a version of an alleged work by Wittgenstein, and that it is *the* one edited text in the *Philosophical Grammar*—are still often made, and they stem, not least, from reading Kenny's essay (See Schulte 2013). If one thinks so, Kenny's argument seems indeed captivating: The 768-page Big Typescript with a table of contents showing the structuring of 19 sections and 140 chapters gives the impression of a work that is nearly ready for press. Comparing the Big Typescript with the printed *Philosophical Grammar*, the likeliness as well as significant differences are obvious, especially in the first part of the edition. Kenny became aware of these differences when consulting the microfilm of Wittgenstein's papers for his translation and noticed that they were not immediately apparent from Rhees' editorial postscript to the edition (Kenny 1977, 41). Hence, Kenny suggested describing the differences between the Big Typescript and *Philosophical Grammar* in a translator's introduction and to replace Rhees' table of contents with the table of contents from the Big Typescript (Kenny to Rhees, 27 August 1972). Rhees, however, rejected this idea. Kenny accepted Rhees' veto for the printing of the English edition, but the text-critical essay by Kenny later appeared in a commemorative volume for von Wright.

In his editorial note, Rhees clearly stated that he regarded the Big Typescript as an intermediate product and that he wanted to implement Wittgenstein's revisions in it (Wittgenstein 1974, Note in Editing). Kenny, however, thought the resulting *Philosophical Grammar* neither manifested Wittgenstein's revisions nor showed the specifics of how and where Rhees as editor had interfered in Wittgenstein's text. Kenny further argued that there was no point in time when, or passage in which, Wittgenstein's text editing could have been regarded as completed. Every decision for a specific version of a text would therefore be subject to the editor's arbitrary decisions (Kenny 1977, 47). Kenny concluded: "The most prudent editorial policy would have been to print the original Big Typescript as it stood rather than to seek for a definitive revision of it" (Kenny 1977, 52). Thus, while Kenny's essay began as a text-critical aid, it turned into a global attack on Rhees' edition. This attack especially seemed to concern the exclusion of the chapter "Philosophy", which amounts to almost 30 typewritten pages in the Big Typescript (Ts 213, 406r–435r). These 30 pages and two other chapters were left out of the

Philosophical Grammar, and Rhees did not even mention the exclusion in his editorial note, as Kenny stressed (Kenny 1977, 45–47).[3]

Kenny's essay made it seem as though Rhees' edition would fight a losing battle. In a case such as this, a third-phase account in the sense described above might be especially valuable. Such an account would aim at understanding the context in which *Philosophical Grammar* was constituted and give us insight into Rhees' reasons for his editorial decisions. This third-phase account would succeed, if it enabled a new understanding of the volume that seems hopelessly indefensible when appealing only to principles of editorial philology. Rhees' reply to Kenny can serve as Ariadne's thread in this hermeneutic venture:

Dear Kenny,

On page 52 of your <u>Acta Philosophica Fennica</u> article you say

… the existence of Volume XII must surely support the contention ((must it?)) that the most prudent editorial policy would have been to print the original Big Typescript <u>as it stood</u> ((my underscoring)) rather than to seek for a definitive revision of it.

To whom is this addressed? To people who have been working with and among Wittgenstein's manuscripts for many years, in an attempt—not to produce a crochet of references and tables which some call 'scholarship' but to make Wittgenstein's discussions available in readable form to those who were interested in philosophy: who wanted to follow him in the development of his methods, the growth of his understanding of certain crucial points, and so on? Or is your remark addressed to people whose interest in Wittgenstein is antiquarian?

So you don't understand my question. No; I suppose not.

'… the <u>most prudent</u> editorial policy …' And now <u>I</u> don't understand.

I did not even try to <u>have</u> an editorial policy. Unless this be one: In any editing I have done I have asked myself again and again what Wittgenstein would have wanted. This has guided me in what I have decided to leave out and in what I have decided to include. A few days before his death Wittgenstein was speaking to me about the work of editing his manuscripts. This had constantly been in his mind, and was so especially then. He said, 'I trust you absolutely, and I trust Miss Anscombe absolutely … ' And he might have said of someone else that he 'did not altogether trust him', or perhaps of someone that he did not trust him at all: meaning, of course, that he trusted, or did not trust the person's <u>judgment</u> in deciding what should be published. For it was plain that he expected or took it as obvious that there would have to be selection, and so there would have to be decisions. —The very brief statement in his Will reads: 'I intend and desire that Mr Rhees, Miss Anscombe and Professor von Wright shall publish as many of my unpublished writings as they think fit…' Where, I suppose, part of the sense of the phrase '<u>as they think fit</u>' falls in with what I have just called <u>judgment</u>. I do not say Wittgenstein was wise or perceptive in entrusting this to just the three people he did. I have thought more often than you have that he blundered in naming me among them. But, <u>whoever</u> was entrusted with it, this was sort of work that Wittgenstein 'intended and desired' those so entrusted to carry out. If you say: 'But look, you never <u>know</u> what Wittgenstein himself would have decided …'—I would say: Hold your horses.—What is obvious in such a statement ('you

---

[3] This is one of the observations that is often referred to for suggesting that Wittgenstein's literary heirs arbitrarily intervened when making their editions and therefore transmitted a censored or even manipulated picture of Wittgenstein; another is Anscombe and Rhees' addition of "Part II" in the *Philosophical Investigations* (Wittgenstein 1953). For notes on this addition in the correspondence of Wittgenstein's literary executors, see Erbacher (2015, 170–172).

can never know …') <u>is</u> obvious, and would never need saying. But if you mean that having known Wittgenstein for some time (I knew him pretty well for 15 years) and having been with him while he was working on and revising his manuscripts—having seen him cut out certain things (sometimes to my bewilderment) and change the order or passages; having seen him change one version for another (this was with the earlier versions of the Philosophische Untersuchungen), and heard him treat the same materials in his lectures; remembering <u>especially</u> the reasons he often did give for cutting out, revising and shortening what he said was '<u>foul</u>'; so that I could see something of the same way of working and the same standards in some of the crossings out and revisions in manuscripts—if you want to say that I '<u>cannot</u>' look to this for guidance when I am working on what he has written, then the matter must rest there.

[…]

Your phrase, in your rhetorical question: 'to seek for a <u>definitive revision</u> of it'—is playing to the gallery. I never imagined I was seeking for a definitive revision of it. But I had reasons for what I did. (Rhees to Kenny, 2 March 1977)

In his essay, Kenny publicly criticized Rhees for having selected and composed the *Philosophical Grammar* without philological certainty; Rhees responded to this in a private letter (as was typical for him), saying that he certainly had reasons for doing what he did. It becomes clear, however, that his reasons were not those of a professional editorial philologist but instead related to his understanding of the texts: Rhees thought Wittgenstein had entrusted him with publishing these texts because he was a friend and colleague who had won some insight in Wittgenstein's working method through observation and discussion. While this encapsulates Rhees' self-understanding as one of Wittgenstein's literary executors, it also reveals the conditions under which Rhees created the *Philosophical Grammar* and excluded the chapter "Philosophy".

4.2   It Seems to Me that It is Important to Show…

… that 'the later Wittgenstein' is a continuation of the same discussions which we have in the Tractatus. (Rhees to von Wright, 10. February 1963)

4.2.1   A Pupil's Approach to Editing His Teacher's Papers

In his letter to Kenny, Rhees points out that the reasons for his editing were connected to his familiarity with Wittgenstein's life and work. This familiarity had developed over many years. In fact, the first documentation of their philosophical encounter dates to 1933, when the 28-year-old Rhees moved to Cambridge to write his PhD thesis. On the suggestion of his supervisor George Edward Moore, Rhees attended Wittgenstein's classes and reported on them to his first philosophical mentor Alfred Kastil in Innsbruck:

He continuously speaks in similes (which are only partly actual examples), and says about himself that he always thinks in similes. If something does not become clear, he does not try to give an explanation in simple words but instead looks for a new simile.

> This method, though, is in accordance with his philosophical position, according to which the answers to the most important philosophical questions cannot be given through propositions or theories, but can only be "shown" by means of similes "or symbolic forms." Therefore, he says that he may be the right man for philosophy. (This is again, I believe, only naivety, not a sign of vanity.) But this is why his lectures do not show a clear thread.
> [...]
> I hear that only after having heard him [Wittgenstein] for a fairly long time one starts to recognize how much one gets from him. That I am willing to believe. But life is short; and the question is whether I would not profit even more if I used the time for something else (e.g., for studying Marty's works). And at the moment, it seems to me that this question has to be answered in the affirmative. (Rhees to Kastil, 5 November 1933)

This letter concerning Wittgenstein's philosophizing is especially interesting with regard to Rhees' production of *Philosophical Grammar*. Its date reveals that Rhees' first impression of Wittgenstein coincided with the time when Wittgenstein was revising the Big Typescript. Rhees would later understand these revisions as pointing to the unfinished book he edited as *Philosophical Grammar*. However, the letter also makes clear how disconcerting Wittgenstein's philosophizing was for Rhees at that time. Yet more than 30 years later, it was the conveying of precisely this philosophizing that motivated Rhees to prepare the *Philosophical Grammar* in the way he did, also his decision to exclude the Big Typescript's chapter "Philosophy" from it.

In the 1930s, however, Rhees continued his own philosophical studies, namely an elaboration of Brentano's fragmental theory of the continuum. The extant parts of Rhees' essay on this topic show that he maintained his own style of thinking and writing despite Wittgenstein having cast a philosophical spell over him (Rhees 2017; cf. Brentano 1968, 1976; Rhees 1970, 104–147). Nevertheless, or maybe therefore, Rhees became Wittgenstein's confidant and privy to his plans for publishing. In the summer of 1938, when Wittgenstein decided not to attend the "Fourth International Congress for the Unity of Science" in Cambridge, he confided in Rhees, mentioning his reasons for the decision:

> I'm sure you'll think me a beast for changing my mind again about attending that bl… congress. But the truth is, I'm glad I have changed my mind. It was an awful thought to go and sit there among logical positivists and the like; even your presence couldn't make up for all the nastiness. I couldn't however make up my mind not to go until this morning I had an idea which I can't very easily explain to you in writing. The gist of it is that I am thinking of publishing something before long after all so as to end the constant misunderstandings and misinterpretations. I very much want to talk the business over with you. (Wittgenstein to Rhees, 13. July 1938: in Wittgenstein 2008, letter 227)

Shortly afterwards Wittgenstein asked Rhees to translate the text for a bilingual volume to be entitled "Philosophische Bemerkungen—Philosophical Remarks" (Wittgenstein 2001, 20). By early 1939, however, Wittgenstein gave up on the plan. At the same time, Rhees stopped his elaborating of Brentano's theory and left academic philosophy to take a job as a welder in a factory in Swansea. Nevertheless, Wittgenstein thought Rhees (in contrast to other students) was suited for philosophy, which seemed not to be insignificant for Rhees' eventual decision to accept a job as lecturer at the University of Swansea. Wittgenstein visited Rhees in Swansea repeatedly and for longish periods of time.[4] During one of these visits, Wittgenstein gave up working on the remarks on the foundations of mathematics that he had intended as the second part of his "Philosophical Investigations" and devoted himself to investigating psychological concepts (Wittgenstein 2001, 23). He continued working on this topic until the end of 1948. This was when he resigned from his professorship in Cambridge and withdrew to Ireland to complete his book. Rhees visited Wittgenstein in Ireland, and they discussed the work on the book.

This may suffice to give an idea of the quality of the relationship between the two thinkers. Rhees experienced the changes in Wittgenstein's philosophy over many years, also witnessing the development of the corresponding written drafts. Wittgenstein, for his part, granted Rhees a special position, which is also instantiated by the fact that he appointed him not only as literary executor but also as executor of his will.[5] With regard to the question of publishing, Rhees was familiar with Wittgenstein's concern about readers' possible misunderstandings of his philosophy, and Rhees took this concern as one of his guidelines for editing. This can be seen, for example, in his insistence to publish *Remarks on the Foundations of Mathematics* (Wittgenstein 1956) right after the publication of the *Philosophical Investigations* (Wittgenstein 1953). Rhees would have regarded any other second publication after the *Philosophical Investigations* as giving a distorted picture of Wittgenstein's philosophy (see Chap. 1). A second concern Rhees had inherited from Wittgenstein was the latter's desire to ward against unauthorized and false portrayals of his philosophy. This was the main reason for the third publication from Wittgenstein's *Nachlass*, namely *The Blue and Brown Books* (Wittgenstein 1958), which consist of dictations that had been circulating for some time and were in danger of appearing as a pirate edition. These motives for publishing the first editions from Wittgenstein's papers—to prevent misunderstandings and to ward against unauthorized publications—foreshadow the specific method Rhees developed for editing, and which would come to full flower in the 1960s and reach its climax in the *Philosophical Grammar*.

4.2.2 Rhees' Disclosure of Wittgenstein's Writings from the Early 1930s

A decade after the publication of *Philosophical Investigations*, Rhees was dissatisfied with how the posthumous volumes of Wittgenstein's writings were being received. To von Wright, he noted laconically: "The reception of the Untersuchungen has been disappointing. And the Bemerkungen über die

---

[4] For records of their conversations, cf. Wittgenstein (1966) and Wittgenstein, Rhees and Citron (2015).

[5] For a discussion of this fact see Erbacher (2016).

Grundlagen der Mathematik have been largely neglected" (Rhees to von Wright, 5. September 1962). One reason why readers might have been missing the philosophical depth of the *Philosophical Investigations* was, he thought, that the long discussions from which the text had resulted had not been sufficiently clarified or disclosed:

> I do not think people will begin to appreciate the Untersuchungen until they see the discussion from which it has come. It would not be enough, just to print it together with the Tractatus.[6] This would suggest that the relation between them is much simpler than in fact it is. People would still not guess the magnitude of the development which there has been. They would not see—as they do not see—what has happened: they would not see what the Untersuchungen are saying. (Rhees to von Wright, 5. September 1962)

With this disillusioned thought, Rhees devoted himself to studying Wittgenstein's writings from the early 1930s, that is, the time when Wittgenstein resumed philosophical writing, after having completed the Tractatus a decade earlier. The literary executors attended to two items from these early years: one was the so-called Moore Volume,[7] which consisted of excerpts from works produced in 1929 and 1930 that had been glued together into one collection; the second was the Big Typescript, which gathered together Wittgenstein's remarks from 1929 to 1933 (cf. stemma in Wittgenstein 2000a; Schulte 2013, 84). Rhees, who loved copying texts with his typewriter, typed out the Moore Volume (he sometimes referred to it as MM), and by doing so, learned increasingly to appreciate the remarks, as he reported to von Wright: "I have been more and more impressed by the MM as I have been typing it" (Rhees to von Wright, 10 February 1963).[8] Rhees also searched Wittgenstein's notebooks to find the handwritten precursors to the typewritten remarks that had been collected in the Moore Volume. Thus, reversely engineering Wittgenstein's writing practice, Rhees gradually recognized the movements in Wittgenstein's scripts.

While Rhees was working on Wittgenstein's Moore Volume in Swansea, Brian McGuinness was editing Friedrich Waismann's *Nachlass* in Oxford. Waismann's notes showed that Wittgenstein had conversations with members of the Vienna

---

[6] After discussions with Nikolai Bachtin, the older brother of Mikael Bachtin, Wittgenstein wanted to publish the *Tractatus* and the *Philosophical Investigations* together (cf. Wittgenstein's preface for the *Philosophical Investigations*). Corresponding attempts by the literary executors in 1951 failed because of legal objections (cf. Erbacher/Krebs 2015). The only edition that fulfils this wish of Wittgenstein is Wittgenstein (1990).

[7] Ts 209, first published in Wittgenstein (1964). Most of the here-quoted letters date to the time before names for the single *Nachlass* items became established through von Wright's (1969) catalogue. The Moore Volume acquired its name because at the time of Wittgenstein's death, it was in the possession of George Edward Moore. Bertrand Russell had initially used it in 1930 to write a report about Wittgenstein's work during the first years of his fellowship at Trinity College Cambridge.

[8] MM = Moore Volume, cf. Erbacher, Jung and Seibel (2017); I thank Joachim Schulte for recollecting Rhees' love of using writing machines.

Circle around the time when he composed the Moore Volume (cf. Wittgenstein 1967a; Iven 2015; Schulte 1982). McGuinness and Rhees exchanged their insights, and Rhees eventually included some of Waismann's material as appendices to his edition of the Moore Volume. Rhees thought that publishing the Moore Volume together with drafts that had emerged from Wittgenstein's discussions with Waismann would make it easier for readers to understand Wittgenstein's remarks from the time he resumed philosophical writing, and that it could clarify his relation to the logical positivism of the Vienna Circle:

> They [the remarks in the Moore Volume] give a statement of the view which Wittgenstein was putting forward in 1929 and the first half of 1930. It was a view which was very influencial [sic] at the time, although it was not understood. It influenced Schlick, and I think it influenced Carnap; and perhaps some others. People are <u>still</u> unclear about the influence of Wittgenstein on the Wiener Kreis, and they try to ascribe this influence to the Tractatus. This generally leads them to read the Tractatus wrongly. I think the MM[9] is interesting because it shows both the source of the impetus of much of the earlywork of the logical positivists, and also how hopeless it was to look for a clue to Wittgenstein's views in their misunderstandings of him. (Rhees to von Wright, 10 February 1963)

While typing out the Moore Volume, Rhees studied the Big Typescript. Reading the two scripts side by side revealed the drastic and far-reaching changes that Wittgenstein's thinking had undergone after his conversations with the members of the Vienna Circle. Rhees saw that Wittgenstein, when composing the Moore Volume, already had moved away from the view that trying to explicate what is essential to language would lead to the construction of a phenomenological language. However, in the Moore Volume, as Rhees wrote to von Wright, immediate experience was still seen as "the source of sense or meaning, in some analogy to the way in which Elementarsätze are the source of it in the *Tractatus*" (Rhees to von Wright, 14. January 1964). But in the Big Typescript, Rhees read that it would generally be grammar that determines meaning, and in particular:

> the grammar of a sign is not something which you have before you all at once, or something immediately 'given'. This might naturally raise the question of how the meaning <u>is</u> 'given', or in other words: how we learn it. When we distinguish meaning and bearer of a name, it is clear that we cannot get the meaning just by being given a reproduction or Abbild [picture] of what it applies to. The meaning of the sign is something you learn as you learn the different 'facets' of its grammar.
> That is: <u>Understanding</u> a word is connected with <u>learning</u> the meaning of a word. It is not something that is shown by 'logical analysis'. And the learning of a word is 'spread out in time'.
> This is perhaps the biggest difference between <u>Philosophie</u> and the <u>Bemerkungen</u>.[10] (Rhees to von Wright, 14. January 1964)

---

[9] MM = Moore Volume.

[10] Philosophie = Big Typescript, Bemerkungen = Moore Volume; cf. Erbacher, Jung and Seibel (2017).

Rhees was so captivated by seeing how Wittgenstein's new ways of thinking emerged that he had to force himself to stop exploring the details of his discoveries: "All of this interests me so much that I want to go on, but I must turn it off" (Rhees to von Wright, 10. February 1963). Studying these scripts showed him that the Moore Volume began with a rethinking of the *Tractatus*, leading to a result that was then replaced by the grammatical investigations of the Big Typescript. This in turn cleared the path to the language-game method of the *Blue and Brown Books* and to the *Philosophical Investigations*. If Rhees was to succeed in making visible these intermediate cases in the trajectory from the *Tractatus* to the *Philosophical Investigations* and the *Remarks on the Foundations of Mathematics*, readers would perhaps be put in a position to recognize "what the Untersuchungen really are; and similarly for the Bemerkungen über die Grundlagen der Mathematik" (Rhees to von Wright, 5. September 1962).

Thus, Rhees' editions of the Moore Volume and the Big Typescript were meant to hinder the simplistic idea of there being two seemingly distinct and divergent philosophical persona—an "early" and a "late" Wittgenstein—with the early represented by the *Tractatus* and the late by the *Philosophical Investigations*. Contrary to such a simplification, the new editions were supposed to make clear that the "late Wittgenstein" emanated from the philosopher's reflection over the *Tractatus*. This provided Rhees with his editorial intention: "It seems to me that it is important to show that 'the later Wittgenstein' is a continuation of the same discussions which we have in the Tractatus" (Rhees to von Wright, 10. February 1963). To this end, Rhees asked for a leave of absence from his post as lecturer at the University of Swansea.

4.3   Perhaps You Are Inclined to Ask:…

> … why can you not just print the big typescript as it stands, ignoring all and every correction or revision.
>
>   Lord. If you do want to ask this, I will try to answer in another letter. I really think this is impossible—and I mean that: I do not mean just inadvisable. (Rhees to von Wright, 8 November 1965)

4.3.1   Wittgenstein's Philosophizing as Clarificatory Writing

Rhees' insights into the movement from the *Tractatus* to the Moore Volume, the Big Typescript, the *Blue and Brown Books* and the *Philosophical Investigations* suggest that the progress of Wittgenstein's philosophizing was not a matter of relinquishing old thoughts and moving on to new ones, but rather a way of thinking that increasingly questioned terminology and the thought-leading pictures built into the terms he used. The term "progress" may thus already invoke a misleading picture of his work, as Wittgenstein himself reflected in notes he made for a preface for his book in 1930:

> This book is written for such men as are in sympathy with its spirit. This spirit is different from the one which informs the vast stream of European and American civilization in which all of us stand. That spirit expresses itself in an onwards movement, in building ever larger and more complicated structures; the other in striving after clarity and perspicuity in no matter what structure. The first tries to grasp the world by way of its periphery—in its variety; the second at its centre—in its essence. And so the first adds one construction to another, moving on and up, as it were, from one stage to the next, while the other remains where it is and what it tries to grasp is always the same. (Wittgenstein 1975, Foreword, cf. Ms 109,204[4]–208[3])

The philosophizing that strives for clarity and transparency constantly reflects on its own guiding concepts, for instance "progress", "analysis", "meaning" and so on. This reflexivity corresponds with a writing practice that tries to clarify itself through working over its results again and again. In this way, Wittgenstein's manuscripts and typescripts are the material traces of a philosophizing that strives for clarification. While typing out these scripts, Rhees began to recognize that Wittgenstein systematically practiced such clarificatory writing in his notebooks, manuscripts and typescripts:

> In my very rough designations, I now distinguish between 'manuscript books' and 'notebooks'. The manuscript books are the large, hard covered books, with the entries invariably (I think) in ink. And their material is generally taken from some of the small pocket notebooks. For instance, the notebook which I dated as 1931 in the first lot of four which I sent you, has been transferred in large measure to Band VII. The 'manuscript books' are nearer to a finished draft. (Rhees to von Wright, 22. August 1965)

These are among the first classifications for studying the internal relations in Wittgenstein's *Nachlass*: Wittgenstein frequently wrote drafts of remarks in notebooks and then copied a selection to manuscripts and manuscript-volumes and then re-dictated selections from these. The resulting typescripts provided starting points for further revisions, which could be corrections of expressions or new compositions. Wittgenstein sometimes had the new compositions re-typed, thus creating yet another starting point for even further revisions. The Big Typescript went through such stages in an exemplary way (cf. stemma in Wittgenstein 2000a and Schulte 2013, 84).[11]

Due to this work method, the same or similar remarks appear over and over again in the different items in Wittgenstein's *Nachlass*. However, this does not mean that they, in each instance, form the same philosophical discussion and only show stylistic changes to one and the same thought. Just as a word or a proposition can vary in meaning in different contexts of use, so also can Wittgenstein's remarks vary in meaning depending on the textual context in which they are used.

---

[11] For a classic study on the working and writing practice of Wittgenstein, see Pichler (1994).

Hence, while Wittgenstein was trying to capture in his remarks the context-sensitivity of meaning, he developed varied contexts in which to put his remarks, treating the practice as a new method of clarificatory writing that showed what he said. Rhees became aware of the philosophical significance of this aspect of the form of Wittgenstein's writings while studying the Moore Volume alongside the Big Typescript:

> At one time we thought that if Philosophie were published, then it would be idle to publish the Philosophische Bemerkungen (the Moore volume), since the larger book seems to contain everything that there is in the Bemerkungen, in a better arrangement, together with important later developments.
>
> Now it does contain a great deal of the Bemerkungen, and it contains these passages verbatim. (Quite often they are in quotes in this manuscript, by the way.) But I do not think this is a reason against publishing both. It is also true that Philosophie has some things WHICH have been taken verbatim, or very nearly, into the Untersuchungen. This does not mean that Philosophie is just an earlier draft of the Untersuchungen; and I find nothing awkward in the repetition of the passages: I see them differently in the different contexts, and I think I understand them better. And I would say this with more emphasis of the passages from the Bemerkungen which are repeated in Philosophie. Except for very small clusters which are kept together as they were before, the passages have a quite different arrangement in the later typescript. This is partly a revision, I agree. On further reflexion Wittgenstein decided that they ought to go in that order. But much else had gone on in him as well. And his reasons for thinking that they ought to go in that order, often went with a different view of the question he was discussing in them. So that I think it is not generally a revised version of the same discussion, but a different discussion.
>
> [...]
>
> Certain philosophical differences can be brought out best by treating the same material in different ways—as in these two books.[12] (Rhees to von Wright, 14. January 1964)

How Wittgenstein made a philosophical difference by treating one and the same remark in different ways can be seen by looking at his use of quotation marks, as Rhees mentioned in his letter. Remarks that Wittgenstein had written down as a philosophical proposition or part of a theoretical thought in an earlier composition could be placed in quotations marks in a later step of the clarificatory writing, having now the function of an example of the sentences that philosophers are inclined to state while philosophizing. Rhees recognized that the relation between remarks in the Moore Volume and the Big Typescript could have this function: "Quite often the passages from the MM appear in the BM in quotation marks, because Wittgenstein is treating them as material for discussion and not as a view which he is putting forward" (Rhees to von Wright, 10. February 1963).[13] In this way, a new written form of clarification evolved along with Wittgenstein's new thought that

---

[12] Philosophie = Big Typescript, (Philosophische) Bemerkungen = Moore Volume; cf. Erbacher, Jung and Seibel (2017).

[13] MM = Moore Volume, BM = Big Typescript; cf. Baker (2002, 66): "What BT and BB tries to get rid of is 'meaning' and 'understanding', not meaning and understanding. Less obviously, but no less crucially, the topic of PI § 202 is not following a rule, but 'following a rule'. In such cases, differences in mere punctuation turn out to be BIG differences!".

the meaning of a word could be clarified by looking at its grammar: logical analysis and logical notation could no longer show in a single picture what the meaning of a word and the sense of a proposition were, but the grammar (in Wittgenstein's sense) of a word could only be shown and clarified by examples of use in sentences and be nuanced through comparing varying examples.[14] Such investigations into the grammar of a word through varying examples are necessarily spread out in time, they form threads of philosophical discussions. Wittgenstein's writings would increasingly take the shape of such discussions, in which word uses were not always indicated by quotation marks, but shown with ever more sophisticated techniques of presentation. Thus, Rhees discovered that, when reading Wittgenstein's papers, it was not always easy to detect which function a given sentence had in the grammatical investigation, but that it was crucial to read it as part of a philosophical discussion.

4.3.2 Finding Intermediate Cases: Rhees' Co-Creative Editing

Because Rhees' copy of the Big Typescript was scribbled over with corrections and notes in Wittgenstein's hand, Rhees recognized that it was not as finished a work as the typographic appearance of the clean typescript may suggest, even to Wittgenstein's literary executors.[15] When Rhees transferred these corrections into a new typescript, he discovered that the emerging remarks resembled passages in one of Wittgenstein's manuscript volumes. Therefore, in this case, the *manu*script was not a preliminary stage of the *type*script but a later version. Hence, after Rhees had finished editing the Moore Volume,[16] he began typing out the handwritten volumes that belonged to the context of the Big Typescript. In the summer of 1965, he discovered to his great surprise that one of the manuscript volumes—namely the "Band X" (Ms 114)—contained not only some corrected remarks but that they were arranged into an entirely new composition. Wittgenstein wrote this new composition under the heading "Umarbeitung" ("Revision"). This Revision continued beyond the end of the one manuscript volume up to the beginning of the next (Ms 114ii, 30–228 up to Ms 115i, 1–117). In a letter to von Wright, Rhees drew some conclusions from this discovery:

> The important point is: a) this is an Umarbeitung of the big typescript, not of the Philosophische Bemerkungen, Do not ask me how I was so stupid before. But I discovered this when I was trying to make a version of the big typescript, taking account of the

---

[14] For the development of Wittgenstein's notion of grammar, see Uffelmann (2018).

[15] See Schulte (2013, 84); due to carbon copies, not only one, but three versions of the Big Typescript exist. The top copy shows different corrections than do the carbon copies. To see how decisive the corrections in the typescript could be, compare Ts 213,250r[2] (http://www.wittgensteinsource.org/BFE/Ts-213,250r_f) and Ts 213,249v[1] (http://www.wittgensteinsource.org/BFE/Ts-213,249v_f). I thank Sarah Uffelmann for this example.

[16] Rhees' edition appeared in 1964, cf. Wittgenstein (1964).

corrections between the lines and on the opposite pages, and I was referring fairly often
to Band X, which I took to be the manuscript Band. It became clear again and again that
what was in Band X is a <u>later</u> version than the typed one. (The material in the typescript
is not all of one time—or should I say: it contains views which are not of a piece. I do not
know to what extent it was typed all at a stretch. And I have a suspicion that it was meant
as the <u>raw material</u> for a book; but this is not important just now).
  b) The Band X Umarbeitung is not just a series of revisions. It is a continuous book:
Even more than a revised statement of many or most of the passages, it is a <u>new ordering</u>
of the material. It is coherent and forceful, and—for me as I type it—extremely interesting. (Rhees to von Wright, 8 November 1965)

After further study, Rhees saw his intuition confirmed—that it was not the Big
Typescript but the "Umarbeitung" that could be regarded as close to a finished
work: "Wittgenstein did regard the Umarbeitung as a coherent statement at that
time, although it was not rounded off" (Rhees to von Wright, 11. September
1966). Rhees was therefore convinced that the Revision had to be the text that
he ought to edit, rather than the Big Typescript. The Revision also indicated the
title of the envisaged edition: "<u>If</u> I can produce a book at all, I think it should be
called '<u>Philosophische Grammatik</u>'. This is what Band X is called" (Rhees to von
Wright, 8. November 1965).

But things were not as straightforward as Rhees had thought: when he began
systematically to type out the Revision, he found references to further revisions
in another manuscript that Wittgenstein called "zweite Umarbeitung" ("Second
Revision").[17] Thus, Rhees now had to cope with at least four layers of an outline
for a work: the Big Typescript as it was typed, the handwritten revisions in it, the
resulting Revision, as well as its revision in the Second Revision. Rhees described
the editorial entanglement he had gotten himself into to his good friend Maurice
O'Connor Drury, who had also been a close friend of Wittgenstein:

What I hoped would be the chief work in this period—what I had hoped was a manuscript with corrections and variants which need to be edited—has now turned out to be not
Siamese twins but Siamese quadruplets. And I wish I would see how to make it plain what
this quartet is saying. (Rhees to Drury, 7. November 1965, quoted from chapter 1)[18]

Dedicated to fulfilling this ambition, Rhees retired for good from his post at the
University of Swansea in order to concentrate on publishing Wittgenstein's writings. Excerpts of letters from this time and traces of his editorial work give an
idea of how he immersed himself in the material.[19] For almost every day, there are

---

[17] The Second Revision is in Ms 140, a manuscript volume called "Grosses Format".

[18] This description of Rhees' editing fits Cora Diamond's recollection of her editorial work
in cooperation with Rhees: Rhees gave to Diamond four sets of notes taken by students at
Wittgenstein's 1939 lectures on the foundations of mathematics; Diamond remembers that, while
preparing from these sets one text, she 'needed to learn to hear Wittgenstein's voice' (from an
unpublished draft to APA Dewey Lecture 2019).

[19] Rhees' Nachlass is kept at Richard Burton Archives at the University Swansea. According to
his student D. Z. Phillips, the estate contains about 16,000 pages. Phillips made many of Rhees'
philosophical writings available in posthumous editions, since Rhees, like Wittgenstein, had

dated pages with philosophical and exegetical notes that evolved simultaneously to his editorial work. This philosophical and exegetical examination that accompanied his editing was more than a reading aid: Rhees reconstructed, stroke by stroke, Wittgenstein's clarificatory writing. Given how Rhees repeatedly worked over Wittgenstein's remarks, it became a form of writing that corresponded to Wittgenstein's own philosophical clarification process. By copying his teacher's typescripts and manuscripts and by carrying out his corrections, Rhees came to know the craft of Wittgenstein's philosophizing as it manifested itself in writing, and he re-enacted Wittgenstein's philosophical development by going through the layers of revision. After more than three years of this philosophical, editorial and literary re-enactment, the typewritten text emerged that would be published under the title *Philosophical Grammar.*

Rhees initially planned that the edition should consist of two volumes, the first called "Satz, Sinn des Satzes" and a second "Über Logik und Mathematik" (the latter not being a part of Wittgenstein's Revision). This envisioned disposition suggests more clearly than the structure of the Big Typescript that the *Philosophical Investigation*'s division into two parts has roots stretching back further than to its first version from 1936. Unfortunately, Rhees' twofold disposition fell victim to the cost of printing.[20] But when one visualizes this division, it shows morphologically the transition from *Philosophical Remarks* to *Philosophical Investigations.* Thus, through his philosophical re-composing, Rhees created the *Philosophical Grammar* as an intermediate case that makes it possible to see connections between a foregoing and a following work. Crafting and publishing this intermediate case contributed to a perspicuous representation of Wittgenstein's development as a philosophical writer (cf. Wittgenstein 1953, §122).

Given its genesis, *Philosophical Grammar* may be called an apocryphal work or a philosophical co-creation. But in co-creating it, Rhees most carefully followed his understanding of the texts he edited and his insights into the development of Wittgenstein's compositions. Today, philosophical-philological accounts of the status of the Big Typescript support Rhees' main decision to edit the *Philosophical Grammar* rather than the Big Typescript as an alleged work of Wittgenstein (See Schulte 2013; Stern 2018). Some philological observations can also be made concerning Rhees' decision not to include the Big Typescript's chapter "Philosophy". For instance, there are comparatively few handwritten corrections in this chapter in the Big Typescript, and it is not included in Wittgenstein's Revision in Band XI (See Ms 115i, 117). The remarks in this chapter may thus belong to a stage in Wittgenstein's thinking from before the Big Typescript, but not to a stage that

---

published very little during his lifetime. Nevertheless, he wrote daily about philosophical questions and corresponded with colleagues.

[20] The correspondence between Rhees and the publisher concerning the printing of the *Philosophical Grammar* can be found in the Rush Rhees Collection at the Richard Burton Archives.

followed it. And it was just such a stage that the *Philosophical Grammar* was supposed to show. Indeed, to Heikki Nyman, von Wright's assistant who later wanted to publish the chapter "Philosophy" on its own, Rhees wrote: "The remarks in this chapter belong to a limited time—I do not think any of them was [sic] written later than the first half of 1932" (Rhees to Nyman, 21. April 1982). Rhees' conjecture was partly confirmed when another dictation by Wittgenstein was discovered some years later. This "Diktat für Schlick" (Ts 302) presumably follows the conclusion of the Revision. Although this dictation includes a section on method, it notably differs from the chapter "Philosophy" in the Big Typescript, making it plausible that Wittgenstein indeed did not want to transfer the chapter from the Big Typescript into the Revision. This coincides with Rhees' view, as he told von Wright, that the remarks in the chapter "Philosophy" and the practiced method in *Philosophical Grammar* are partially "incongruous" (Rhees to von Wright, 26. August 1982). More than any philological investigation, this was for Rhees the decisive argument. This points back to Rhees' understanding of the text that is inextricable from his editing. Thus, it is Rhees' understanding of Wittgenstein's philosophizing that may further illuminate his reasons for leaving out the chapter "Philosophy".

4.4 But Nothing One Could Formulate as 'the General Method of Philosophy'…

> … the use of Beispiele. If someone asks, 'What use of Beispiele?', we can answer again only by giving Beispiele. (Rhees to von Wright, 26. August 1982)

4.4.1 Philosophizing as Activity that Shows Itself

Wittgenstein's philosophizing served to clarify the language that is used when philosophizing. The written form of this clarificatory work is manifested in his manuscripts that show the repeated questioning and working over of his remarks. The remarks thus become material for clarifying the thinking rather than fixed results. Even in the *Tractatus,* he expressed this idea of philosophy as a clarificatory activity (TLP 4.112). He continued with this orientation throughout his philosophical career but developed various forms of clarification (See Erbacher 2015). As a clarificatory activity, philosophizing resembles an art (skill) to be learned. Mastery of this art is demonstrated when one successfully clarifies the language one uses when philosophizing. This understanding of philosophizing was one reason why Rhees left out the chapter "Philosophy" in the *Philosophical Grammar,* as he explained to von Wright:

> You will agree that you cannot tell anyone what philosophy is, if he has never been near enough the water to get his feet wet. And it is impossible to tell anyone what Wittgenstein's conception of philosophy is, if he has made no long or serious study of what Wittgenstein has written. It would have been impossible for Wittgenstein himself to

do this. And the remarks in that section of Typoskript 213 can have force or sense only against the _Hintergrund_ of the philosophizing which Wittgenstein does, or has done. Wittgenstein used to say something in this sense to people who wanted to come to his lectures. It is why he used (for example) to speak of the work of philosophy as the work of changing one's way of looking at things, _durch lange Übung_. (Rhees to von Wright, 22. January 1976)

Rhees appeals in this letter to his experience of Wittgenstein's lectures, an experience that von Wright shared, since he and Rhees both attended the lectures on the foundations of mathematics in 1939 (Wittgenstein 1976). Rhees referred again to this mutual experience in another letter a few years later:

> The point, of course, is that this chapter assumes that you already _know_ what sort of discussions Wittgenstein called 'philosophy'. If someone who _didn't_ know asked you, 'What was Wittgenstein's conception of philosophy?', you would not tell him: 'Read this that's called 'Philosophie', and you'll know.'
> [...]
> You were present at W.'s lecture in 1939 (on _Foundations of Mathematics_) when he said, 'What we are studying here is a _way of investigating_ certain questions.' (He added, for Turing, 'And it is a way that goes very much against the grain of some people.') Again and again he would say that what he was trying to show or teach was a _method_. To understand what it was he called 'doing philosophy' I should have to have got _some_ idea of the method of his discussions. When I have, then I shall also begin to understand what he would call the _result_ of a philosophical investigation.
> But nothing one could formulate as 'the general method of philosophy'. The use of Beispiele.
> If someone asks, 'What use of Beispiele?', we can answer again only by giving Beispiele.
> The _Brown Book_ as one example. (Rhees to von Wright, 26. August 1982)

Explanations like these leave no doubt that Rhees thought Wittgenstein's method of philosophizing was significant: he understood that Wittgenstein's classes and writings served to teach a method. However, one could master this method only by practicing on examples, not through theorizing about it. As Rhees noted in the above letter, he regarded Wittgenstein's writings as examples of how he practiced his method.[21] With this in mind, Rhees wrote to Nyman concerning "Philosophy" in the Big Typescript:

> When you say it is 'the longest statement of Wittgenstein on the nature of philosophy', I want to ask: Is it longer than the _Untersuchungen_? You will say this is unfair. But if someone asked me, 'What is the nature of philosophy?' it would have more sense to refer him to the _Untersuchungen_ than to this chapter from TS 213. (Rhees to Nyman, 21. April 1982)

According to Rhees, Wittgenstein's works as a whole, rather than the remarks in the chapter "Philosophy", showed what philosophizing meant for him. The way to

---

[21] Or later "methods", cf. Conant (2011).

recognize Wittgenstein's different methods was by comparing his works. Rhees' *Philosophical Grammar* instantiates precisely this understanding, as he explicitly stated in his editorial postscript:

> Many things in the *Blue Book* are here (and they are better expressed). There are passages also which are in the *Philosophical Remarks* and others later included in the *Investigations*. It would be easy to give the reference and page number for each of these. We decided not to. This book should be compared with Wittgenstein's earlier and later writings. But this means: the method and the development of his discussion here should be compared with the *Philosophical Remarks* and again with the *Investigations*. The footnotes would be a hindrance and, as often as not, misleading. When Wittgenstein writes a paragraph here that is also in the *Remarks*, this does not mean that he is just repeating what he said there. The paragraph may have a different importance, it may belong to the discussion in a different way. (Wittgenstein 1974, Note in editing)

Footnotes, comments, references to passages in related manuscripts and other elements of a text-critical apparatus were deliberately excluded, not only from the *Philosophical Grammar*, but from all volumes edited by Wittgenstein's literary heirs. They did so not because they were unable to include them, but because they thought that such a philological apparatus might not instigate the kind of use of the books that Wittgenstein had had in mind. Rhees probably thought the philological distraction might even lead readers into the very confusions about philosophizing that Wittgenstein wanted to dissolve with his writings. Rhees' friend Drury supported him in this judgement concerning Wittgenstein's orientation that provided the "soil" for his writing.

4.4.2 Drury's Support

While working on *Philosophical Grammar*, Rhees and Drury exchanged views on Wittgenstein's "philosophical orientation", as Drury called it:

> The higher conception here is that what is eternal in philosophy can have no permanent or precise statement in words, it has to be shown not said. And so every generation has to do its philosophy over again, for what has shown the truth to one person or one age will become opaque to another. Hence it is that although Wittgenstein is not concerned with 'progress', he does say that 'if my remarks do not bear a stamp which marks them as mine, I do not want to lay any further claim to them as my property'. And again 'I should not like my writing to spare other people the trouble of thinking'.
> [...]
> I am mentioning these memories because I think the tradition has grown up that Wittgenstein regarded himself as one who had made progress beyond all previous metaphysicians. It is this idea of progress in philosophy that bedevils everything. What Wittgenstein taught me was this. That only through the pain of my own thinking, langen Zweifeln, la longue meditation, would the eternal truths of philosophy shew themselves. I would not find them written out for me in any book, however great the stature of its author. (Drury to Rhees, presumably October 1965)

Drury pointed out the importance of differentiating Wittgenstein's philosophizing from the idea of progress that animates Western civilization and its sciences.
Indeed, Wittgenstein's clarificatory philosophizing often treated the confusion
associated with an undue application of scientific thinking beyond its appropri-
ate realm. Drury remembered that Wittgenstein found an outstanding example of
such mislead and misleading scientific thinking in James G. Frazer's *The Golden
Bough*:

> Once Wittgenstein asked me to read to him part of 'The Golden Bough'. Frazer always
> treated the myths and customs he had so assiduously collected with a certain condescen-
> tion [sic]. He said we must not despise them for their errors because they represented the
> first rudimentary thoughts from which later science was to spring. But, as Wittgenstein
> pointed out, these ancients had indeed already their science. Agriculture, irrigation,
> weapon making, etc.: they were able to survive under conditions where we would now
> perish. No, these myths these customs, had nothing to do with the beginning of science.
> They were the expression of a belief and a longing for something other than the bread and
> comforts of daily existence. And in so far as we have now lost these common myths and
> common customs, so much are we the poorer. The belief that the further progress of scien-
> tific discovery and invention will bring us any nearer to the relief of our deepest needs, is
> a superstition worse than anything Frazer cast his pity on. (Drury to Rhees, Spring 1966;
> cf. Drury 1984, 2017; Wittgenstein 1967b)

Drury wrote in a similar way in another letter:

> He said that although Frazer roamed over the whole world in describing magical prac-
> tices, he never put one of them in their right context. Namely that these practices took
> place among people who had already got important and difficult scientific achievements
> to their credit. Making weapons out of refractory material, agriculture, irrigation, etc. The
> magical practices must be looked at against this background, then they take on a different
> appearance. Frazer refers to the Australian aborigines as being 'in the most backward state
> of human society' and as 'the rudest savages as to whom we possess accurate informa-
> tion'. But could Frazer make, still less use, a boomerang? Place Frazer in the Australian
> bush and he would appear to these 'rude savages' as a complete ignoramus. (Drury to
> Rhees, 15. May 1967)

For Drury just as for Rhees, Wittgenstein's remarks on Frazer's work pointed to
his entire philosophical orientation that impeded Western academic and progress-
oriented thinking. In the early 1930s, Wittgenstein had even considered starting
his book with this theme.[22] Inspired by this, Rhees considered creating a preface for Philosophical Grammar out of a series of remarks Wittgenstein had written about Frazer's Golden Bough. At the same time, however, he remembered
Wittgenstein's warning against the danger of a long preface and decided against

---

[22] Ms 110,177[5–6] (http://www.wittgensteinsource.org/BFE/Ms-110,177_f): "Ich glaube jetzt
daß es richtig wäre mein Buch mit Bemerkungen über die Metaphysik als eine Art der Magie
zu beginnen. Worin ich aber weder der Magie das Wort reden, noch mich über sie lustig machen
darf".

using the remarks as a preface (Rhees to von Wright, 10. February 1963).[23] Instead, he published a composition of Wittgenstein's remarks on Frazer's Golden Bough to give a detailed representation of Wittgenstein's discussion.[24] Since some of the remarks on Frazer are part of the chapter "Philosophy" in the Big Typescript (Ts 213, 433–435), this editorial handling can give a hint on how Rhees wanted to see the chapter published. For it was not Rhees' intention to withhold the chapter "Philosophy" in the Big Typescript, but to include it in a way that would avoid misunderstandings:

> May I emphasize once again: I am not saying that those remarks in 213 should not be published. —If you do publish them, I should pray that you might write a fairly long introduction: calling attention, for instance, to other remarks or passages by Wittgenstein which throw more definite light on what doing philosophy was for him: to what he says in Untersuchungen about his own errors in Tractatus, for instance, and especially to what he says about the difficulties in coming to recognize these; to what he says about the importance of method—and to the fact that the section here which is called 'Die Methode in der Philosophie' gives you no idea and no example of what Wittgenstein's method was (e.g., the difference which he held important between the method of the Brown Book and the method of the Untersuchungen);
>   [...]
> The thousands of times people have quoted "the fly in the fly-bottle", as if W. meant it to be illuminating just by itself. It is excellent as the final 'bar' as it were characterizing the whole performance. It seems to me the same is true of most of the remarks in that section of 213.
> From 213 you'd hardly guess why or how method was important in philosophy—in later years the 'übersichtliche Darstellung' does not have the central place which he seemed to give it in 1931—nor would you understand what he meant by calling his earlier method wrong or defective: what is there about philosophical perplexity and the work of philosophy that leads him to think (though his soul groans within him) that he must start over again and (since he has abandoned notions which were central earlier) that he must follow in certain ways a different method. (Rhees to von Wright, 22. January 1976)

This shows that Rhees considered it his duty to make editions of Wittgenstein's writings for those who—just as he himself while editing—wanted to study Wittgenstein's method as shown in his works. It was only for readers who were willing to make this effort that he did his editorial work. For Rhees, it would be missing the point to make editions that did not serve these readers, or that gave an impression of a work whose genesis could be put in a philological apparatus. Drury shared this opinion:

> Forty years ago Wittgenstein's teaching came to me as a warning against certain intellectual and spiritual dangers by which I was strongly tempted. These dangers still surround

---

[23] Cf. Erbacher, Jung and Seibel (2017) and Ms 109, 208 (http://www.wittgensteinsource.org/BFE/Ms-109,208_f).

[24] Rhees' edition of the remarks on Frazer (=Wittgenstein 1967b) has also gone through the second critical phase in the history of editing Wittgenstein (Wittgenstein 1993) and has entered the third phase (Westergaard 2015).

us all. It would be a tragedy if well meaning commentators should make it appear that these writings were now easily assimilable into the very intellectual milieu they were largely a warning against. (Drury to Rhees, Spring 1966, cf. Drury 2017)

This understanding of Wittgenstein's philosophical orientation forms an important aspect of the background of Rhees' reading of Wittgenstein's texts and therewith of his editorial handling of them. However, young scholars who had gotten hold of the Cornell microfilm wanted to make up their own minds when studying the sources, instead of accepting the paternalism of editions that had been constituted through so much philosophical co-creation.[25] This clash of generations also formed the background for Rhees' reaction to Kenny's criticism on the *Philosophical Grammar*, with which this investigation began.

4.5   You Say You Think 'Readers Might Find It Helpful'...

… and if I could agree with you on this there would be no trouble. (Rhees to Kenny, 27. February 1973)

4.5.1   Back to Kenny

Thus far in this chapter, the focus has been on trying to understand Rhees' reasons for his way of editing. Editorial decisions that could at first seem incomprehensible from a philological point of view—namely not to print the Big Typescript as it stood and to exclude the chapter "Philosophy"—served as an entry point for the investigation. If the present constructive contextualization of Rhees' editing has succeeded, readers should now be in a better position to understand Rhees' response to Kenny's proposal to print his (Kenny's) text-critical examination as an introduction to the English edition of the *Philosophical Grammar*. Let us therefore return to the exchange between Rhees and Kenny.

After Kenny sent a draft of his introduction to Rhees in February 1972, Rhees became distrustful and complained to his friend Peter Winch, saying that Kenny spoke as if he had worked his way through a wealth of material that mattered for the selection and composition of the *Philosophical Grammar*. But Rhees, having studied Wittgenstein's papers in the way described in earlier sections in this chapter, suspected that Kenny had not actually followed Wittgenstein in his moves of clarifying revising; if this was so, Rhees would have regarded Kenny's introduction an instance of "Oxford glibness", as Rhees put it in a letter to Peter Winch (Rhees to Winch, 23. February 1973). He therefore rejected Kenny's proposal:

Dear Kenny,

---

[25] I thank David Stern for this recollection.

Forgive me for being so long in thanking you for the draft of the note you had in mind for your translation. I did not want to answer without trying to understand better, if I could, what you were after. But I find I still cannot go along with it.—By 'it' I mean chiefly: 1) your idea of including the table of contents which Wittgenstein drew after he had completed the arrangement (as it stands) of the TS 213; and (2) the including of more detailed references to manuscript books and typescripts, as on your page 2 and 27.

You say you think 'readers might find it helpful'. And if I could agree with you on this there would be no trouble.

With regard to the table of contents: The readers would be presented with a table of contents which is not the table of contents of the book they have in their hands. Or—which makes it worse, if anything—which is partly identical with the table of contents of the book—namely that of Part II—and partly not. They would naturally suppose that the table of contents which you were printing gave them an übersichtliche Darstellung of the contents of the book. But it does not. It will not help them to find in the book the topics which are mentioned in it.—Then: they'll find another table of contents given. I should think they would wonder what is going on; and that they will be discouraged from reading the book itself.

It will not help them to find their way. On the contrary.

Insofar as it stimulates readers to ask further questions at all, it will deflect their attention from what Wittgenstein is saying to a study of the 'codices'. I think this influence would be deplorable. It would be in line with what is already happening as copies of the Cornell microfilms are being more and more widely distributed.—I am saying dogmatically what must seem to you an expression of prejudice and nothing more. It is not simply that. But I do not know how to try to make you see what I mean in a few sentences. And I should probably make nothing clear if I went on at more length.

When I speak of 'what is already happening' I think partly of the products of certain pseudo-scholars who have come up with 'discoveries' from the Cornell manuscripts; and who have prepared a 'work', carefully annotated with references to the numbers of the 'Cornell Volumes', etc., etc. That is part of the world we live in, and not worth worrying too much about. But there is a tendency among more serious philosophers to erect fences between the readers and what Wittgenstein is saying. A sarcophagus. But we can tell whose sarcophagus it is, because there are all these inscriptions. And now about the inscriptions, you see …

I am reminded of the pedantic and humourless detail about the conditions of the manuscripts that appears in the posthumous editing of Husserl's writings.

Wittgenstein would have loathed it. (Rhees to Kenny, 27. February 1973)

After receiving this message from Rhees, Kenny tried to shed further light on his intentions:

I think that the general philosophical public feels rather about the Wittgenstein Nachlass as the Roman plebs felt about Caesar's will. There are these triumvirs, and we only have their word for what is in the will. Who knows whether Caesar may not have left us all his gardens on both sides of the Tiber? (Kenny to Rhees, 20. March 1973)

Against the background of what has been said on the foregoing pages, it should be no surprise that Rhees did not change his mind after this reply. However, thanks to Kenny's persistence, Rhees wrote a more definite statement regarding his understanding of his duty as Wittgenstein's literary executor:

You say that 'the general philosophical public' is suspicious of what has been published of Wittgenstein's writings apart from the Tractatus, since they have only the word of the literary executors that this is what Wittgenstein wrote.—The only place I have met anything of the sort was in an article by Stephen Toulmin; and even this was not quite what you describe. But I do not read much, and I am sure you are speaking of something you have met.—On the other hand, I do not think it is important.

When I am trying to decide what to publish (or to give an opinion): what to include and what to leave out, how best to present it—one question I generally have in mind is: What will make it easier to see what Wittgenstein is saying?

But that question is subordinate to another, namely: 'What would Wittgenstein have wanted? Would he have wanted it this way? Is this faintly like what he would have done or have wanted us to do?' I think this is more in my thoughts than anything else. NOT: 'What does the general philosophical public want?'

[...]

Suppose I told the general philosophical public to go and have a look for himself—and suppose he did so. The chances are he would come away more suspicious than ever. He can say now: 'You are misleading us when you say this is what Wittgenstein wrote. He wrote lots of other things.'—And I think you have said this, in a more educated and intelligent way. And I've thought that if you had Alladin's lamp you'd want to show people all the other things at once. If this is unjust to you, I beg pardon.

It would be no help towards an understanding of Wittgenstein's ideas and discussions if the whole lot had been published at once; even if it had been physically possible. Some of those who think it wrong for editors to work as editors do not even study what has been published. Do you know anyone of the general philosophical public who has studied the Philosophische Bemerkungen?

'Why should we read this when we do not even know if Wittgenstein wrote it?'

Are you seriously impressed by such a remark when you meet it?

Would you expect the speaker to work as he'd have to work to understand it if ever he did know that Wittgenstein wrote it? (Rhees to Kenny, 22. March 1973)

This dissuaded Kenny from his plan to publish his introduction, and when the English edition of the *Philosophical Grammar* appeared, Rhees heartily congratulated Kenny. However, as has already been mentioned, Kenny let his introduction be published three years later. Rhees did not react to this publicly but wrote a private letter, which ended with the words: "I have no doubt, by the way, that your article will be praised as a piece of fine scholarship" (Rhees to Kenny, 2. March 1977).

4.5.2   The Meaning of Editing and Editorial Cultures

Rhees' own understanding of decent philosophical research can be found in the same commemorative volume for von Wright that includes Kenny's essay (Rhees 1977). Rhees, in his article, introduces his interpretation of Wittgenstein's remarks on Frazer. The simultaneousness of these two contributions illustrates the conflict between two phases in the history of making Wittgenstein's writings available. Today, the accounts of the text-critical second phase are often held as editorial common sense. For example, in writing about the work of Wittgenstein's original literary heirs, Venturinha says that their "peculiar editorial methodology immediately reveals that there was no real concern among the Wittgenstein editors to be faithful to the sources" (Venturinha 2010, 2).

This statement is characteristic for advocates of the critical phase. The present attempt to offer a constructive contextualization could possibly show that Rhees was deeply concerned about being faithful to Wittgenstein's texts. This faithfulness, however, was to Wittgenstein's philosophical purpose for his writings. As executor of his will and as a literary executor, Rhees wanted to serve just this purpose. He saw it as the duty which Wittgenstein's will had imposed on him. This shows that proponents of the different phases of editing had different understandings of what "faithfulness" towards the texts meant. Such different understandings extent also to many other terms: "scholarship" is one example, such as Rhees used it in his letter to Kenny. Another example is the following sentence that Rhees wrote to Drury about the problem of misunderstanding Wittgenstein's intentions:

> And there is a danger that a misunderstanding of Wittgenstein's 'intentions' will stand more and more in the way, so that his works are never read as they were written. (Rhees to Drury, 6. November 1966)

This sentence could have also been stated by advocates of critical editorial philology, in the same phrasing but with the exact opposite meaning. Such different meanings of the same terms show that the two phases in the history of editing Wittgenstein's writings indeed belong to different academic cultures. It is in these academic cultures the different terms have different meanings. This is why those who want to understand Rhees' way of editing without embedding it in his philosophical life and work and instead judging his editorial decisions according to the principles of editorial philology, are likely to apply standards that were foreign to Rhees himself. Although there are, as shown above, good philological reasons for Rhees' editing of *Philosophical Grammar*, the application of this type of measurement would be analogous to, for example, Frazer's scientist view of other cultures, or to scientists who identify the rationality of human conduct in society as "bad" scientific thinking.[26]

Last but not least, the story of Rhees and Wittgenstein's Philosophical Grammar shows that the differences in the meaning of central terms in the first and second phase of editing Wittgenstein's Nachlass also come to expression in the different ways of comprehending what it means to create a "perspicuous representation" of Wittgenstein's writings. The editors' different readings of this phrase—a phrase that belongs to the self-understanding of the edited texts—are materialized in the editions of the two phases (Wittgenstein 1953, §122). The editing of both phases can thus be seen as part of the philosophical activity that the writings seek to inspire. By approaching the editions in this way, it is eventually possible to see also the third phase in the history of editing Wittgenstein as

---

[26] Garfinkel (1967) uses this example in "'Good' organizational reasons for 'bad' clinic records", which has inspired the title of this chapter.

belonging to this continuous effort. Whereas the first phase consisted of a unity of philosophizing and editing inspired by first-hand experience of philosophizing with Wittgenstein, critical editions of the second phase dis-united and gradually replaced the canonical editions of the first phase. Through reconstructing the work of both phases, a partial reconciliation is achieved in the third phase, which consists of producing perspicuous representations of the editorial ways of dealing with Wittgenstein's writings. The works of all three phases help readers find paths through the writings of Wittgenstein. If today's technically empowered readers take up this challenge, they may practice or re-construct Wittgenstein's method, as Rhees had done while editing the papers. They may then exercise the ultimate authorization that Wittgenstein originally had entrusted only to his literary executors. Neither Wittgenstein nor the editors of the first or second phase may have anticipated or wished readers to have this authorization. However, it may satisfy another intention of the author: "Anything your reader can do for himself leave to him" (Wittgenstein 1980, 77e, cf. Ms 137,134b[5], http://www.wittgensteinsource. org/BFE/Ms-137,134b_f).

Acknowledgements This chapter has been created within the scope of the SFB 1187 "Media of Cooperation" at the University Siegen. It is a translated and heavily revised version of Erbacher (2017). The letters of Rush Rhees in the National Library of Finland (NLF) and at the von Wright and Wittgenstein Archive at the University of Helsinki (WWA) were quoted with permission from Volker Munz, who represents copyright holders in this case. Permission to quote from the letters of Rush Rhees in the Richard Burton Archive at the University Swansea (RBA) was granted by Volker Munz and the Richard Burton Archive. The letter from Rush Rhees to Alfred Kastil was quoted with permission from Volker Munz and the Franz Brentano Archive. Anthony Kenny granted permission to quote from his letter. The letters from Maurice O'Connor Drury were quoted with permission from the Drury Archive at Mary Immaculate College, Limerick. I thank all participants of the "Creation of Wittgenstein" workshop in Kilpisjärvi for their helpful and illuminating comments. I thank Julia Jung and Anne dos Santos Reis for their editorial help, and Arlyne Moi for her copy-editing. Erhard Schüttpelz is especially thanked for inspiring many of the thoughts that are developed in the introduction and concluding remark.

List of Archival Sources

Editorial note: the letters here have been quoted in a normalized transcription without keeping line breaks and page breaks. The orthography of the original has been kept; obvious orthographic mistakes have been corrected within this scope. Corrections and additions by the authors have been implemented in the transcription.

Drury to Rhees, presumably October 1965, The Drury Archive, Mary Immaculate College Library, Limerick.

Drury to Rhees, Spring 1966, The Drury Archive, Mary Immaculate College Library, Limerick.

Drury to Rhees, 15. May 1967, RBA, UNI/SU/PC/1/1/3/4.

Kenny to Rhees, 27. August 1972, RBA, UNI/SU/PC/1/2/6/4.

Kenny to Rhees, 20. March 1973, RBA, UNI/SU/PC/1/2/6/4.

Rhees to Drury, 6. November 1966, RBA, UNI/SU/PC/1/1/3/4.

Rhees to Kastil, 5. November 1933, Franz Brentano-Archiv, Estate Alfred Kastil, K.1.96.1, 000.616-000.622.

Rhees to Kenny, 9. September 1972, RBA, UNI/SU/PC/1/2/6/4.

Rhees to Kenny, 27. February 1973, RBA, UNI/SU/PC/1/2/6/4.

Rhees to Kenny, 22. March 1973, RBA, UNI/SU/PC/1/2/6/4.

Rhees to Kenny, 2. March 1977, WWA, WWA documents\Wittgenstein's Nachlass\Filing cabinet\Rush Rhees III.

Rhees to Nyman, 21. April 1982, WWA, WWA documents\Wittgenstein's Nachlass\Filing cabinet\Rush Rhees III.

Rhees to Winch, 23. February 1973, RBA, UNI/SU/PC/1/2/6/4.

Rhees to von Wright, 5. September 1962, NLF, COLL.714.200-201.

Rhees to von Wright, 10. February 1963, NLF, COLL.714.200-201.

Rhees to von Wright, 14. January 1964, NLF, COLL.714.200-201.

Rhees to von Wright, 22. August 1965, NLF, COLL.714.200-201.

Rhees to von Wright, 8. November 1965, NLF, COLL.714.200-201.

Rhees to von Wright, 11. September 1966, NLF, COLL.714.200-201.

Rhees to von Wright, 22. January 1976, WWA, WWA documents\ Wittgenstein's Nachlass\Filingcabinet\Rush Rhees II.

Rhees to von Wright, 26. August 1982, WWA documents\Wittgenstein's Nachlass\Filingcabinet\Rush Rhees III.

Wittgenstein's Testament, 29. January 1951, copy at WWA.

References

Baker, Gordon P. 2002. Quotation-marks in Philosophical Investigations Part I. *Language & Communication*, 22(1): 37–68.

Brentano, Franz. 1968. *Kategorienlehre*. ed. Alfred Kastil. Hamburg: Felix Meiner Verlag.

Brentano, Franz. 1976. *Philosophische Untersuchungen zu Raum, Zeit und Kontinuum*. With a preface by Stephan Körner and Roderick M. Chisholm, with annotations by Alfred Kastil. Hamburg: Felix Meiner Verlag.

Conant, James. 2011. Wittgenstein's Methods. In *The Oxford Handbook of Wittgenstein*, eds. Oskari Kuusela and Marie McGinn, Oxford: Oxford University Press, 620–645.

Drury, Maurice O. 1984. Conversations with Wittgenstein. In *Recollections of Wittgenstein*, ed. Rush Rhees, Oxford: Oxford University Press, 97–171.

Drury, Maurice O. 2017. *The Selected Writings of Maurice O'Connor Drury—On Wittgenstein, Philosophy, Religion and Psychiatry*. Ed. John Hayes. London: Bloomsbury.

Erbacher, Christian. 2015. *Formen des Klärens—Literarisch-philosophische Darstellungsmittel in Wittgensteins Schriften*. Münster: mentis.

Erbacher, Christian. 2016. Die Wittgenstein-Editionen im Kontext. Über editorische Defizite und ihre konstruktive Kontextualisierung. In *editio, eds*. Rüdiger Nutt-Kofoth and Bodo Plachta, Vol. 30, 197–221.

Erbacher, Christian. 2017. "Gute" philosophische Gründe für "schlechte" Editionsphilologie. Zur Philosophischen Grammatik von Ludwig Wittgenstein und Rush Rhees damals und heute. In *Textologie. Theorie und Praxis eines neuen Ansatzes*, eds. Martin Endres, Alois Pichler and Claus Zittel. Berlin/Boston: De gruyter, 257–297.

Erbacher, Christian. 2019. 'Good' Philosophical Reasons for 'Bad' Editorial Philology? On Rhees and Wittgenstein's. In *Philosophical Grammar, Philosophical Investigations*, 42(2): 111–145.

Erbacher, Christian, Jung, Julia and Seibel, Anne. 2017. The Logbook of Editing Wittgenstein's "Philosophische Bemerkungen". *Nordic Wittgenstein Review*, eds. Martin Gustafsson, A. M. Søndergaard Christensen and Y. Neuman, 6(1): 105–147.

Erbacher, Christian and Krebs, Sophia V. 2015. The First Nine Months of Editing Wittgenstein— Letters from G. E. M. Anscombe and Rush Rhees to G. H. von Wright. *Nordic Wittgenstein Review*, eds. Martin Gustafsson, Anne-Marie Søndergaard Christensen and Yrsa Neuman, 4(1): 195–231.

Garfinkel, Harold. 1967. *Studies in Ethnomethodology*. Englewood Cliffs/NJ: Prentice Hall.

Iven, Mathias. 2015. Er "ist eine Künstlernatur von hinreissender Genialität". In *Wittgenstein-Studien, eds.* Wilhelm Lüttersfelds, Stefan Majetschak, Richard Raatzsch and Wilhelm Vossenkuhl, Vol. 6, Nr. 1, 83–174.

Kenny, Anthony. 1977. From the Big Typescript to the *Philosophical Grammar. Acta Philosophica Fennica—Essays on Wittgenstein in Honour of G.H. von Wright*, ed. Jaakko Hintikka, Amsterdam: North-Holland Publishing Company, 41–53.

Pichler, Alois. 1994. Untersuchungen zu Wittgensteins Nachlaß. http://wittgensteinrepository. org/agora-wab/article/view/2951/3622. Accessed: 29. May 2017.

Pichler, Alois. 2010. Towards the New Bergen Electronic Edition. In *Wittgenstein After his Nachlass* ed. Nuno Venturinha, Basingstoke: Palgrave Macmillan, 157–172.

Pichler, Alois and Bruvik, Tone M. 2014. Digital Critical Editing: Separating Encoding from Presentation. In *Digital Critical Editions, eds.* Daniel Apollon, Claire Bélisle and Philippe Régnier. Illinois: University of Illinois Press, 179–199.

Rhees, Rush. 1970. *Discussions of Wittgenstein*. London: Routledge and Kegan Paul.

Rhees, Rush. 1977. Wittgenstein on language and ritual. *Acta Philosophica Fennica—Essays on Wittgenstein in Honour of G. H. von Wright*, ed. Jaakko Hintikka. Amsterdam: North-Holland Publishing Company, 450–485.

Rhees, Rush. 2017. On Continuity: Rush Rhees on Outer and Inner Surfaces of Bodies. *Philosophical Investigations*, ed. Christian Erbacher and Tina Schirmer. 40(1): 3–30.

Schulte, Joachim. 1982. Bedeutung und Verifikation: Schlick, Waismann und Wittgenstein. *Grazer Philosophische Studien, eds.* Johannes Brandl, Marian David, Maria Reicher and Leopold Stubenberg, Vol. 16/17, 241–253.

Schulte, Joachim. 2013. The Role of the Big Typescript in Wittgenstein's Later Writings. In *The Textual Genesis of Wittgenstein's Philosophical Investigations*, ed. Nuno Venturinha, 81–89.

Stern, David G. 1996. The Availability of Wittgenstein's Philosophy. http://www.academia. edu/310356/The_Availability_of_Wittgensteins_Philosophy. Accessed: 30. May 2017.

Stern, David G. 2017. Reflections on Editing Moore's Notes in Wittgenstein: Lectures, Cambridge 1930–1933. In *Belgrade Philosophical Annual 2017*, eds. James R. Connelly, Andrej Jandrić and Ljiljana Radenović. Vol. 30, 225–234.

Stern, David G. 2018. Wittgenstein in the 1930's. In *The Cambridge Companion to Wittgenstein*, second edition, eds. Hans D. Sluga and David G. Stern. Cambridge: Cambridge University Press, 126–151.

Uffelmann, Sarah. 2018. *Vom System zum Gebrauch. Eine genetisch-philosophische Untersuchung des Grammatikbegriffs bei Wittgenstein*. (= On Wittgenstein. vol. 3), Berlin/ Boston: De Gruyter.

Venturinha, Nuno. 2010. *Wittgenstein After His Nachlass*. Basingstoke: Palgrave Macmillan. v.

Wright, Georg H. 1969. The Wittgenstein Papers. *The Philosophical Review*, ed. Michelle Kosch, 78: 483–503.

Westergaard, Peter K. 2015. On the Ketner and Eigsti Edition of Wittgenstein's Remarks on Frazer's "The Golden Bough". *Nordic Wittgenstein Review*, eds. Martin Gustafsson, Anne-Marie Søndergaard Christensen and Yrsa Neuman, 4(2): 117–142.

Wittgenstein, Ludwig. 1921. Logisch-philosophische Abhandlung. In *Annalen der Natur- und Kulturphilosophie*, ed. Wilhelm Ostwald, Vol. 14, 185–262.

Wittgenstein, Ludwig. 1922. *Tractatus Logico-Philosophicus*. Ed. C. K. Ogden, trans. C. K. Ogden and Frank P. Ramsey. London: Kegan Paul, Trench, Trubner.

Wittgenstein, Ludwig. 1929. Some Remarks on Logical Form. In *Proceedings of the Aristotelian Society Supplementary*. Vol. 9, 162–171.

Wittgenstein, Ludwig. 1953. *Philosophical Investigations/Philosophische Untersuchungen*. Ed. G. E. M. Anscombe and Rush Rhees, trans. G. E. M. Anscombe. Oxford: Basil Blackwell.

Wittgenstein, Ludwig. 1956. *Remarks on the Foundations of Mathematics/Bemerkungen über die Grundlagen der Mathematik*. Eds. Georg H. v. Wright, Rush Rhees and G. E. M. Anscombe, trans. G. E. M. Anscombe. Oxford: Basil Blackwell.

Wittgenstein, Ludwig. 1958. *Preliminary Studies for the Philosophical Investigations. Generally Known as The Blue and Brown Books*. Oxford: Basil Blackwell.

Wittgenstein, Ludwig. 1964. *Philosophische Bemerkungen*. Ed. Rush Rhees. Oxford: Basil Blackwell.

Wittgenstein, Ludwig. 1966. *Lectures and Conversations*. Ed. Cyril Barrett. Oxford: Basil Blackwell.

Wittgenstein, Ludwig. 1967a. *Ludwig Wittgenstein und der Wiener Kreis*. Ed. Brian McGuinness. Oxford: Basil Blackwell.

Wittgenstein, Ludwig. 1967b. Bemerkungen über Frazers The Golden Bough. *Synthese*, ed. Rush Rhees, 17: 233–253.

Wittgenstein, Ludwig. 1969. *Philosophische Grammatik*. Ed. Rsuh Rhees. Oxford: Basil Blackwell.

Wittgenstein, Ludwig. 1974. *Philosophical Grammar*. Ed. Rush Rhees, trans. A. Kenny. Oxford: Basil Blackwell.

Wittgenstein, Ludwig. 1975. *Philosophical Remarks*. Ed. Rush Rhees. Oxford: Basil Blackwell.

Wittgenstein, Ludwig. 1976. *Wittgenstein's Lectures on the Foundations of Mathematics Cambridge 1939*. Ed. Cora Diamond. Ithaca, USA: Cornell University Press.

Wittgenstein, Ludwig. 1980. *Culture and Value*. Ed. Georg H. v. Wright. Oxford: Basil Blackwell.

Wittgenstein, Ludwig. 1989. *Logisch-philosophische Abhandlung. Tractatus logico-philosophicus. Kritische Edition*. Eds. Brian McGuinness and Joachim Schulte. Frankfurt am Main: Suhrkamp.

Wittgenstein, Ludwig. 1990. *Tractatus Logico-Philosophicus. Philosophische Untersuchungen*. Ed. Peter Philip. Leipzig: Reclam.

Wittgenstein, Ludwig. 1993. *Philosophical Occasions*. Eds. James Klagge and Alfred Nordmann. USA: Hackett.

Wittgenstein, Ludwig. 1994a. Philosophische Bemerkungen. In *Wiener Ausgabe*, ed. Michael Nedo, Bd. 1. Vienna: Springer.

Wittgenstein, Ludwig. 1994b. Philosophische Betrachtungen, Philosophische Bemerkungen. In *Wiener Ausgabe, ed.* Michael Nedo, Vol. 2. Vienna: Springer.

Wittgenstein, Ludwig. 1995a. Bemerkungen, Philosophische Bemerkungen. In *Wiener Ausgabe*, ed. Michael Nedo, Vol. 3. Vienna: Springer.

Wittgenstein, Ludwig. 1995b. Bemerkungen zur Philosophie, Bemerkungen zur philosophischen Grammatik. In *Wiener Ausgabe*, ed. Michael Nedo, Vol. 4. Vienna: Springer.

Wittgenstein, Ludwig. 1996. Philosophische Grammatik. In *Wiener Ausgabe*, ed. Michael Nedo, Vol. 5, Vienna: Springer.

Wittgenstein, Ludwig. 2000a. The Big Typescript. In *Wiener Ausgabe*, ed. Michael Nedo, Vol. 11, Vienna: Springer.

Wittgenstein, Ludwig. 2000b. *Wittgenstein's Nachlass. The Bergen Electronic Edition*. Ed. The Wittgenstein Archives at the University of Bergen. Oxford: Oxford University Press.

Wittgenstein, Ludwig. 2001. *Philosophische Untersuchungen. Kritisch-genetische Edition.* Ed. Joachim Schulte in collaboration with H. Nyman, E. v. Savigny and G. H. v. Wright. Frankfurt am Main: Suhrkamp.

Wittgenstein, Ludwig. 2008. *Wittgenstein in Cambridge. Letters and Documents 1911–1951.* Ed. Brian McGuinness. Oxford: Wiley-Blackwell.

Wittgenstein, Ludwig, Rhees, Rush and Citron, Gabriel. 2015. Wittgenstein's Philosophical Conversations with Rush Rhees (1939–50): From the Notes of Rush Rhees. In *Mind,* ed. Gabriel Citron, 124(493): 1–71.

"Among the Omitted Stuff, There Are Many Good Remarks of a General Nature"

On the Making of von Wright
and Wittgenstein's *Culture and Value*

5.1   Constructively Contextualizing the Making of *Culture and Value*

Georg Henrik von Wright's work as one of Ludwig Wittgenstein's literary executors is informed by his concern to preserve the historical documents of Wittgenstein's writings and to make them available for research. This concern is most strikingly reflected in von Wright and Norman Malcolm's initiative to produce a complete microfilm copy of Wittgenstein's papers. Together with von Wright's (1969) corresponding catalogue, the microfilm provided the main source for most of the subsequent historical and philological research into Wittgenstein's writings, leading to large-scale editorial projects such as the Wittgenstein Archives at the University of Tübingen in the early 1980s, and the Wittgenstein Archives at the University of Bergen, which made Wittgenstein's *Nachlass* available in its entirety through the *Bergen Electronic Edition* (Wittgenstein 2000a). Von Wright's own editorial work also increasingly bore traces of critical philology. He became convinced that it would be best to publish Wittgenstein's manuscripts and typescripts with as little editorial intervention as possible and eventually published some of them "in toto" (cf. Wittgenstein 1992, preface). With help from assistants, he traced remarks in the *Philosophical Investigations* to their manuscript sources and thus reconstructed the book's pre-versions (cf. Maury 1981, 1994; chapter 1). In addition to these Wittgenstein editions in a strict sense, von Wright published contextual sources written by Wittgenstein and his friends, such as letters and memoirs (e.g., Wittgenstein 1969a, 1973, 1974, 1983, 1994a; Pinsent 1990), and a series of scholarly essays that shed light on the historical context of Wittgenstein's work (von Wright 1955, 1971, 1979, 1992a). These essays have become classics in the study of how Wittgenstein gradually distilled more finished versions of

---

This chapter is a revised version of Erbacher 2015a and 2017.

© The Author(s), under exclusive license to Springer-Verlag GmbH, DE, part of
Springer Nature 2023
C. Erbacher, *The Happy Afterlife of Ludwig W.*, Beiträge zur Praxeologie /
Contributions to Praxeology, https://doi.org/10.1007/978-3-662-66155-0_5

his work from his notes. Together, they can be read as the factual backbone of Wittgenstein's work-biography (von Wright 1982). The sum of all these pioneering achievements became the point of departure for the critical-genetic edition of the *Philosophical Investigations* (Wittgenstein 2001), a book that can be seen as a high point of the scholarly text-genetic approach that von Wright developed as an editor of Wittgenstein's writings.

Due to this scholarly and source-oriented approach to editing Wittgenstein's papers, von Wright's edition *Culture and Value* (Wittgenstein 1977, first English edition Wittgenstein 1980; from now on abbreviated CV) seems at first sight not to fit. CV is a collection of aphoristic remarks which Wittgenstein wrote on general topics such as religion, music, literature, history and art, but in contrast to the other volumes that von Wright edited, it was von Wright himself who assembled the passages from various places in the Nachlass, according to his own personal taste and judgment. This was an untypical editorial procedure for him, and it may raise suspicions if measured against today's philological 'gold standard' of scholarly critical editing. It may be accused of being "unfaithful" (Venturinha 2010, 1) to the sources, possibly even misleading concerning Wittgenstein's philosophy, as has happened in some cases of editions sourced from Wittgenstein's Nachlass (cf. Stern 1996). However, what may appear as an editorial deficit from the perspective of critical editorial philology, can provide a fruitful starting point for an investigation from another perspective: by inquiring into von Wright's reasons and motives for creating and publishing his selection, we may gain insight into von Wright as an editor and his understanding of Wittgenstein's philosophy. For this, it is necessary to understand his editing process not exclusively as a series of context-less philological operations but as philosophically relevant acts that took place in specific working contexts, through cooperation with friends and colleagues and with an elaborated understanding of the edited materials. This may be called *constructively contextualizing*, as it takes into account the relevant historical context for constructing a helpful understanding of the editorial intentions that critical text philology identifies as editorial biases (cf. Erbacher 2016, 2019, chapter 4). This step from a 'critical' to a 'post-critical' investigation of editions from Wittgenstein's writings is what this paper tries to achieve for the case of von Wright and Wittgenstein's CV.

Taking seriously the editorial intentions for CV, it is important to note right away that the book was never intended as a presentation of a philosophical work by Wittgenstein. Despite it often being treated as such, von Wright did not regard his collection of general remarks as directly belonging to Wittgenstein's philosophical writings, as he made unmistakable clear in his preface to CV. Whether Wittgenstein himself ever contemplated composing a book of remarks on broader cultural topics is an issue of debate (cf. Rothhaupt and Vossenkuhl 2013; Rothhaupt 2013, 2017). While working on and revising his texts, Wittgenstein marked sections that may be read as remarks on culture, and he transferred such remarks into fair copies (e.g., Ms 168[1]; cf. Rothhaupt 2017). But scholars have questioned whether the philological evidence suffices to conclude that Wittgenstein worked on a selection of cultural remarks as part of his philosophical work or even that he planned a book containing such a selection (Majetschak 2013; Stern 2013). In any case, with regard to Wittgenstein's literary executors, there is no indication that they thought the selection in CV would resemble anything Wittgenstein would have wanted to publish as his contribution to philosophy. Hence, the literary executors did not regard CV as another work by Wittgenstein, but as a collection of remarks illuminating his intellectual orientation. The editor, Georg Henrik von Wright, was convinced that CV tells "us more than any other written source about Wittgenstein's intellectual character and view of life, and also how he regarded his relationships with his times" (von Wright 1982, 203). According to von Wright, CV thus shows Wittgenstein as an intellectual phenomenon ("geistige Erscheinung"), which is "to view his personality and work in relation to phenomena outside the strictly professional sphere of philosophy—for example, trends in contemporary literature or art, or political and social ideas" (von Wright 1982, 2). Making readers aware of this intellectual orientation was, for von Wright, related to correcting a dominant picture of Wittgenstein in the reception of his works (mainly in the Anglo-Saxon world), where the *Tractatus* and the *Philosophical Investigations* had become pillars in the canon of professional analytical philosophy:

> The vogue of 'Wittgensteinianism' of the first two postwar decades was rather narrowly 'professional'. It disregarded the broader cultural perspectives. An explanation for this is perhaps the fact that whereas Wittgenstein's influence then was mainly in the Anglo-Saxon world, his background was central European. The portrait of the man implicit in the writings of his British and American pupils and followers was—as an Italian writer put it—that of a cultural illiterate. Partly as a consequence of the gradual reception of Wittgenstein's philosophy by the German-speaking and Latin worlds this portrait is now being corrected. The publication of the *Vermischte Bemerkungen* (1977) will, I hope, contribute to a better understanding both of Wittgenstein's roots in European culture and of his significance to our times. (von Wright 1982, 2–3)

From the perspective of strict, critical text philology, this quote may be read as showing an editor's agenda for steering the reception of Wittgenstein's philosophy by producing a collection of remarks that was neither made nor planned by the author. By contrast, from the perspective of a constructive contextualization, it may be read as an invitation to try to *understand the understanding* that motivated this editorial intention. The hermeneutical endeavor that involves the latter alternative may be of special interest for the practical reflexivity of working practices in philosophy, as it aims to conceive of von Wright's making of the book—a book that was meant to show Wittgenstein as an intellectual

---

[1] Identification of Nachlass items follows the numbering system that was introduced by von Wright (1969).

phenomenon—as an intellectual phenomenon in its own right. As such, to fathom the connection between work in philosophy and its broader cultural context would not only be von Wright's editorial intention when making CV, but also the leitmotif for the constructive contextualization of his making of that edition. Naturally then, the starting point for this editorial story is the editor's lived experience with Wittgenstein's work and how it was embedded in his broader cultural life.

5.2   Knowing Wittgenstein as a Man Entrenched in Great Culture

In stating his hope that CV will contribute to a better understanding of Wittgenstein's cultural roots, von Wright makes a distinction between a strictly professional philosophy and a broader cultural perspective. This distinction is present from the very beginning of von Wright and Wittgenstein's friendship, as von Wright remembered it. Von Wright met Wittgenstein for the first time in the spring of 1939, when he was a doctoral student from the University of Helsinki and lived in Cambridge for a study sojourn. Philosophically, the 23-year-old was convinced that logical positivism would be his "gateway to serious philosophizing" (von Wright 1989, 5). Having inspired proponents of the Vienna Circle, and being inspired by them in return, Wittgenstein would surely have had something to say about von Wright's philosophical orientation. Yet, as von Wright reports, they did not talk about philosophy during their first meeting (von Wright 2001, 72–77). They talked instead about Nordic architecture and the landscape Wittgenstein had learned to love during periods of work that had been crucial for the development of both the *Tractatus* and the *Philosophical Investigations*. But von Wright's geographical origin may not have been the only non-philosophical aspect of interest to Wittgenstein. Being raised in the spirit of the continental European educational elite, von Wright's broader cultural background matched that of Wittgenstein: while von Wright's professional home was logical positivism, his "spiritual home", as he once put it, was the literature of Goethe and Schiller, of Schopenhauer and Nietzsche (von Wright 1989, 8). To this list of German authors, we may add the nineteenth century art historian and humanist Jakob Burckhardt and the philosopher of history Oswald Spengler, who Wittgenstein counted among the few authors who had influenced him (CV, 19; Ms-154,16r_f).[2] Burckhardt's books, for example, were in von Wright's suitcase when he travelled as a student through Italy with Göran Schildt (von Wright 2001, 59–67). As if walking in Goethe's footsteps, the two young intellectuals travelled in a first-class compartment to follow the traces of great past cultures. Strongly influenced by Spengler's *Untergang des Abendlandes* (*Decline of the West*), which he had found in his

---

[2] Single remarks from Wittgenstein's Nachlass are identified by the sigla used in www.wittgensteinsource.com; these sigla function at the same time as the URL for accessing the facsimile of that remark, in the present case: http://wittgensteinsource.org/BFE/Ms-154,16r-f.

father's library,[3] von Wright experienced this journey in a mood colored by what he called his "early Spenglerism" (von Wright 1989, 8), that was:

> to view history as a sort of tableau vivant, to be looked at in awe and contemplated like a work of art. In the details of history one should try to discern the typical, the 'morphological similarities', the recurrent patterns. The great changes, the crises and revolutions of history, are like earthquakes and other catastrophes in nature. They cannot be judged under the moral categories of justice and rightness. But they may, like life as whole, be seen in the light of 'tragedy'. (von Wright 1989, 8)

Though "rightness" was not a category for this detached contemplation of world history, "greatness" certainly was. This is the element von Wright absorbed from Burckhardt's writings:

> the admiration of *greatness*—greatness of achievement but also of personality (Goethe, Leonardo). Greatness is an unpredictable chance element in history; it is largely through greatness that the typical and recurrent gets its individuality. (von Wright 1989, 8)

Von Wright's early Spenglerism was thus not a matter of cultural pessimism, which is often associated with the title of Spengler's book, but a glowing appreciation of past cultures and great personalities. Resonating with that was the belief in a nobility of spirit completed by education and social-spiritual formation—Bildung (cf. von Wright 1947). Wittgenstein, though he may have been sympathetic to that ideal, probably did not share a romantic optimism about it. In fact, von Wright was shocked by what he experienced as Wittgenstein's cultural pessimism:

> This grim pessimism was, at times at least, coupled with a positive wish for destruction. I remember Wittgenstein saying: 'I am all for chaos.' When in the Summer month 1939 I expressed my horror before the impending war, he said that not one but four or five great wars was what mankind needed.[4]

Quite understandably, the doctoral student was shattered to hear this, especially since military airplanes over Cambridge simultaneously portended the outbreak of a new war. According to von Wright, Wittgenstein *"lived"* the decline of the West (von Wright 1982, 212). Yet, this lived experience of the cultural decline resulted "not only in his disgust for contemporary civilization, but also in his deep awe and understanding of this civilization's great past" (von Wright 1982, 212). This reverence for the greatness of past cultures resembles the mood of von Wright's early Spenglerism and may have provided silent but firm grounds for a common

---

[3] Von Wright read the German original of Spengler (1922; 1923). The historical copies from the library of von Wright's father and with von Wright's annotations are kept at The von Wright and Wittgenstein Archives at the University of Helsinki (WWA).

[4] Draft for the opening lecture of the 2nd Wittgenstein Symposium in Kirchberg (1977, 9). The recollection was published later in a revised version in von Wright (1990, 1995a).

understanding, even though they did not talk explicitly about Spengler (cf. von Wright 2001, 127).

Von Wright and Wittgenstein's appreciation of greatness surely extended to great literary authors, for example the already mentioned Goethe. Regarding the time after World War II, when von Wright had become Wittgenstein's successor as professor of philosophy at Cambridge, von Wright remembered Wittgenstein sometimes stayed at his house, and that their conversations centered upon cultural topics and literature:

> When Wittgenstein was with us, he and I had daily talks, sometimes on things he was working on, sometimes on the logical topics which were mine at the time, but most often on literature and music, on religion, and on what could perhaps be termed the philosophy of history and civilization. Wittgenstein sometimes read to me from his favourite authors, for example, from Grimm's *Märchen* or Gottfried Keller's *Zuericher Novellen*. The recollection of his voice and facial expression when, seated in a chair in his sickroom, he read aloud Goethe's *Hermann und Dorothea* is for me unforgettable. (von Wright 1989, 15)

Recollections like this show that von Wright understood his acquaintance with Wittgenstein as a friendship with a philosopher who related his thinking and being to great history, music, literature and art. Likewise, von Wright surmised, in his autobiography, that their mutual affinity originated from these shared non-philosophical interests and a shared taste rooted in a central European culture, a culture that was in a state of dissolution (von Wright 2001, 74). This character of their friendship may account for why, already shortly after Wittgenstein's death, von Wright wanted to write about Wittgenstein with a view to their "conversations, of his likes and dislikes in literature and art, etc." (Wright to Friedrich August von Hayek, 22. February 1953; cf. Erbacher 2015b). This intention eventually led to von Wright's now-classic biographical sketch, which concludes by saying "It would be surprising if he [Wittgenstein] were not one day ranked among the classic writers of German prose" (von Wright 1982, 33). This statement was partly a preventative measure, to ward against a one-sided and purely professional reception. Von Wright continues:

> Those who approach Wittgenstein's work will sometimes look for its essence in a rational, matter-of-fact dimension, and sometimes more in a supra-empirical, metaphysical one. In the existing literature on Wittgenstein there are examples of both conceptions. Such "interpretations" have little significance. They must appear as falsifications to anyone who tries to understand Wittgenstein in all his rich complexity. They are interesting only as showing in how many directions his influence extends. I have sometimes thought that what makes a man's work *classic* is often just this multiplicity, which invites and at the same time resists our craving for a clear understanding. (von Wright 1982, 34)

This contrast—of, on one hand, seeing Wittgenstein as a great author belonging to a cultural tradition, and on the other hand, interpreting him in the context of professional philosophy—is present in many of von Wright's recollections. That von Wright was so aware of this contrast may have to do with his intellectual life being shaped by both the practice of professional philosophy, which he pursued from his early positivistic days onwards, and by his friendship with Wittgenstein, a great philosopher with whom he shared broader views on culture and literature. This distinction—between professional philosophy and a broader cultural context in von Wright's thinking and conception of his acquaintance with Wittgenstein—is relevant for the whole editorial story of CV. As we will see in the next stage of this story, the shared cultural background helped von Wright to perceive more clearly the literary quality of Wittgenstein's remarks. He came across them when he read through the manuscripts that the literary executors had inherited. But distinguishing between professional philosophy and a broader cultural perspective may also partly account for his hesitation to publish remarks which seemed to have a general character rather than a philosophical one.

5.3 Making the First Selection of General Remarks but not Publishing it

Von Wright became aware of the special beauty of some of Wittgenstein's remarks when he stayed at Cornell University as a guest of Norman Malcolm. The two men first met at Cambridge in 1939, but they became friends only when attending Wittgenstein's very last lecture in 1947 (von Wright 1992b, 215 and 1995b). Immediately after Wittgenstein's death, they began what would develop into a lifelong friendship cultivated through regular visits and written correspondence. Having resigned from his chair at Cambridge one year after Wittgenstein's death, and fearing that his home country, Finland, which he had moved back to, could be incorporated into the Soviet Union, von Wright proposed that Malcolm should act in his place as literary executor, if he ended up being isolated from the West:

> As you probably know, Ludwig Wittgenstein in his will gave to Rhees, Miss Anscombe and me the copyright in his unpublished writings with the wish that we shall publish as many of them as we think fit.
>   Should it now—for some reason or other—happen that the other executors will not be able to consult and contact me about the editing and publication of the manuscripts, I should like them to consult you and you to exercise the same authority as regards their publication as I possess according to the will. I completely trust your judgment in the matters concerned, and I know that Wittgenstein would have done so too. (von Wright to Malcolm, 25. November 1952)[5]

This was probably as much a measure to ensure continued work on Wittgenstein's writings as it was an expression of trust. It might also have signaled that von Wright did not want the fact that Wittgenstein had appointed him a literary

---

[5] Von Wright also reports about this wish and about legal aspects related to it to Anscombe in a letter from 12. November 1952. Interestingly, Wittgenstein had used a very similar phrase when talking to Rhees a few days before his death: "I trust you absolutely, and I trust Miss Anscombe absolutely." (cf. Chap. 2).

executor and not Malcolm to become a barrier between them. In any case, their friendship grew stronger in the subsequent years. Not long after von Wright's proposal, Malcolm invited him to Cornell University. At that time, von Wright's biographical sketch (1955) of Wittgenstein appeared for the first in English in *The Philosophical Review*, then edited by Malcolm. Staying at Cornell, von Wright taught a course on the Tractatus. Six students attended, so did also five staff members, among them, Malcolm himself, Max Black and John Rawls.[6] In contrast to earlier rather discouraging experiences in trying to explain Wittgenstein's thought,[7] the course on the Tractatus at Cornell was an exhilarating experience, as he wrote to Elizabeth Anscombe:

> I give seminars in which I try to explain the Tractatus. I have learned a lot from them and I have the feeling that now I am beginning to understand the book. It is even more wonderful than I had thought. And one of the most wonderful things about it is that it is absolutely straightforward. No metaphors, no allusions, no mystery. The difficulty is to avoid twisting his words, to avoid putting an "interpretation" on them. (von Wright to Anscombe, 6. June 1954)

With his enthusiasm for the poetic clarity of the Tractatus, von Wright got the inchoate idea to compile a collection of general remarks drawn from Wittgenstein's manuscripts. He had brought to Cornell photographs of some manuscripts and was intent on typing out the passages that Rhees, Anscombe and he had chosen for the volume that would appear as Remarks on the Foundations of Mathematics (Wittgenstein 1956). It was the first time von Wright was centrally involved in editing a volume from Wittgenstein's Nachlass.[8] Transcribing the selection was an unedifying experience at times, as he noted to Anscombe: "the work was awful. I am constantly tormented by the question: Do we do the right thing, or not?" (Anscombe to von Wright, 4. July 1954). Still, while continuing to transcribe the selected passages, he was struck by the beauty of some remarks in the manuscripts:

---

[6] Von Wright's list of attendees is kept at WWA among von Wright's lecture drafts.

[7] In 1952, for example, he reported to Anscombe about two lectures he had given at the Philosophical Society of Helsinki: "How far I am myself from understanding these things properly I realized both in the course of writing the paper and by watching the reaction it provoked. The discussions which followed revealed that I had implanted in most hearers' minds the very misunderstandings I think it is most important to guard against. I was very much discouraged and depressed." Letter from von Wright to Anscombe, 12. November 1952.

[8] Though von Wright was centrally involved in creating good working conditions for the literary executors, for instance by clarifying legal questions, applying for funding and negotiating with publishers, and though he supported Anscombe and Rhees by proofreading, the preparation of the typescript and the editing of the *Philosophical Investigations* (Wittgenstein 1953) was done by Anscombe and Rhees (cf. Erbacher and Krebs 2015). The decisions for the selection printed in the *Remarks on the Foundations of Mathematics* were made in only ten days, during the executors' meeting in Austria in the summer of 1952 (cf. Chap. 1).

> Among the omitted stuff, there are many good remarks of a general nature. I have omit-
> ted them in order to avoid—as I think we should—creating the impression that the book,
> which we publish, is a collection of aphorisms. Perhaps some of the omitted remarks can
> be published on some other occasion. (von Wright to Anscombe, 6. November 1954)[9]

This first observation of "some good remarks of a general nature" may be seen as
the germ of CV. At that time, however, it did not occur to von Wright that these
remarks might be related to Wittgenstein's writings on the foundations of mathematics. Indeed, it took ten more years for the germ of CV to sprout, and yet
almost another decade for von Wright to fully recognize the flower's philosophical
significance.

In the first half of the 1960s, Rhees systematically investigated the writings
from Wittgenstein's first years after his return to Cambridge in 1929 (cf. Erbacher,
Jung and Seibel 2017). Both Rhees and von Wright were fascinated to discover
that the writings in those manuscripts provide a bridge between the Tractatus and
Philosophical Investigations. The first volume from those writings was Rhees'
edition Philosophische Bemerkungen (Wittgenstein 1964), which was intended
as the first of two "intermediate cases" (Philosophical Investigations, § 122) in
the morphology of Wittgenstein's thinking.[10] The typescript of Philosophische
Bemerkungen (Ts 209) stems from 1929/1930, the same time as Wittgenstein's
Lecture on Ethics (Ts 207, edited in Wittgenstein 1965). This caused Rhees to
wonder if he ought to add the Lecture on Ethics to Philosophische Bemerkungen,
or, alternatively, to combine it with a collection of remarks of a general nature.
Von Wright addressed this consideration in a letter to Anscombe:

> You may remember that Rhees in a letter raised the question of what to do with the lecture
> on Ethics. Chronologically it belongs in the period of the Philosophische Bemerkungen.
> Published as an Appendix to the Bemerkungen—with extract from Waismann's notes—it
> would appear rather "out of place". Rhees seems to feel the same, since he mentioned
> the possibility of publishing a separate volume consisting of general remarks on aesthet-
> ics, ethics, religion, etc. and including the Ethics lecture in it. This idea of a volume of
> "general remarks" is worth taking seriously. There are, for example, a number of remarks
> in the typescript of October 1948 to March 1949 which might go into such a volume and
> also in the typescript of last writings (i.a. the whole Notebook IV). We must discuss the
> problem when we meet. (von Wright to Anscombe, 11. June 1964)

The literary executors indeed discussed the issue during their next meeting in the
summer of 1964, and they appointed von Wright to go through all the manuscripts

---

[9] I thank Lassi Jakola for directing my attention to this passage.

[10] Rhees' editing of *Philosophische Bemerkungen* may called "philosophical", since he based
his editorial decisions concerning selection and composition on his philosophical understanding of Wittgenstein's texts; just like the *Philosophical Investigations* identify the finding and
inventing of intermediate cases as an important part of the philosopher's work, Rhees' editions
Philosophische Bemerkungen and *Philosophische Grammatik* have been philosopher's works
that allowed to see connexions between the *Tractatus* and the *Philosophical Investigations* (cf.
Erbacher 2019, chapter 4).

in the Nachlass in order to make a selection for a volume of general remarks. Yet when he actually started making this selection, he soon became sceptical about the project and about ever publishing it, as he wrote to Anscombe in March 1965:

> I have started to make a selection of "aphorisms" and "general remarks". My impression so far is that the job is next to hopeless and will result in nothing publishable. But it can nevertheless be nice to have the selection made for one's own (and your and Rhees's) sake. (von Wright to Anscombe, 10. March 1965)

Only six days later, von Wright saw his first doubts confirmed:

> I have been working on the selection now, but I am very pessimistic about the eventual publishability of anything. (von Wright to Anscombe, 16. March 1965)

He nevertheless continued searching the manuscripts, as he wrote to Anscombe:

> As I think I told you in an earlier letter, I have been selecting "general remarks", but become rather pessimistic about their publishability in one volume. In any case I am going to complete the job and compose a volume for you and Rhees, and me. It may be nice to have it in typescript, even it is unsuitable for publication. (von Wright to Anscombe, 20. April 1965)

After three and a half months, von Wright completed his task. The resulting first selection of general remarks amounts to two big folders containing more than 1,500 passages from about 60 items in Wittgenstein's Nachlass. The typed selection is entitled thus (Quoted from von Wright's copy of his selection kept at WWA):

> A collection of remarks by Ludwig Wittgenstein
>   on questions connected with
>   his Life and Work; the Nature of Philosophical Inquiry;
>   Art, Religion and the "Philosophy of Life"; the I, the
>   Will, and the World; and various other General Topics

Von Wright sent a copy of this collection to each literary executor. In an accompanying letter, he explained the rationale for his selection:

> I have proceeded on a "maximum principle": selecting generously and with a view to then sieving the selected material. I doubt whether my present view of the matter is definitive: but it is against, rather than for, publishing anything at all. [...] Perhaps some of us will some day have a really good idea of how to make a selection that can justifyable [sic] be published. (von Wright to Anscombe, 28. June 1965)

A note attached to the collection shows that the missing "justification" for a publication had to do with the assumed hiatus between Wittgenstein's philosophical work and his general remarks:

> One can make a broad distinction between remarks which are of Wittgenstein's philosoph-
> ical work and remarks which are "detached" or "detachable" from it. [...] To the "detach-
> able" remarks belong a great number of reflexions on art and religion. —Question: Could
> a collection be published consisting of only "detachable" remarks? Or would such a col-
> lection be too far removed from the rest of Wittgenstein's work to be of interest? (von
> Wright, A collection of remarks by Ludwig Wittgenstein).

While von Wright, in 1954, did not question whether it was right to separate the remarks of a general nature from those on the foundations of mathematics, he now wondered whether if there could be a justification to publish them by themselves. For the time being, the literary executors did not see such a justification and thus did not publish them. This decision was in line with other cases where the literary executors excluded passages from publication-typescripts which they regarded as not belonging to Wittgenstein's philosophical work. One of these cases is the edi-torial project that von Wright turned to after he had made the first selection of gen-eral remarks, namely, the project that developed from his and Malcolm's idea to deposit copies of Wittgenstein's writings at Cornell University. The way in which Wittgenstein's private non-philosophical remarks were then discussed and handled sheds light on the hesitations to publish the general non-philosophical remarks in CV, especially as some of the former were eventually treated as part of the latter.[11]

5.4 Turning to Another Project: Microfilming the Whole Nachlass

In their extensive correspondence, von Wright regularly informed Malcolm about plans and activities in connection with publishing Wittgenstein's writings. It was therefore natural for von Wright to tell Malcolm about his excitement over read-ing the Moore Volume and the Big Typescript. Receiving such news, Malcolm was anxious to learn more about these works, especially since they might forge links between the *Tractatus* and the *Philosophical Investigations*. His interest also stemmed from his desire to write about the relation between Wittgenstein's early and late philosophy in an encyclopaedia article (cf. Malcolm 1967). Thus, in the summer of 1963, when Anscombe gave guest lectures at Cornell, Malcolm raised the question of whether it would be possible for Cornell University to make photocopies or a microfilm of Wittgenstein's writings from the middle period (Malcolm to von Wright, 6. June 1963). This proposal, which, accord-ing to Malcolm (Malcolm to von Wright, 6. June 1963), Anscombe considered a good idea, may be seen as the first mention of what would later become the Cornell Microfilm. Rhees, however, objected vehemently to Malcolm's proposal (Rhees to von Wright, 7. July 1965). He reminded von Wright that Malcolm's notes to Wittgenstein's lectures from 1939 had been published without Malcolm's

---

[11] The revised edition of CV (Wittgenstein 1994b) lists more than 50 coded remarks in von Wright's published collection.

permission and without him being told it was going to happen. Rhees feared that if the material went to Cornell, a similar situation would arise. He was certain that the manuscripts contained a lot of material Wittgenstein would not have wanted to have in general circulation. Rhees explained his concerns to von Wright:

> When such material is published, many writers ("publish or perish") refer to it as though it were on the same level as those remarks which Wittgenstein <u>did</u> give as his consid-ered statements for publication. These writers bounce back and forth between the pub-lished statements and the posthumously published notes as suits their own thesis: showing their "new interpretation", etc. I have noticed this again and again in connexion with the <u>Notebooks 1914–1916</u>, which are often treated as though they were a part of the <u>Tractatus</u>. (Rhees to von Wright, 7. July 1965)

Rhees thought this was certainly not what Wittgenstein wanted them to do with his papers, as he put sharply:

> When I spoke to Wittgenstein about the task ten days before his death he was particularly anxious that care should be taken in what was published and how it was presented. This is vague, I know. But I am certain he would have said "no" to "Just circulate everything".
> [...]
> If Wittgenstein had thought we were going to be careless about letting this material get into the hands of all and sundry, ahead of any publication from it, then I do not think he would have entrusted us with the material. (Rhees to von Wright, 7. July 1965)

This issue became even more sensitive inasmuch as Wittgenstein had written down not only tentative philosophical remarks but also remarks in a special code. The literary executors had already seen such coded remarks in Wittgenstein's note-books from World War I (Mss 101–103). These notebooks begin with diary-like entries written when Wittgenstein enlisted as a soldier. Six days after the first entry, he started inverting the alphabet when expressing disgust over the coarse meanness of his comrades. Throughout the preserved war notebooks, he used the code when writing notes about private matters, his health and mood, thoughts about friends and about the progress of his philosophical work. When von Wright and Anscombe published their edition of these notebooks (Wittgenstein 1961), they excluded these coded entries, thus creating a precedent for not publishing the remarks that seemed to them to be unrelated to Wittgenstein's philosophical work. Besides being a matter of piety, in light of the content of some of the coded remarks, their appearance could be taken as a reason for regarding them as not belonging to the philosophical work. After all, Wittgenstein had distinguished the coded entries from his notes on logic precisely by using the code, also by strictly keeping the coded notes on the left-hand pages while writing his philosophical notes on the right. In his later manuscripts, Wittgenstein repeatedly used this code again, albeit less systematically (cf. Somavilla 2010). Like the coded entries in the war notebooks, the ones in his later manuscripts appear initially to be private and of no philosophical importance. Naturally then, a question arose: What should be done about the coded remarks if whole ledgers would be copied and made avail-able? Rhees in particular did not want them to be published:

> I wished (and do) that W. had not written those passages. I do not know why he wanted to; but I think I do understand in a way, and I understand then also why he chose this ambiguous medium. I fear especially that if they are published they will be published by themselves—not in the contexts (repeat: contexts) in which they were written; so that what was a minor and occasional undertone to Wittgenstein's life and thinking, will appear as a dominant obsession. (Rhees to von Wright, 17. December 1966)[12]

Malcolm suggested covering up the coded passages during the photographing—if they were the main reason for not giving a set of manuscript copies to Cornell University (Malcolm to von Wright, 21. September 1965). However, the literary executors first wanted to know exactly what Wittgenstein had written in code before they made any decision about having them copied. In autumn 1965, von Wright was given the task of deciphering the coded remarks in their entirety, as he reported to Malcolm:

> We discussed the question of copies for Cornell. Our feeling was that the final decision on the question should be taken when the writings in code have become deciphered in their entirety. This, I am afraid, will take me the whole of this academic year. Then, depending upon the over-all impression which the decoded text makes upon us, there are two possibility [sic]. One is to photograph everything, and the other to omit the text in code. For a great many reasons—scholarly, technical, and economic—the first possibility is by far the more attractive one. But I find it difficult to make a prediction at this stage, both because there is still a lot to be decoded and because different people may judge the final situation differently. (von Wright to Malcolm, 13. October 1965)

Indeed, von Wright started siding with Rhees after he had deciphered the coded passages; hence he wrote to Rhees:

> In the course of the Term I have completed the decoding of all the MSS of which I have copies. I am now convinced that your restrictive attitude to the question of taking copies of the whole <u>Nachlass</u> without discrimination for libraries was fully justified. (von Wright to Rhees, 15. December 1965)

The next spring, however, von Wright and Malcolm discussed once again the possibility of depositing copies of the Wittgenstein Nachlass in the Cornell Library. Von Wright now became convinced that it would be right to have the entire Nachlass microfilmed with the help of Cornell University, since it "would solve, once and for all, the problem of taking copies of the originals. The existence of the microfilm, moreover, would be a safeguard of the preservation of the Nachlass in case of disaster" (von Wright to Rhees, 28. April 1966). But it took much effort to persuade Rhees to agree to the idea.[13] After long and heated negotiations, a two-step procedure for dealing with the coded passages was agreed upon: first,

---

[12] What Rhees feared here is precisely what happened when the coded passages from the war notebooks later appeared as Wittgenstein's "secret diaries" (Wittgenstein 1985a, b; 1991a, b).

[13] Von Wright and Rhees' exchange of letters between 1963–1967 are documents of these negotiations.

a microfilm without omissions was produced under von Wright and Malcolm's supervision. Of this microfilm, one Xerox-copy was made. This copy was then given to the literary executors for striking out the passages they considered inappropriate for the public, especially all the coded remarks. In a second step, Cornell University Library produced another microfilm of this examined copy. Scholars would gain access only to the film without the coded remarks. In addition, other research institutions were allowed to purchase copies of the second film from Cornell University Library (cf. von Wright 1969).

The episode of producing a covered-up version of the Nachlass on microfilm, together with editorial decisions not to publish the coded entries and the decision not to publish the first selection of general remarks, all testify to the fact that the literary executors felt it was their duty *not* to publish what they regarded as not belonging to Wittgenstein's philosophical work, or not contributing to its understanding. In the case of the general remarks, however, von Wright changed his opinion about their significance when he re-read them in times of cultural, philosophical and personal change. In particular, he experienced a blurring of the formerly strict distinction between Wittgenstein's philosophical remarks and his broader notes on culture. This happened at the same time as von Wright's professional philosophizing blurred with his personal involvement in political and cultural issues. It is, again, the correspondence with Malcolm that provides the opportunity for these changes to enter the editorial story of CV.

5.5   Re-Reading Wittgenstein Under Changed Conditions

The correspondence between von Wright and Malcolm is as much a philosophers' exchange of ideas on philosophical themes as it is a conversation between friends who talk about personal, political and cultural affairs. This correspondence therefore offers valuable insights into the context of von Wright's editorial work on Wittgenstein's papers. A clue to the changes that accompanied von Wright's editorial work in the mid-1960s is found in a letter from February 1965, written while deciphering the remarks in Wittgenstein's personal code:

> I am proceeding with the decoding-job—as a sort of "psychotherapy" for myself. Now when I have got used to it I can do it rather quickly, and there is no question that we cannot finish the job in another two or three months.
> [...]
> I spoke above of "psychotherapy". This was no mere joke. Because of the emotional upset, I have been practically unable to do any creative work now for two months. In order to not aggravate my depression, I try to concentrate on semi-mechanical and routine jobs. Otherwise I should have a feeling of being completely useless,—as indeed the newspapers tell me I am. (von Wright to Malcolm, 8. February 1965)

The background for these depressing circumstances was that von Wright, in his function as chancellor of the Academy of Finland, experienced a political threat to the academy (cf. von Wright 2001, 175–194). He noted to Anscombe:

> We have had a somewhat gloomy time here. The Academy of Finland has been violently attacked by the president of the republic and his attacked [sic] seconded by strong fire, particularly in the leftist newspapers. It is not clear what are the objectives, but prima facie they seem to be to bring the scientific and artistic activity under some form of political control. This, needless to say, opens up very sad prospects for the country's future. These sinister developments have depressed me very much and I have not been able to do any work now for more than a month. (von Wright to Anscombe, 18. January 1965)

What von Wright expressed in this letter in a rather polite form, he put more frankly in a letter to Malcolm:

> Something extraordinary has happened here. The Academy of Finland has practically since it was founded, been the object of attack from various political quarters, chiefly leftist. [...] Now the President of the Republic, probably in a fit of bad temper and under the influence of evil and stupid advisors, decreed—hear and try to believe it—that the whole institution should be dissolved and abolished. (von Wright to Malcolm, 2. January 1965)

In his next letter, von Wright told Malcolm the situation had become even worse:

> You say you hope the uproar over the Academy has subsided. It has not. The press is becoming impatient that we have not already been "dissolved"; we are accused of being reactionaries, out of touch with scientific development and a burden on the nation. I know that I _ought not_ to [sic] pay attention to all this nonsense, but to my shame I must confess that it worries me terribly. I feel disappointed at my country's backwardness and immaturity, and I know that I shall for the future feel alienated from it. I am not planning to take any immediate action, but I am seriously considering the possibility of breaking up from here for good after a year or two. Should Jaakko Hintikka decide not to return to Finland, it is almost certain that I should follow his example. (von Wright to Malcolm, 8. February 1965)

The political attack on the Academy of Finland, and, indeed, on himself, represented a point of transition in von Wright's life. More than once, he considered immigrating to the USA. Malcolm supported this idea and offered to negotiate a permanent post for him at Cornell University.[14] Von Wright ended up not leaving his country, but he clearly cultivated his relationship with Malcolm and strengthened his ties to the USA. He accepted a professor-at-large position at Cornell, and his and Malcolm's cooperation on "Wittgensteinian themes" (cf. von Wright 1995b) intensified. On his regular visits to the USA during these years, von Wright experienced the cultural change that took place during the Johnson administration. He experienced the civil rights movement and the escalation of the Vietnam War, both of which affected him. The USA had been for him the example of a good democracy and a free society, but this conviction was radically shaken when he witnessed Johnson's decision to begin heavy bombing in Vietnam (Note from a conversation with Anita and Benedict von Wright). This shock came to expression

---

[14] These considerations are mentioned in several letters from von Wright to Malcolm, e.g., in the letters from 21. December 1967 and 14. January 1968.

in an article von Wright wrote during a visit to Cornell University in 1967. In this article, which was published under the title *The War against Vietnam* (von Wright 1967), he expressed anger over the annihilation of Vietnamese civilians by American bombing; he was convinced that no outcome of the bombing could justify its continuation. By publishing this article, von Wright sent his fellow Finns a fervent call to action. Here spontaneous emotions were conveyed with a directness rarely sensed in his otherwise well-tempered publications. Indeed, the article was originally not meant for publication. Only when von Wright returned to Finland did he think about submitting it to a newspaper. Afterwards, he was, more than many of his academic colleagues, open to discussing the demands of the younger generation. He was curious to learn about how young people saw life and wanted to improve it (Note from a conversation with Anita and Benedict von Wright). Von Wright underwent, so to speak, his own '1968 revolution' at the age of 52. On the other side of the political spectrum, however, his struggle with the political left about the Academy was aggravated, especially after he had succeeded Alvar Aalto as president of that institution: von Wright suddenly found himself in a personal duel with the president of Finland (von Wright 2001, 241–252).

With regard to the eventual publication of CV, it is important to understand that von Wright's involvements in practical political issues during that period of cultural change affected his understanding of philosophy and its role in society. He made this interaction between cultural change, personal life and philosophy explicit in a letter to Anscombe just before she was to visit him:

> You may find that I have changed a lot. Some years ago I began to take interest in things which I had before regarded with indifference. One could call them "political and social" questions. It was, chiefly, the Vietnam war and my repeated visits to the United States which woke me up. Whether my new consciousness has been in any way "futile" or whether it has only "tormented" me, I feel quite unable to tell (yet). Another thing which has much changed is "my" philosophy. This too is partly a shift in interests, but even more in opinions—and since "opinion" is a very poor term her one must I think really use the more pretentious term "philosophy". Many of my colleagues would speak of these changes as a "deterioration". They may be right. But I am sure that deterioration is not, so to speak, in the new direction my thoughts have taken, but possibly in the fact that I am too old to be able to do any decent philosophy of a different kind from the work I had been doing before.—To add just one last comment: I slowly begin to feel and understand that the two changes I mentioned have something to do with another. (von Wright to Anscombe, 29. June 1969)

To Malcolm he had written in a similar vein, and with a view to Wittgenstein:

> This last winter my "view of the world", and particularly of the future of man and human society, have undergone great changes. I feel like becoming a different person myself. I am on my way somewhere, but do not yet know the destination. External events have of course greatly contributed to this—in the first place by making me aware of the world round me in a way I never was before. I think I told you in an earlier letter that I have come to a new understanding also of the great pessimism which was Wittgenstein's. (von Wright to Malcolm, 13. April 1968)

Von Wright's new understanding of Wittgenstein's pessimism—one may call it his 'later Spenglerism' to contrast it with the cultural optimism connected to the young von Wright's early Spenglerism—is also reflected by the fact that in his letters, he began using the phrase "the darkness of our time", alluding to Wittgenstein's preface to the Philosophical Investigations (Wittgenstein 1953). Von Wright (1990, 1995a) regarded an earlier version of that preface as an oppositional response to Carnap's (1928) preface to Der logische Aufbau der Welt, which expressed the conviction that positivistic philosophy served the spirit of progress in its time. Resonating thus with Wittgenstein's views of contemporary Western civilization—views which von Wright had been astounded by thirty years earlier—the general remarks came again to the fore of his mind, as he noted to Malcolm three months after the letter quoted directly above: "I have been thinking a little about a possible collection of Wittgenstein's 'general remarks'. My view of the selection has become a little more definite." (von Wright to Malcolm, 4. July 1968). This renewed interest in Wittgenstein's general remarks coincided with von Wright's new reading of Wittgenstein's philosophical works that made connections to historical and social developments:

> The Wittgensteinian mood of the so-called ordinary language philosophy of the 1950s left me completely cool. My neo-Wittgensteinianism, if it can be called by that name, is related to changes which my thinking as a whole has undergone since the mid-1960s: to my awakening interest in Hegel and Marx, to my questioning of the political and social *Weltbild* with which I had been brought up and lived, and to my search for a new humanist orientation. (von Wright 1989, 41)

Von Wright's new philosophical orientation brought him into contact with the Yugoslavian Praxis-group that sought to develop a humanist Marxism. In 1973, von Wright took part in one of their summer-schools on the island of Korčula. When the group and their journal Praxis were forbidden a year later, von Wright was a leading force in protesting against this political censorship (von Wright 2001, 250–254). By this time, he had clearly departed from the narrow professional philosophy that had been advocated by the protagonists of logical positivism. Instead, he turned towards a philosophy that developed a critical perspective of Western civilization. At the same time, a new 'continental' philosophy moved to the front stage of academic philosophy. Along with these philosophical changes came a fresh interest in Wittgenstein, recognizing that his philosophy had a central European pedigree. Allan Janik, for example, wrote as early as in 1966 about traces of Schopenhauer in Wittgenstein's writings. Around 1968, Janik started working on a book that would embed Wittgenstein's thinking in the intellectual sphere of Viennese modernity: Wittgenstein's Vienna (Janik and Toulmin 1973). Von Wright liked and supported this work that showed the importance of seeing the biographical context of Wittgenstein's work.[15] A shock for the literary

---

[15] See the correspondence between von Wright and Janik, which is partly kept at the NLF, COLL.714.98. Janik's papers have recently been acquired by the Brenner Archives at the University of Innsbruck.

executors, on the other hand, was the biographical essay "Wittgenstein" (Bartley 1973) that attributed scandalous homosexual practices to him. Anscombe (1974) and Rhees (1974) denounced such speculations, which, to the best of their knowledge, were unwarranted. Von Wright wondered whether it would be right to honor the author of that essay with so much attention, but he liked the remarks in Rhees' article about knowledge of a man's private life and how it might relate to understanding his work (cf. von Wright to Rhees, 15. April 1974). The wondering about this relation was also the context in which Wittgenstein's general remarks gained renewed interest and came to be seen as possibly illuminating for understanding his philosophical works. The final impulse that made von Wright resume the idea to publish Wittgenstein's general remarks came during a visit from Christopher Nyíri, another proponent of investigating Wittgenstein from a cultural point of view. In late 1974, von Wright wrote to Malcolm about Nyíri's (cf. Nyíri 1988) visit:

> In November a Hungarian scholar by the name of Nyíri visited us and read a paper to our research seminar on Wittgenstein in the "perspective" of Marx, Freud, and Musil. [...] A consequence of N's visit was that I resumed the work which I, as you remember, started years ago on editing a collection of Wittgenstein's "general remarks". I re-read the material and was deeply impressed. I must now set myself to do the work. It is an immense job and I am sure that I shall experience much frustration in the course of doing it. But fortunately I can find two junior people here to help me with the more "technical" aspects of the task. (von Wright to Malcolm, 12. December 1974)

5.6 Making a Second Selection that Could Justifiably Be Published

One of the "junior people" whom von Wright mentioned when informing Malcolm about his resumption of editing the general remarks was Heikki Nyman. Von Wright told Rhees about Nyman's contribution to correcting the remarks in the first selection:

> In doing this work I have relied heavily on the assistance of a certain Mr Heikki Nyman. He has translated several of Wittgenstein's works into Finnish, knows the material extremely well, and has in my opinion a very good judgement. He also knows German well. He has, among other things, checked all the selected remarks against their manuscript sources which, as you can imagine, resulted in a very great number of corrections in the text which I typed out earlier—and also in some additions. When the stuff is published, due acknowledgement ought to be made to Mr Nyman. (von Wright to Rhees, 17. December 1975)

Von Wright and Nyman consulted together to determine which remarks should be excluded from the original selection. In a first step, they cut the number of repetitions and already-published remarks. Then they excluded remarks of a purely personal nature and, as Nyman remembers, remarks that referred to living persons, such as the following[16]:

> Philosophers like Wisdom, Ayer and others. They show off with a bundle of stolen keys // show you keys which they have stolen//, but they can't open doors with them. (Ms-138,17a_f)[17]

Apart from these cuttings, von Wright initially did not want to interfere much in the first selection, as is confirmed in a letter to Rhees:

> It will essentially be a "collection of materials" with no attempt at ordering or sieving the stuff. The presentation will be chronological.—I reread the remarks recently and was struck by their beauty and depth. (von Wright to Rhees, 13. December 1974)

Rhees, who was deeply concerned about not producing misunderstandings of Wittgenstein's philosophy through their editions, and about not publishing something Wittgenstein probably did not want them to publish, was very interested in how von Wright would decide whether a remark was good enough to be published and whether philosophical remarks should be included in the selection:

> I am interested that you are going to prepare a volume of 'general remarks'. One or two questions come to my mind. These are expressions of curiosity, simply. They are not matters on which at some point I might raise "objections" I shall do nothing of the kind. If I seem to express an opinion here, it is simply meant as part of a question, that is all.
>
> Some years ago we used to speak of 'Wert-Fragen', when we spoke of collecting quasi parenthetical remarks in the manuscripts. The term 'general remarks' is of wider scope. Does it mean that you intend to include the various remarks about the nature of philosophy—about das 'was der Philosoph immer tut', 'die Art der Fragen in der Philosophie', similies characterizing the work of philosophy, and so on? You have included these in your original typescript. And I have wondered why. It is often hard to draw a line between such remarks and more detailed but still general discussions of philosophical method, which often form a part of his investigation of some important question. And further: they seem to be of a fundamentally different sort from those other remarks about Lebensprobleme, Einstellung (oder Verhalten) im Leben, about Ethik ("Subjektivität", Willensfreiheit, Verantwortung …), Kultur und Künste (Musik, Architektur, Dichtung, Malerei) und Religion. I say "fundamentally" because the remarks about the nature of philosophy could themselves be subjects of philosophical discussion, often; as Lebensprobleme could not.
>
> You say you will produce the material "with no attempt at …sieving the stuff". The question this raises is more difficult still. It always starts me asking what Wittgenstein himself would have wanted. What he would have destroyed, if it came to that. From my memory of them (Which I have not refreshed recently) I would say that some of the remarks are 'all right, but ordinary'—daß sie keinen Stempel an sich tragen, der sie als die seinen kennzeichnet. Diese würden dann die Luft verbrauchen, welche dem lebendigen

---

[16] Recollection of Mr. Nyman in a conversation with A. Maury. I thank A. Maury for passing on my questions to Mr. Nyman.

[17] Translation by Christian Erbacher. The German original reads: "Philosophen wie Wisdom, Ayer, u.a. Sie prahlen mit //zeigen Dir// eine[mln] Bund gestohlener Schlüssel Bund //Schlüssel den sie gestohlen haben//, aber sie können keine Türen damit öffnen."

> Blühen der eigentlichen ('gestempelten') Bemerkungen dienen sollte.—But I do not think
> this is a question on which discussion is possible, and I am not trying to discuss it. (Rhees
> to von Wright, 10. January 1975)

Von Wright understood the difficulties Rhees saw in producing a collection of
Wittgenstein's general remarks:

> I am sensitive to the comments you make on my plans for a collection of "general
> remarks". For me too it is very much of a problem, whether one should include remarks
> about the nature of philosophy in general and the more personal remarks about the nature
> of W's own work. These remarks are very numerous; perhaps it would be a good idea
> to exclude them altogether. However, I also find them on the whole very interesting and,
> when they have an auto-biographical touch, very moving. Another great difficulty for me
> is whether one should attempt a "sieving" of the stuff. You are quite right when you say
> that the inclusion of too many less original remarks may have a suffocating effect on the
> really excellent ones. On the other hand: should the editor also pass value-judgements on
> the stuff, or should he limit his task to that of presenting a collection of materials.
>
> I think that none of the difficult questions here can be answered until one has produced
> a more surveyable collection than the one we already have omitting all the already printed
> ones and cutting down the repetitions (which are very numerous). You will hear from me
> about this, when I think I have made some progress. (von Wright to Rhees, 16. January
> 1975)

As it turned out, von Wright also excluded a number of hitherto unpublished passages stemming from the chapter "Philosophie" in the so-called Big Typescript
(Ts 213, edited in Wittgenstein 1969b and 2000b), which von Wright had originally included in his first selection. As these belonged to the remarks Rhees had
also omitted from his edition of Philosophical Grammar (Wittgenstein 1969b; cf.
Kenny 1976; Erbacher 2019, see chapter 4), they remained unpublished for several
more years. However, there were also some additions to von Wright's first selection, in particular, some coded remarks commenting on the philosophical work or
which von Wright regarded as beautiful aphorisms. After one year, the number of
remarks was reduced to about a third of those included in the first selection. Von
Wright reported to Rhees and Anscombe on the sieving process:

> From the material included in the "old edition" I have, following the advice given by
> Rhees and in agreement with my own view of the matter, omitted a) remarks of a purely
> personal nature, b) comments by Wittgenstein on the progress of his own work, c) reflec-
> tions on the nature of philosophy, and d) remarks which belong in the broader context
> of philosophical argument. Some remarks which may be classified under these headings,
> however, I have not omitted. (von Wright to Rhees, 17. December 1975)

Von Wright considered the new selection publishable in principle (von Wright
to Siegfried Unseld, 10. February 1976). Since he thought it would be especially
difficult to translate the literary quality of the remarks, and since they would be
of prime interest to a German audience, he proposed publishing them first solely
in German. Rhees and Anscombe agreed. Von Wright then wrote straightaway to
Siegfried Unseld, director of the publishing house Suhrkamp, asking him whether

he would be interested in a volume of Wittgenstein's "General Remarks" (von Wright to Unseld, 10. February 1976). Unseld immediately replied that he would, without any hesitation, be willing to publish them (Unseld to von Wright, 24. February 1976).

Von Wright sent Unseld the 'new edition' of about 500 remarks under the title "Allgemeine Bemerkungen" in March 1976 (von Wright to Unseld, 5. March 1976). Unseld was fascinated by the collection and suggested to publish it as *Vermischte Bemerkungen*.[18] This proposal for the title pleased von Wright, perhaps since it could be understood as an allusion to the posthumously published *Vermischte Schriften* of Georg Christoph Lichtenberg, perhaps also because Lichtenberg was one of the authors whom both Wittgenstein and von Wright very much liked.[19] Since von Wright expected the selection to appeal to a "very wide audience", he and Unseld envisaged publishing the new book in the series "Bibliothek Suhrkamp" (Unseld to von Wright, 26. March 1976; von Wright to Anscombe, July 1976). The books in this series were available for a decent price and set the intellectual agenda in Germany for a long time. Hence, Unseld's support and enthusiasm for CV contributed to making Wittgenstein's writings not only accessible but also popular in Germany. When the volume was finally published, Unseld wrote to von Wright:

> I took the volume into my hand again and wanted to re-read the one or other passage that I knew already from the manuscript, and I was deeply fascinated again by the wisdom of some of the remarks. These remarks one cannot only read, one can live with them. (Unseld to von Wright, 7. September 1977)[20]

Von Wright too regarded the remarks as more than beautiful aphorisms, as he pointed out in his preface to CV:

> I am all the same convinced that these notes can be properly understood and appreciated only against the background of Wittgenstein's philosophy and, furthermore, that they make a contribution to our understanding of that philosophy. (Wittgenstein 1980, preface)

---

[18] The title "Vermischte Bemerkungen" appears in the correspondence between von Wright and Unseld for the first time on 19. March 1976. According to Mr Nyman, in a conversation with A. Maury, it was Unseld's suggestion to call the selection "Vermischte Bemerkungen" instead of "Allgemeine Bemerkungen". How the title "Culture and Value" for the English edition came about is not clear, but it was not von Wright's suggestion, as can be seen from his correspondence with the translator Peter Winch, kept at NLF, COLL.714–267.

[19] Von Wright had written an essay about Lichtenberg as a philosopher already after the return from his study sojourn at Cambridge (von Wright 1942).

[20] Translation by Christian Erbacher. Unseld's original letter is written in German, and the passage reads: "Ich habe jetzt wieder den Band zur Hand genommen und wollte noch einmal das eine oder andere, das mir schon aus der Lektüre des Manuskripts bekannt war, nachlesen, und wieder hat mich die Lebensweisheit mancher Bemerkungen tief in Bann geschlagen. Diese Bemerkungen kann man nicht nur lesen, mit ihnen kann man leben."

Von Wright spelled out the ideas expressed in this prefatory note in more detail in his opening address at the International Wittgenstein Symposium in Kirchberg (Austria) in August 1977. Just in time, for it was there that he received the first printed copies of CV. In his lecture—later published as Wittgenstein in Relation to His Times (cf. von Wright 1982, 201–216)—he announced the appearance of CV to the philosophical community and explained how he regarded the collection's significance for understanding Wittgenstein's philosophy. He still held that the remarks in CV did not belong to Wittgenstein's philosophical work, but he now proposed that they may make readers see Wittgenstein's philosophical work in the right relation to his times. Von Wright argued that Wittgenstein had seen human life and human artefacts entrenched in structures of a social nature, which he had called "forms of life". Language games could be seen as embodiments of forms of life. Thus, malfunctions or distortions in language games would signal malfunctions in the way people lived. Consequently, Wittgenstein's work on misleading ways of speaking would amount to a fight against distortions in the language games that were rooted in a sick way of living (cf. von Wright 1982, 206–208). Wittgenstein's writings may thus be read as subversive philosophy targeting current Western civilization. If so, however, it seemed important to von Wright to add that his fight against distortions of language games was, not aiming at changing people's way of speaking. In order to change it, one would have to change the way of life that entrenches the particular way of speaking. And, as von Wright pointed out in his lecture: "It is vain to think that by fighting the symptoms one can cure illnesses" (von Wright 1982, 208). Thus, Wittgenstein may have diagnosed the sickness of his times, he may even have shown how a therapy may work, but he did not carry out therapy, for the therapy would have consisted of changing the way the 'patient' lived. As von Wright put it, Wittgenstein "wished these ways of life changed—but he had no faith that he or his teaching would change them" (von Wright 1982, 206).

As von Wright noted, the civilization-critical orientation of Wittgenstein's philosophizing could be seen most strikingly precisely there where one would expect it the least: in his remarks on the foundations of mathematics. In-between his treatment of set-theory, there would appear passages on the "sickness of a time" (von Wright 1982, 208). These passages, von Wright now stressed, truly belong there: "To Wittgenstein set-theory was a cancer rooted deep in the body of our culture and with distorting effects on that part of our culture which is our mathematics" (von Wright 1982, 208). This sentence indicates how much von Wright's reading of the remarks had actually changed during the past 25 years. After all, the manuscripts on the foundations of mathematics were precisely the context from which von Wright decidedly omitted the "remarks of a general nature" when he was first struck by them in 1954. In contrast to his opinion at that time (i.e., that the general remarks ought to be separated from Wittgenstein's philosophical work), von Wright now presented an interpretation according to which the general remarks encourage one to read even Wittgenstein's remarks on the foundations of mathematics as animated by his criticism of the contemporary Western way of life.

5.7 Inspiring the Next Generations with a Documentary Approach

Von Wright's lecture at Kirchberg opened up for a reading of Wittgenstein's writings as showing their socio-cultural embeddedness, their 'entrenchment in structures of a social nature', and the author's entrenchment in the same. This level of self-reflection in Wittgenstein's writings becomes tangible especially when taking into account some of the passages that the literary executors had long excluded from their editions but which were then assembled in CV. Read in their light, Wittgenstein's philosophical writings can no longer be regarded as intending to state eternal philosophical truths, but rather as showing a man's philosophizing in and responding to his specific intellectual environment. Hence, at the end of his lecture, von Wright concluded that Wittgenstein's "way of seeing philosophy was not an attempt to tell us what philosophy, once and for all, *is*, but expressed what it, for him, in the setting of his times, had to be" (von Wright 1982, 216). This suggests that each era needs its own philosophy—a message that not only may address the spirit of the times but is likely to encourage subsequent generations to go their own way. Indeed, the 1977 Kirchberg Symposium signalled that the 'baton' of editing Wittgenstein was about to be passed to younger scholars. This conference gathered, on the hand, Wittgenstein's pupils and heirs who had worked for more than 25 years to make his writings publically available, above all von Wright and Anscombe, but also Malcolm or Anscombe's husband Peter Geach (cf. Leinfellner et al. 1978, 545–550). On the other hand, scholars like Allan Janik, Anthony Kenny, Brian McGuinness, Tore Nordenstam and Joachim Schulte, who came to Kirchberg that year, became leading forces in the next rounds of editing Wittgenstein. Janik remembers this historic conference in the literal meaning of the word:

> Anyone who attended the second annual Wittgenstein Symposium is not likely to forget it. For a young scholar it was mighty impressive to see everybody who was anybody on the Wittgenstein scene gathered together for a week, discussing, socializing and generally enjoying each other's company (it would be simpler to list who was not there from the international Wittgenstein community than to make a long list of those who were present). The philosophical highlight of the meeting was G.H. von Wright's presentation of the Vermischte Bemerkungen. Since only a few of the people present were aware that Wittgenstein's Nachlass contained such texts, the little book was a bombshell. I can still remember staying up well into the night devouring its pages. (Janik 2007, 94)

Von Wright's presentation of CV at Kirchberg impressed even those who were already familiar with Wittgenstein's 'general remarks', such as Schulte:

> I was quite familiar with many of the remarks quoted by von wright, but I was none the less deeply impressed by his way of posing his questions, the sober enthusiasm with which he spelled out the context in which he placed Wittgenstein's observations, and above all the historical perspective which he brought to bear on the latter's writings—a perspective I have slowly learned to appreciate as an indispensable ingredient in fruitful Wittgenstein studies. (Schulte 2016, 188)

The excitement von Wright kindled with his lecture and his edition of CV is paradigmatic for his work as one of Wittgenstein's literary executors. His devotion to preserving and publishing Wittgenstein's papers inspired large-scale editorial projects that would follow in the footsteps of Wittgenstein's literary heirs. For example, there are the critical scholarly editions of Wittgenstein's main works (Wittgenstein 1989, 2001), the complete electronic edition (Wittgenstein 2000a) and the complete correspondence (Wittgenstein 2011)—projects that continued editing Wittgenstein in the historically informed and source-oriented spirit that von Wright had developed. This also holds true for the new reading edition (PU 2003) that was made from the critical-genetic edition of the PI (PU 2001). Quite in accordance with the orientation of von Wright's work reported in this chapter, the editor of that volume, Schulte, expresses his hope that the still-existing hiatus between the "analytical" and "cultural" (PU 2003, 295) reception may be bridged, such that an understanding can be achieved which does justice to what von Wright, already in 1955, had called the "multiplicity" of Wittgenstein and "all his rich complexity". Just as in von Wright's work, one senses a merger here between editorial philology and an apprehension of the cultural dimension of Wittgenstein's writings. As this paper has tried to show, von Wright's selecting and publishing Wittgenstein's remarks on general topics evolved in the spirit of just this merger. Thus, being an editor's selection with a clear editorial intention, CV may go against the grain of much of critical editorial philology. But the motivation to document the historical Wittgenstein is that which unites CV with much of von Wright's other editorial work on Wittgenstein's writings.

In conclusion then, von Wright's work as one of Wittgenstein's literary executors, including his studies and CV, may be called *documentary*, indicating the aim to understand all of Wittgenstein's writings as documents of a rich and complex, but unified philosophical pattern.[21] The editions and publications coming together in this documentary approach can be grouped into three kinds of documents: (1) editions of Wittgenstein's writings, (2) editions of contextual material such as letters and memoirs and (3) scholarly investigations. CV is indeed a special publication when seen against the background of this grouping, but not because it stands in contrast to von Wright's other work as one of Wittgenstein's literary executors. Rather, CV partakes in all three kinds of sources that are characteristic for his documentary approach: CV (a) consists of *remarks* that can be found among Wittgenstein's philosophical writings, and yet (b) which are, in the editor's opinion, contextual material that (c) he selected in order to bring out a specific dimension of Wittgenstein's writings. Thus, CV, though being an edition of Wittgenstein's writings, resembles, in its function, von Wright's editions of letters and memoirs as well as his scholarly work on Wittgenstein's biography and on the origins of the *Tractatus* and the *Philosophical Investigations*. CV may therefore

---

[21] This concept is borrowed from Harold Garfinkel, who introduced 'the documentary method of interpretation' for investigating what sociological researchers, lay and professional, actually do (cf. Garfinkel 1967, 76–103).

be regarded as a hybrid—an edition *and* a contextual study of Wittgenstein's writings—that is meant to allow readers to see Wittgenstein's life and work as a unified whole. It thereby shows von Wright's documentary intention like no other single edition made from Wittgenstein's Nachlass.

Von Wright not only developed a documentary approach as an editor of Wittgenstein's writings, but he also prepared the grounds for applying this approach to studying the editorial work itself. By donating his archives and his correspondence to the University of Helsinki and the National Library of Finland (Wallgren and Österman, 2014), he provided the sources that enable scholars to investigate the history of editing Wittgenstein in its 'rich complexity' and 'multiplicity'. These resources contain a wealth of details for critical philological research, but they additionally allow themselves to be understood as documents of a human story of philosophical inheritance and of the making of a philosophical classic. Their potential has here been explored, inasmuch as they are the main sources for the present account.

Acknowledgements I am especially indebted to Benedict and Anita von Wright for generously sharing their recollections and for permission to quote from von Wright's unpublished letters. I thank Volker Munz, who represents the copyright holders of the letters by Rhees that are quoted here, and who granted permission to quote from Rhees' letters. For permission to quote from Siegfried Unseld's letter, I thank Suhrkamp Verlag. I thank the National Library of Finland and the von Wright and Wittgenstein Archives at the University of Helsinki for providing access to letters and archival materials. Furthermore, I thank Bernt Österman and Thomas Wallgren for fruitful discussions on the topic and for the opportunity to present drafts of this paper at a research seminar at the University of Helsinki. Likewise, I thank the University of Bergen for the opportunity to present an earlier version of this paper. For comments and responses at these presentations, I am grateful to all participants of these presentations. For comments on an earlier version of this essay, I thank Allan Janik. I thank André Maury for a personal interview and for transmitting my questions to Heikki Nyman. For language corrections, I thank Tina Schirmer and Arlyne Moi; for help in final editing, I thank Anne Seibel and Julia Jung. Last but not least, I am indebted to the anonymous reviewers of SATS for their comments that significantly improved the paper.

The main research undergirding this chapter has been funded by the Research Council of Norway, as part of the project "Shaping a Domain of Knowledge by Editorial Processing: The Case of Wittgenstein's Work" (NFR 213080). First sketches of the present text were crafted under the aegis of the program "Joint Nordic Use of WAB Bergen and VWA Helsinki", funded by Nordforsk. Preparation of the study and early presentations were part of a mobility program funded by the Alexander von Humboldt Foundation. The substantial revision and elaboration of the earlier German version of the text has been funded by the Deutsche Forschungsgemeinschaft (DFG) as part of the Collaborative Research Centre "Media of Cooperation" (SFB 1187) at the University of Siegen (Germany).

List of Archival Sources

Editorial note: the archival materials cited in this chapter have been quoted in a normalized form, that is, corrections, deletions, repetitions and so forth have not been preserved in the transcription.

Anscombe to von Wright, 4. July 1954, The National Library of Finland (NLF), COLL.714.11-12.

Draft for the opening lecture for the 16th Wittgenstein Symposium in Kirchberg 1977 (Austria), WWA, WWA\Von Wright materials\Manuscripts etc.\ Kirchberg 1977.

Malcolm to von Wright, 21. September 1965, NLF, COLL.714.142-148.

Malcolm to von Wright, 6. June 1963, NLF, COLL.714.142-148.

Rhees to von Wright 17. December 1966, WWA, WWA documents\ Wittgenstein's Nachlass\Filing cabinet\Rush Rhees I (1975–1998).

Rhees to von Wright 7. July 1965, NLF, COLL. 714.200-201.

Rhees to von Wright, 10. January 1975, WWA, WWA documents\ Wittgenstein's Nachlass\Filing cabinet\Rush Rhees III (1975–1998).

Spengler, Oswald. 1923. Der Untergang des Abendlandes, Vol. 1. München: C. H. Beck; Spengler, Oswald. 1922. Der Untergang des Abendlandes, Vol. 2. Munich, C. H. Beck, WWA, WWA\Von Wright related Publications\Books from von Wright's Home Library\Spengler\The Decline of the West.

Unseld to von Wright, 24. February 1976, WWA documents\Wittgenstein's Nachlass\Filing cabinet\Suhrkamp.

Unseld to von Wright, 26. March 1976, WWA documents\Wittgenstein's Nachlass\Filing cabinet\Suhrkamp.

Unseld to von Wright, 7. September 1977, WWA documents\Wittgenstein's Nachlass\Filing cabinet\Suhrkamp.

Von Wright, A Collection of Remarks by Ludwig Wittgenstein, The von Wright and Wittgenstein Archives at the University of Helsinki (WWA), WWA documents\Wittgenstein's Nachlass\Wittgenstein Materials\Additional Material\ G1\A collection of remarks.

von Wright to Anscombe, 10. March 1965, NLF, COLL.714.11-12.

von Wright to Anscombe, 11. June 1964, NLF, COLL.714.11-12.

von Wright to Anscombe, 12. November 1952, NLF, COLL.714.11-12.

von Wright to Anscombe, 16. March 1965, NLF, COLL.714.11-12.

von Wright to Anscombe, 18. January 1965, NLF, COLL.714.11-12.

von Wright to Anscombe, 20. April 1965, NLF, COLL.714.11-12.

von Wright to Anscombe, 28. June 1965, NLF, COLL.714.11-12.

von Wright to Anscombe, 29. June 1969, NLF, COLL.714.11-12.

von Wright to Anscombe, 6. June 1954, NLF, COLL.714.11-12.

von Wright to Anscombe, 6. November 1954, NLF, COLL.714.11-12.

von Wright to Anscombe, July 1976, NLF, COLL714.11-12.

von Wright to Friedrich August von Hayek, 22. February 1953, WWA documents\Biographical\2. Hayek, Sjögren, National Biography.

von Wright to Malcolm, 12. December 1974, NLF, COLL.714.142-148.

von Wright to Malcolm, 13. April 1968, NLF, COLL.714.11-12.

von Wright to Malcolm, 13. October 1965, NLF, COLL.714.142-148.

von Wright to Malcolm, 14. January 1968, NLF, COLL.714.142-148.

von Wright to Malcolm, 2. January 1965, NLF, COLL.714.142-148.

von Wright to Malcolm, 21. December 1967 NLF, COLL.714.142-148.

von Wright to Malcolm, 25. November 1952, WWA, WWA\Von Wright materials\Manuscripts etc.\Letter to Malcolm 25. November 1952.

von Wright to Malcolm, 4. July 1968, NLF, COLL.714.142-248.

von Wright to Malcolm, 8. February 1965, NLF, COLL.714.142-148.

von Wright to Rhees 15. April 1974, Richard Burton Archives at the University of Swansea (RBA), UNI/SU/PC/1/3/1/10.

von Wright to Rhees 28. April 1966, NLF, COLL. 714.200-201.

von Wright to Rhees, 13. December 1974, WWA, WWA documents\Wittgenstein's Nachlass\Filing cabinet\Rush Rhees II (1972–1974).

von Wright to Rhees, 15. December 1965, NLF, COLL. 714.200-201.

von Wright to Rhees, 16. January 1975, WWA, WWA documents\Wittgenstein's Nachlass\Filing cabinet\Rush Rhees III (1975–1998).

von Wright to Rhees, 17. December 1975, NLF, COLL.714.200-201.

von Wright to Rhees, 17. December 1975, WWA, WWA documents\Wittgenstein's Nachlass\Filing cabinet\Rush Rhees III (1975–1998).

von Wright to Unseld, 10. February 1976, WWA documents\Wittgenstein's Nachlass\Filing cabinet\Suhrkamp.

von Wright to Unseld, 5. March 1976, WWA documents\Wittgenstein's Nachlass\Filing cabinet\Suhrkamp.

References

Anscombe, G. E. M. 1974. "'Wittgenstein' [Letter to the Editor]." *Times Literary Supplement*, 4 Jan. 1974: 12.

Bartley, William Warren. 1973. *Wittgenstein*. London: Quartet Books.

Carnap, Rudolf. 1928. *Der logische Aufbau der Welt*. Leipzig: Felix Meiner.

Erbacher, Christian. 2015a. Editionspraxis, Philosophie und Zivilisationskritik: Die Geschichte von Wittgensteins *Vermischten Bemerkungen*. In *Wittgenstein-Studien* 6: 211–236.

Erbacher, Christian. 2015b. Friedrich August von Hayeks unvollendete 'Skizze für eine Biographie über Ludwig Wittgenstein'. In *Mitteilungen aus dem Brenner-Archiv* 34: 83–100.

Erbacher, Christian. 2016. Die Wittgenstein-Editionen im Kontext—Über editorische Defizite und ihre konstruktive Kontextualisierung. In *Editio* 30: 197–221.

Erbacher, Christian. 2017. 'Among the omitted stuff, there are many good remarks of a general nature'—On the making of von Wright and Wittgenstein's. In *Culture and Value, Northern European Journal of Philosophy* 18(2): 79–113.

Erbacher, Christian. 2019. 'Good' Philosophical Reasons for 'Bad' Editorial Philology? On Rhees and Wittgenstein's. In *Philosophical Grammar, Philosophical Investigations*, 42(2): 111–145.

Erbacher, Christian, Julia Jung and Anne Seibel. 2017. The Logbook of Editing Wittgenstein's 'Philosophische Bemerkungen'. In *Nordic Wittgenstein Review* 6(1): 105–147.

Erbacher, Christian, Sophia V. Krebs. 2015. The First Nine Months of Editing Wittgenstein—Letters from G. E. M. Anscombe and Rush Rhees to G. H. von Wright. In *Nordic Wittgenstein Review* 4(1): 195–231.

Garfinkel, Harold. 1967. *Studies in Ethnomethodology*. Englewood: NJ, Prentice Hall.

Janik, Allan and Stephen Toulmin. 1973. *Wittgenstein's Vienna*. New York: Simon and Schuster.

Janik, Allan. 2007. Remembering Kirchberg 1977. In *Wir hofften jedes Jahr noch ein weiteres Symposium machen zu können. Zum 30. Internationalen Wittgenstein Symposium in*

Kirchberg am Wechsel, eds. C. Kanzian, V. Munz and S. Windholz, 94–95, Austria: Ontos Verlag.

Kenny, Anthony. 1976. From the BIG Typescript to the Philosophical Grammar. In *Essays on Wittgenstein in Honour of G.H. von Wright, Acta Philosophica Fennica*, ed. J. Hintikka, 28: 41–53, Helsinki: University of Helsinki.

Leinfellner, Elisabeth, Leinfellner Werner, Berghel, Hal and Hübner, Adolf. 1978. *Wittgenstein and his Impact on Contemporary Thought*. In Proceedings of the Second International Wittgenstein Symposium. Wien, Hölder—Pichler—Tempsky.

Majetschak, Stefan. 2013. 'Kringel' -Sektionen in Wittgensteins Nachlass Kritische Bemerkungen zu ihrer Deutung. In *Kulturen und Werte-Wittgensteins "Kringel-Buch" als Initialtext*, eds. J. Rothaupt and W. Vossenkuhl, 77–98. Berlin: de Gruyter.

Malcolm, Norman. 1967. Wittgenstein, Ludwig Josef Johann. In *The Encyclopedia of Philosophy*, ed. P. Edwards, 327–340. London: The Macmillan Company and The Free Press.

Maury, André. 1981. Sources of the Remarks in Wittgenstein's Zettel. In *Philosophical Investigations* 4: 57–74.

Maury, André. 1994. Sources of the Remarks in Wittgenstein's Philosophical Investigations. In *Synthese* 98: 349–378.

Nyíri, Christopher. 1988. *Am Rande Europas. Studien zur österreichisch-ungarischen Philosophiegeschichte*. Vienna: Böhlau.

Pinsent, David H. 1990. *A Portait of Wittgenstein as a Young Man: From the Diary of David Hume Pinsent 1912–1914* ed. G. H. von Wright, Oxford: Basil Blackwell.

Rhees, Rush. 1974. Review of W. W. Bartley III, 'Wittgenstein'. In *The Human World* 14: 66–85.

Rothhaupt, Josef. 2013. Zur Philologie des Kringel-Buches und seiner Verortung in Wittgensteins CEuvre. In *Kulturen und Werte*, eds. W. Vossenkuhl and J. Rothaupt, 3–76. Berlin, Boston: De Gruyter.

Rotthaupt, Josef. 2017. Wittgensteins 'General Remarks'. In *Wittgenstein-Studien* 8: 103–136.

Rothhaupt, Josef and Wilhelm Vossenkuhl (eds.). 2013. *Kulturen und Werte. Wittgensteins Kringel-Buch als Initialtext*. Berlin, Boston: de Gruyter.

Schulte, Joachim. 2016. Memories of Georg Henrik von Wright. In *Georg Henrik von Wright's book of friends. Acta Philosophica Fennica Vol. 92*, eds. G. Meggle and R. Vilkko, 187–202. Helsinki: Societas Philosophica Fennica.

Somavilla, Ilse. 2010. Wittgenstein's Coded Remarks in the Context of His Philosophizing. In *Wittgenstein After His Nachlass*, ed. N. Venturinha, 30–50. Basingstoke: Palgrave Macmillian.

Spengler, Oswald. 1922. *Der Untergang des Abendlandes*, Vol. 2. Munich: C. H. Beck.

Spengler, Oswald. 1923. *Der Untergang des Abendlandes*, Vol. 1. Munich: C. H. Beck.

Stern, David. 1996. The Availability of Wittgenstein's Philosophy. In *The Cambridge Companion to Wittgenstein*, eds. H. Sluga and D. Stern, 442–476. Cambridge: Cambridge University Press.

Stern, David. 2013. A New Book by Wittgenstein? The Place of the Kringel-Buch in the Wittgenstein Papers. In *Kulturen und Werte-Wittgensteins "Kringel-Buch" als Initialtext*, eds. J. Rothaupt and W. Vossenkuhl, 97–112. Berlin: de Gruyter.

Venturinha, Nuno (ed.). 2010. *Wittgenstein After His Nachlass*. Basingstoke: Palgrave Macmillian.

Von Wright, Georg H. 1942. Georg Christoph Lichtenberg als Philosoph. In *Theoria* 8: 201–217.

Von Wright, Georg H. 1947. Paideia. In *Nya Argus* 40: 229–231.

Von Wright, Georg H. 1955. Ludwig Wittgenstein. A Biographical Sketch. In *The Philosophical Review* 64: 527–545, reprinted in von Wright (1982, 13–34).

Von Wright, Georg H. 1967. Kriget mot Vietnam. In *Hufvudstadsbladet*, 28. November. Online version under: http://filosofia.fi/se/arkiv/text/4533. Accessed: 31. July 2017.

Von Wright, Georg H. 1969. The Wittgenstein Papers. In *The Philosophical Review* 78: 483–503, republished with revisions in von Wright (1982, 35–62).

Von Wright, Georg H. 1971. Historical Introduction: The Origin of Wittgenstein's *Tractatus*. In *Prototractatus. An early version of Tractatus Logico-Philosophicus by Ludwig Wittgenstein*, eds. B.F. McGuinnes, T. Nyberg and G.H. von Wright, 1–34. London: Routledge and Kegan Paul, reprinted in von Wright (1982, 63–109).

Von Wright, Georg H. 1979. The Origin and Composition of Wittgenstein's *Investigations*. In *Wittgenstein: Sources and Perspectives*, ed. C.G. Luckhardt, 138–160. Ithaca, NY: Cornell University Press, reprinted in von Wright (1982, 111–136).

Von Wright, Georg H. 1982. *Wittgenstein*. Minneapolis, MN: University of Minnesota Press.

Von Wright, Georg H. 1989. Intellectual Autobiography. In L. E. Hahn and P. A. Schilpp, eds., *The Philosophy of Georg Henrik Von Wright. Library of Living Philosophers Volume 19* (Chicago, Open Court), 3–58.

Von Wright, Georg H. 1990. Wittgenstein and Twentieth Century. In *Language, Knowledge, and Intentionality: Perspectives on the Philosophy of Jaakko Hintikka, Acta Philosophica Fennica*, eds. L. Haaparanta, M. Kusch and I. Niiniluoto, 47–67. Helsinki: Societas Philosophica Fennica.

Von Wright, Georg H. 1992a. The Troubled History of Part II of the Investigations. In *Grazer Philosophische Studien* 42: 181–192.

Von Wright, Georg H. 1992b. Norman Malcolm. In *Philosophical Investigations 15* (1992b): 215–222.

Von Wright, Georg H. 1995a. Editor's Preface. In *Norman Malcolm: Wittgensteinian Themes*, ed. G. H. v. Wright, vii–xii. Ithaca, N.Y: Cornell University Press.

Von Wright, Georg H. 1995b. Wittgenstein and Twentieth Century. In *Wittgenstein: Mind and Language*, ed. E. Egidi, 1–19. Dodrecht: Kluwer.

Von Wright, Georg H. 2001. *Mitt Liv som jeg minns det*. Helsingfors: Söderström.

Wallgren, Thomas and Bernt Österman. 2014. The von Wright and Wittgenstein Archives at the University of Helsinki (WWA). In *Wittgenstein-Studien* 5: 273–282.

Wittgenstein, Ludwig. 1953. *Philosophical Investigations / Philosophische Untersuchungen*. G. E. M. Eds. Anscombe and R. Rhees. Oxford: Basil Blackwell.

Wittgenstein, Ludwig. 1956. *Remarks on the Foundations of Mathematics / Bemerkungen über die Grundlagen der Mathematik*. Eds. G. H. von Wright, R. Rhees and G. E. M. Anscombe. Oxford: Basil Blackwell.

Wittgenstein, Ludwig. 1961. *Notebooks 1914–1916*. Eds. G. H. von Wright and G. E. M. Anscombe. Oxford: Basil Blackwell.

Wittgenstein, Ludwig. 1964. *Philosophische Bemerkungen*. Ed. R. Rhees. Oxford: Basil Blackwell.

Wittgenstein, Ludwig. 1965. A Lecture on Ethics. In *The Philosophical Review* 74: 3–12.

Wittgenstein, Ludwig. 1969a. *Briefe an Ludwig von Ficker*. Ed. G. H. von Wright, in collaboration with W. Methgal. Brenner Studien 1. Salzburg: Otto Müller.

Wittgenstein, Ludwig. 1969b. *Philosophische Grammatik*. Ed. R. Rhees. Oxford: Basil Blackwell.

Wittgenstein, Ludwig. 1973. *Letters to C. K. Ogden*. Edited with an Introduction by G. H. von Wright and an Appendix of Letters by Frank Plumpton Ramsey. Oxford: Basil Blackwell.

Wittgenstein, Ludwig. 1974. *Letters to Russel, Keynes and Moore*. Edited with an Introduction by G. H. von Wright, assisted by B. F. McGuinness. Oxford: Basil Blackwell.

Wittgenstein, Ludwig. 1977. *Vermischte Bemerkungen*. Ed. G. H. von Wright, assisted by H. Nyman. Frankfurt am Main: Suhrkamp.

Wittgenstein, Ludwig. 1980. *Culture and Value / Vermischte Bemerkungen*. Ed. G. H. v. Wright, in cooperation with H. Nyman. Oxford: Basil Blackwell.

Wittgenstein, Ludwig. 1983. Some Hitherto Unpublished Letters from Ludwig Wittgenstein to Georg Henrik von Wright. In *The Cambridge Review* 104: 56–64.

Wittgenstein, Ludwig. 1985a. Diaris Secrets / Geheime Tagebücher. In *Saber* 5: 24–49.

Wittgenstein, Ludwig. 1985b. Diarios Secretos (y II) / Geheime Tagebücher. In *Saber* 6: 30–59.

Wittgenstein, Ludwig. 1989. *Logisch-philosophische Abhandlung. Tractatus logico-philosophicus*. Ed.s B. McGuinness and J. Schulte. Kritische Edition. Frankfurt a. M.: Suhrkamp.

Wittgenstein, Ludwig. 1991a. *Geheime Tagebücher*. Ed. Wilhelm Baum. Vienna: Turia und Kant.

Wittgenstein, Ludwig. 1991b. *Geheime Tagebücher*. Ed. Wilhelm Baum. Vienna, Turia und Kant, 2nd ed.

Wittgenstein, Ludwig. 1992. *Last Writings on the Philosophy of Psychology / Letzte Schriften über die Philosophie der Psychologie*. Vol. 2. Eds. G. H. v. Wright and H. Nyman. Oxford: Basil Blackwell.

Wittgenstein, Ludwig. 1994a. Ludwig Wittgenstein's Correspondence with Skjolden. In *Wittgenstein and Norway*, eds. G. H. von Wright and K. O. Åmås, 83–162. Oslo: Solum.

Wittgenstein, Ludwig. 1994b. *Vermischte Bemerkungen*. G.H. von Wright, ed. assisted by Heikki Nyman. Neubearbeitung des Textes durch Alois Pichler. Frankfurt a. M.: Suhrkamp.

Wittgenstein, Ludwig. 2000a. *Wittgenstein's Nachlass. The Bergen Electronic Edition*. Ed. Wittgenstein archives at the University of Bergen. Oxford: Oxford University Press.

Wittgenstein, Ludwig. 2000b. *The Big Typescript. Wiener Ausgabe Band 11*. Ed. N. Nedo. Vienna, New York: Springer.

Wittgenstein, Ludwig. 2001. *Philosophische Untersuchungen. Kritisch-genetische Edition*. Ed. J. Schulte, in collaboration with H. Nyman, E.v. Savigny and G. H. v. Wright. Frankfurt am Main: Suhrkamp.

Wittgenstein, Ludwig. 2011. *Gesamtbriefwechsel/Innsbrucker elektronische Ausgabe. 2nd Release*. Eds. A. Coda, G. Citron, B. Halder, A. Janik, U. Lobis, K. Mayr, B. McGuinness, M. Schorner, M. Seekircher and J. Wang. On behalf of the research institute Brenner-Archiv. Charlottesville: Intelex.

The Tragedy of Tübingen

A Story about the Humanities and Technology

6

6.1   Scholarly Prologue

Understood or misunderstood, Ludwig Wittgenstein's philosophical investigations have inspired many scholars, both within and beyond academic philosophy. In some disciplines, his remarks have incited scientific revolutions. His remarks on the language games of 'knowing' and 'proofing' contained the revolutionary seeds for a philosophy of science that showed the limits of Popper's 'Logik der Forschung' (Popper 1935) when the latter was just on the verge of its long career.[1] That it took another generation before Thomas Kuhn (1962; on Wittgenstein's influence, see Isaac 2012, 89–107) cultivated Wittgenstein's philosophical seed to go beyond Popper's paradigm is typical for the delayed distribution and reception of Wittgenstein's thought. (This essay and the history of editing Wittgenstein are contributions to understand the specifics of this delay.) However, once the new philosophy of science was set in motion, the investigation of scientific practices began to prosper in various veins, but with a common recognition of congeniality with Wittgenstein's posthumously published writings. Examples here are the Edinburgh school's sociology of knowledge (e.g., Bloor 1983), science and technology studies (e.g., Sismondo 2009) and ethnomethodological studies of scientific work (e.g., Lynch 1997)—they all found that Wittgenstein had already thought through what they regarded as belonging to their certainties. Of course, they differ in saying exactly what they owe to Wittgenstein because they read

---

[1] Wittgenstein's different investigations regarding '*Sprachspiele*' appear in many of his posthumous editions; *On Certainty* (Wittgenstein 1969) only holds the last investigations regarding this topic, which the 'late Wittgenstein' dealt with repeatedly between 1929 and 1951.

This chapter is a revised and translated version of Erbacher 2019a.

C. Erbacher, *The Happy Afterlife of Ludwig W.*, Beiträge zur Praxeologie / Contributions to Praxeology, https://doi.org/10.1007/978-3-662-66155-0_6

Wittgenstein differently (Bloor 1992, 266–282; Lynch 1992a, 215–265; 1992b, 283–300; Rawls 2011, 396–418). But as Erhard Schüttpelz has perspicaciously noted, they all have the same shortcoming:

> While two generations of scholars have, in exemplary studies, investigated an impressive bandwidth of the publishing processes and media practices in the sciences—from inscriptions in the laboratory and field to the published papers and text books, from the infrastructural and technological standardization to the popularization of science and public experts—the media practices and publication processes in the humanities, and thereby in the very homeland from which the studies of sciences had originated, have been looked at only tentatively. (Media of Cooperation 2015, DFG-proposal for CRC 1187)[2]

Studying the media practices and processes for publishing Wittgenstein's writings promises a remedy here: it would be an investigation into the scholarly practices that praxeologically reflect the history of praxeological thinking.

Thinking radically praxeologically, Wittgenstein's remarks reflect their own genesis. His writings do not postulate a theory, not even a theory of philosophy as practice. Instead, they represent a practice of philosophizing and offer readers companionship in their own philosophical investigations. In order to indicate this use of his remarks, Wittgenstein uses several literary means and techniques of alienation that are supposed to prevent the misuse of his writings as theory (see for example Erbacher 2015). One of Wittgenstein's literary techniques of alienation is to make explicit the genesis of his remarks when he is writing about philosophy.[3] His remarks on philosophy therefore do not answer the question of what philosophy once and for all and essentially is—rather, they replace the question with reflections on how Wittgenstein as an author crafted his writings. Some ethnomethodologists saw this and read Wittgenstein's *Philosophische Untersuchungen* as an ethnomethodological study on philosophizing academically.[4] But also for a sociology of knowledge and a sociology of writing, a reconstruction of the actual genesis of Wittgenstein's writings is possible when the 20,000 pages of his Nachlass are investigated philosophically, philologically and biographically. With this, one gains an understanding of how Wittgenstein's

---

[2]Translation by Christian Erbacher. The German original: *Während zwei Generationen Wissenschaftsforscher in exemplarischen Analysen eine eindrucksvolle Bandbreite unterschiedlicher naturwissenschaftlicher Veröffentlichungsprozesse und Medienpraktiken untersucht haben—von den Inskriptionen im Labor und Feld bis hin zur Publikationsreife und zum Lehrbuch, von den infrastrukturellen wissenschaftlichen und technischen Standardisierungen bis zur Wissenschaftspopularisierung und öffentlichen Expertise—sind die Medienpraktiken und Veröffentlichungsprozesse der Geisteswissenschaften und damit die Erschließung der eigenen Herkunftsregion dieser Forschung nur zaghaft in Angriff genommen worden.*

[3]Wittgenstein's remarks about philosophy have a long history, but they were most powerful in connection with his *Philosophical Investigations* (cf. Wittgenstein 2001).

[4]Lynch in a personal conversation about H. Garfinkel's account of Wittgenstein's *Philosophical Investigations*.

writings came into being through his systematic revisions of notebook entries, transferences into selections and arrangements into larger representations.

Although a comprehensive history of such media practices remains to be written, the sources for it have largely been disclosed. But this does not mean that the basic research for a history of the media practices and publication processes of Wittgenstein's writings has been finished: that history does not end with the death of the author. It can be understood as an ongoing practice akin to Wittgenstein's understanding of philosophizing. Wittgenstein did not seal his writings in one published book; instead, he entrusted three of his students with a collection of fragments and instructed them to publish what they thought fit. Carrying out this order led to the publications that were highly influential for investigating the scientific and scholarly practices mentioned above. Hence, a history of the media practices and publication processes for Wittgenstein's writings must include the making of the posthumous editions of his writings.

A history of the media practices and processes involved in publishing Wittgenstein's writings –it consists not only of an account of Wittgenstein's media practices but also an account of the editors' work in their relevant contexts—will extinguish the genius cult that still exists in some historiographies of philosophy. This cult is partly responsible for the impression that great philosophical works fall from the window of an ivory tower, in completed form, printed and bound, just in order to hit and inspire the next genius philosopher walking by. In actual fact, in the history of philosophy, there are a number of cases in which great philosophers do not publish their thoughts in writing; it takes their pupils and followers to put their teacher's thought into a publishable form. The literary tradition of Western philosophy begins with this case. But it has rarely been possible to look into the black box of such discipulary production processes and to investigate the making of the conditions for scholarly reception in academic philosophy.

In the case of Wittgenstein's writings, we can, at least to some extent, open the black box of discipulary production processes: not only does Wittgenstein's Nachlass include texts in several genealogical stages, but there are many published recollections and a comfortable documentation of the editorial processes that have been applied to his writings over the last 70 years. Through collecting and analyzing these documents, the genesis of Wittgenstein's influential writings can be constructively contextualized (Erbacher 2017b). This process has already begun for the work done by Wittgenstein's three original literary heirs (see Chap. 1, 2 and 5). But since the history of editing Wittgenstein's writings goes beyond the work of these three, and, since the 1970s, has included big international digitization projects, the history of the media practices and publication processes for Wittgenstein's writings turns from being a history told through the personalities of editors into a history of media in twentieth century academic philosophy. This whole history can be structured into three phases: (1) Wittgenstein's own media practices and publication processes (notes, revisions, arrangements, copies, dictations, lectures), (2) the consensually reviewed division of labour of the three literary heirs who worked with analogical means for a canonization of posthumously edited volumes, and (3) the critical deconstruction of the canonical editions through the transition to digital media technology. This deconstruction, which happens through comprehensive digitization in the World Wide Web (WWW) together with software for user-driven forms of representation, eventually dissolves the boundary between the producer and the reader. This history of media practices and publication processes has evolved over 100 years and comes with a steady growth in infrastructures and publics (Erbacher 2019b).

6.1.1   The Topic of This Essay

This essay is concerned with the transition from the first to the second phase in the history of editing Wittgenstein's writings. This is the transition towards digitization and therewith the shift in scholarly generations and scholarly paradigms. The conditions for this transition to digital media were prepared by the older generation of editors and through a change within analogue media, namely by turning from the manuscript form to microfilm in 1969. Norman Malcolm and von Wright enabled the production of the so-called Cornell microfilm that contained almost the entire philosophical Nachlass of Wittgenstein (von Wright 1969, 483–503; see chapter 5). Wittgenstein's unpublished writings thus became accessible at university libraries and research institutions. Together with von Wright's catalogue of the Wittgenstein papers and his writings on the hitherto published editions, the microfilm created a new public for, and a scholarly awareness of Wittgenstein's manuscripts and typescripts. With the possibility to study them independently of the three literary heirs, the discourse on the posthumously published editions changed: while the three literary heirs had always aimed at constituting readable volumes without learned commentary, scholars began to ask for a text-critical discussion of these volumes. Naturally, younger scholars with philological knowledge regarded many editorial decisions of the literary heirs as unfounded.

The conflict between the literary heirs' original approach and a text-critical ambition found a paradigm in the controversy around Rhees and Wittgenstein's volume *Philosophische Grammatik* (see Chap. 5). This volume appeared in 1969, the same year the Cornell microfilm was produced, and it is the pinnacle of Rhees's philosophically co-creative editing (Erbacher 2017a, 257–298). But it was precisely this construction of a new text not found among Wittgenstein's papers that became the target of Anthony Kenny's textual criticism; he argued that Rhees's decision to leave out passages and whole chapters from a source typescript was an arbitrary intervention (Kenny 1977, 41–53). In saying this, Kenny used an investigative topos that announced a new generation of scholars: censorship and manipulation based on old privileges would be displaced by the disclosure of such processes by resolute researchers who strove for more transparency. The shift in attitude was all the more welcome because the literary heirs had covered up certain passages in the Cornell microfilm, mostly those parts written in Wittgenstein's private code and which the literary heirs regarded as being of a purely private nature (Erbacher et al. 2017, 79–113).

The Cornell microfilm thus set in motion a new process of investigation. It made it possible to answer new research questions and thus produced a new generation of scholars who argued on the basis of principles that the new digital medium allowed them to apply. While it was clear to the literary heirs that Wittgenstein had trusted their judgements as philosophers and friends and that he had empowered them to make decisions concerning the selection and arrangement of his remarks, the new generation of scholars appealed to standards of comprehensiveness and neutrality. While discretionary judgement was a central tool for the literary heirs, the new scholars suspected it to be a source of bias. The role of such judgment in the editorial process was supposed to be superseded by ideals of exactness and completeness that had survived from the positivistic historicism of the nineteenth century. These ideals gained fresh power when they now joined forces with computer technology in the humanities. Naturally, in the eyes of Wittgenstein's literary heirs, this resulted in some curious products. For instance, in 1972 Hans Kaal and Alastair McKinnon published a computer-based concordance for the *Philosophical Investigations*; it was admired in philosophical journals, but the three literary heirs could not see the point of it (Kaal and McKinnon 1975):

> Blackwells have yet produced a horrible volume a 'concordance' to Philosophische Untersuchungen. This has been produced by computer and the man who did it has not treated the computer as producing the raw materials for intelligence to work on—he has simply made a book out of the computers production. 16 pages of occurrences of 'sagen', as in 'Man könnte sagen'. The most striking imbecility is that separable verbs when occurring in their divided form appear under the heading of the bare verb. Thus under the heading 'hören' you get 'er hört auf...'. 'Mitteilen' makes two appearances under 'Mitteilen' and under 'Teilen'. 'Ubereinstimmen' under 'stimmen', 'aus-' and 'an-' 'sehen' under 'sehen'; 'wahr nehmen' under 'wahr' and so on. I have told Blackwells they ought to withdraw it at once. I hope you will agree. (Anscombe to von Wright, 1972_1)

The scepticism towards progress and technology that is built into Wittgenstein's thought seems to manifest itself here. Even von Wright, who supported a scientific approach to Wittgenstein's Nachlass, could not defend this product of automatized retrieval and text processing (von Wright to Anscombe, 7 January 1972). But of course, computational text processing had already been applied successfully elsewhere, and it had been established institutionally at some universities. With the *Index Thomisticus* that the Jesuit Roberto Busa produced in cooperation with IBM (1949), and with Wilhelm Ott's programming work at the University of Tübingen that would become the editing software TU-STEP, two milestones had already been reached on the path now called 'digital humanities' (Jones 2016). By launching a regular colloquium on the use of data processing in the humanities, the University of Tübingen became an early centre for this new field.[5] It

---

[5] For information regarding "Kolloquium über die Anwendungen der *EDV* in den Geisteswissenschaften", see: http://www.tustep.uni-Tübingen.de/kolloq.html. Accessed: 09 July 2022. For an early successful example of using TU-STEP for editorial purposes, see Joyce 1984.

therefore does not seem coincidental that Tübingen was the place for the first big project concerned with digitalizing Wittgenstein's Nachlass: the research project *Preservation, Documentation, and Retrieval of Ludwig Wittgenstein's Left-Behind Writings*. Funded by the Thyssen Foundation, this project ran for four years (1978–1982). In the scholarly community, however, it is known less for its achievements than for its failure. This is precisely what makes the project an interesting object for my study: if relevant (infra)structures become visible in situations of disruption, then the analysis of this failed project promises insight into the structures of research, administration and funding institutions, all of which interact as scholarly, technological, personal and bureaucratic factors when new technologies create new objects of investigation (Star 1999, 377–391).

6.1.2   The History of the Wittgenstein Archive as a Tragedy of Scholarly Cooperation

Little is as yet known concerning the dynamics of the breakdown of the Wittgenstein Archive at the University of Tübingen. Nevertheless, the intensity of the still-lively emotions of everyone involved indicates that these dynamics cannot be understood without paying attention to the human dynamics at the archive. This idea is also present in the few published texts dealing with the history of the archive. While scholarly papers discretely mention internal discord, newspaper articles speak of a fruitless investment of one million German marks for an 'editorial operetta', or of a 'gigantomanic paperchase' that was perpetuated by the archive co-leader Michael Nedo's skilful writing of funding applications. The other co-leader of the archive, Professor Hans Jürgen Heringer, has been quoted as saying that the story of the archive is a first-rate ""scholarly crime novel" (cf. Pichler 2008; Kenny 2006, 382–396; Hintikka 1991, 183–201; Osterle 1993; N. N. 1993). That these descriptions are not feuilleton dramatizations can be seen from the project's official Final Report. At its very outset, it stresses that there were continuous troubles with Nedo, who is said to have neither the administrative competencies nor the human qualities to lead such a project (Final Report, 2). According to the Final Report, it was Nedo's attempt to transfer the project to Cambridge that led to a deterioration of trust, resulting in the archive members' conviction that Nedo was unacceptable as a project leader. This is the most frequently-quoted part of the Final Report, and still today it sets the tone for any account of the archive's history.

If one actually attempted to write the archive's history as a scholarly crime novel, it seems clear who would play the role of the scoundrel. But we must be careful! Although all previous constructive contextualizing of episodes from the history of editing Wittgenstein's Nachlass indeed had to centre around the human stories of the editors, and although the story of the Wittgenstein Archive at Tübingen cannot be told without the human stories of its members, it would be grossly inadequate to reduce the story of the archive to a personal dimension. Such a reduction would probably turn into an editorial 'soap opera' and add little to our understanding of scholarly practices in the humanities. By contrast, investigating the breakdown of the archive at Tübingen promises more valuable insights if it shows how the actors act in a complex network of literary, philosophical, technological and institutional conditions. Approached in this manner, the history of the Tübingen Wittgenstein Archive becomes a classic drama in the world of scholarship—one with social, technological and institutional underworlds. It is a drama in which individually reasonable actors veer with increasing velocity from a path of success and suffer a foreseeable catastrophe. This is the drama that shall be sketched here on the basis of newly-gathered archival materials and oral history interviews.

6.2   First Act (1965–1975)

6.2.1   The Birth of the Idea in a Reading Circle

Michele Ranchetti was an ecclesiastical historian with many intellectual passions, one of which was German literature.[6] In the mid-1960s he was particularly fascinated by the 'new' Wittgenstein who seemed to speak about the things about which, according to the *Tractatus,* one had to be silent (Wittgenstein 1965; 1966). The new writings edited from Wittgenstein's Nachlass fascinated Ranchetti so much that he translated them into Italian even before they were published in the original German (Wittgenstein 1967a). In his work as a translator, he was aided by his doctoral student Marino Rosso, who had begun translating the *Philosophical Remarks* that had been edited by Rhees (Wittgenstein 1964). Ranchetti and Rosso found the philological idiosyncrasies and problems of the posthumous editions a most stimulating topic for discussion, and their eagerness grew further when von Wright made known the full extent of the writings that Wittgenstein had left to posterity (von Wright 1969, 83–503). They began to fantasize about producing an index for the whole corpus or to edit a small but nice scholarly edition of one of Wittgenstein's short writings.

These were Ranchetti's thoughts in the early 1970s when he had a research sojourn at the University of Tübingen. The official aim of his time there was to work on his *opus magnum,* a history of catechisms (this history would remain fragmentary). He continued his discussions on Wittgenstein's Nachlass in a reading circle at Tübingen that was also attended by Michael Nedo (Nedo, Oral History Interview).Having originally trained as a toolmaker, Nedo graduated from high school and then studied mathematics, physics and zoology. At the time of

---

[6]The following information about Ranchetti is from an Oral History Interview led by Alois Pichler. Some of Ranchettis translations of German literature are: Freud 1976a, 1976b; Wittgenstein 1980; Celan 1998; Rilke 2005, 2006. For a detailed bibliography see: Pacioni and Romanelli (n. d.), Archivio Michele Ranchetti, https://www.vieusseux.it/inventari/ranchetti.pdf. Accessed 27 September 2018.

Ranchetti's stay at Tübingen, Nedo worked at the Max Planck Institute for Bio-acoustics. Here he had become an expert on research technology for studying the common grasshopper (cf. Willkomm 2022). This technological expertise may have inspired Ranchetti to ask Nedo about the technological requirements for an edition of Wittgenstein's writings on the basis of the Cornell microfilm. Exploring this question, Nedo came to believe that a complete scholarly edition of all of Wittgenstein's writings was badly needed. This was also something von Wright had mentioned in his publication on Wittgenstein's Nachlass (von Wright 1969, 483–503).

In this context, it may be important to note that the boldness needed for big editorial ventures was in the academic air of Germany at that time. The book-seller Dietrich Sattler had just stirred up the established editorial philologists in German university departments: the self-taught editor had shown that the prestigious *Stuttgarter Hölderlin Edition* deviated from Hölderlin's own punctuation and thereby changed the reading of his poems. Sattler's radical textual criticism inspired a new generation of editors (Kermani 2008; Groddeck et al. 2003, 1–55). At the same time, Paul Sappler's edition of Heinrich Kaufringer's works showed that an edition could be prepared and typeset with the computer software TU-STEP that was programmed at Tübingen (Kaufringer 1972 & 1974). In Ranchetti's reading circle, these developments fired the imagination and led to the vision of a completely new basis for the study of Wittgenstein's writings: a computer-based edition of all of Wittgenstein's surviving writings. This was the intellectual dream to which Nedo would devote himself.

6.2.2   Visiting Rhees

Anyone who wanted to work with Wittgenstein's papers at that time needed the approval of the literary executors. Although the actual documents had been given to the Wren Library at Trinity College Cambridge, the three literary heirs still controlled the access to the papers and all questions of publication. Indeed, after the papers had been transferred to the Wren Library, Rhees turned his full attention to the task that Wittgenstein had entrusted to him. He retired from his post at the University of Swansea to conclude his editorial work for *Philosophical Grammar* (see Chap. 4). Afterwards, he moved to London where he and two friends, the Wittgenstein pupil Norman Malcolm and his former colleague at Swansea Peter Winch, collaborated on teaching Wittgenstein's philosophy (cf. Lyas 1999, 4). During this period of his life, he intensified his unmatched intimacy with Wittgenstein's oeuvre. Cora Diamond, who edited notes from Wittgenstein's lectures on the foundations of mathematics under Rhees's supervision, experienced that Rhees lived amongst manuscripts and hand-copied writings, and that he was always minutely prepared for their meetings concerning the editing of notes from Wittgenstein's lectures (Wittgenstein 1976a, for the first German edition, see

Wittgenstein 1978).[7] Such preparedness may also be assumed for the audience that Rhees granted Ranchetti and Rosso in the summer of 1973. Here is Rhees's report of that conversation:

> I was visited by two Italians a few days ago: Professor Ranchetti, of the University of Florence (he translated Wittgenstein's Lecture on Ethics and the notes to his Lectures on Aesthetics into Italian); and Signor Mario Rosso, who has translated the <u>Philosophische Bemerkungen</u> and whom I had 'known' through correspondence about this.
> [...]
> They want to make a "concordance" of <u>all</u> the Wittgenstein papers. They have a copy of the Cornell microfilm. They find this unclear in various parts. And they suspect (this being evidently the mark of a scholar) they suspect that the Cornell microfilm is not complete; and they wanted permission to inspect the manuscripts in Trinity Library.
> [...]
> At first I asked if they meant a general index or <u>Register</u> (we talked in German because Rosso cannot speak English) and I said that this might be worth doing if one had the stamina for it; and if one could find ways to solve the obvious difficulties. I added that it would be a collosal [sic] job. They agreed. They suggested it might take five years. I said "at a minimum". They said also that it would cost money, and Professor Ranchetti was going to Germany to interview the trustees (or whatever they be called) of some German body which gives grants for things of this sort. He seemed fairly confident of getting a grant if there were no barrier from the executors of the Nachlaß Wittgensteins. (Rhees to Anscombe and von Wright, 19 July 1973)

Rhees was impressed by the two Italians during the two hours they discussed Wittgenstein's Nachlass. He was inclined to support their project idea, particularly since they seemed to know that the production of a complete index would take years and since they had thought about how to solve the practical issues. But when they mentioned the use of a computer, Rhees became reluctant and pointed to the recently published concordance by McKinnon und Kaal:

> My spirits sank when they said that one of the expenses would be in the use of a computer. They tried to reassure me. They had seen the still-born concordance by McKinnon out of Blackwell, and they said that what they were proposing would be <u>nothing</u> like that. (Rhees to Anscombe and von Wright, 19 July 1973)

Despite Rosso's attempts to explain the 'cybernetic principles' at the core of their wish to employ a computer for editing purposes, Rhees could not see the use of such technology. However, he wanted to postpone final judgment until he had seen results. Von Wright, who also lacked any idea of how computer technology could be used for editorial work, saw the need for an index covering all the writings of Wittgenstein, so his opinion was that the literary heirs ought to support Ranchetti and Rosso's proposal:

---

[7] Concerning her cooperation with Rhees, Cora Diamond recalls that "I had to learn to hear Wittgenstein's voice".

> If they are keen on making a General Index to all of Wittgenstein's writings—published as well as unpublished ones—and if they can raise the money for the purpose, I think we should let them go ahead, provided that we retain a pretty rigourous [*sic*] control of what they intend to do and what in fact they accomplish. (von Wright to Rhees, 1 August 1973)

This assessment may be taken as a summation of the literary executors' standpoint at the time: they were not against the project of an index, but they would remain cautious until they saw some results. Still, they had a far more decisive attitude towards Ranchetti and Rosso's second proposal, namely to produce a complete edition. Rhees could not see the point of publishing all of Wittgenstein's writings because he already hated some researchers' sensation-seeking sniffing in the Cornell microfilm. He feared that publishing all the writings would result in even more fuss while not helping truly interested readers who wanted access to Wittgenstein's complex discussions. It was precisely this distrust that was the reason why Rhees worked for years on his *Philosophical Grammar* instead of printing the "Big Typescript" as Wittgenstein had left it (see Chap. 4). Now, when Ranchetti and Rosso mentioned their vision of a complete edition, Rhees took his copy of the "Big Typescript" from the shelf and explained the complexly layered structure of Wittgenstein's revisions. Rhees thought it was impossible to transfer this phenomenon into a printed edition, unless one produced a complete set of facsimiles. At this point, Rosso again appealed to the computer: the new data-systems would be able to handle complex text phenomena (e.g., underlinings, deletions, slashes, links and other revision markings). Furthermore, argued Rosso, the best way to prevent scholarly misuse was to make Wittgenstein's writings available so that they could be studied in detail. Maybe Rhees could agree to this in principle, but he did not want to concede anything before seeing some solid evidence that such a project would be feasible and successful. Rhees, it seems, was open to questioning his own editorial principles:

> Ranchetti asked, "At any rate you are not definitely against the project?". I said, "No, not definitely against it; but I cannot say either than I am definitely in favour of it. I see strong arguments in favour of it: your argument that the best protection for scholarship would be to have the complete edition available as a check. I am influenced partly by my feeling that Wittgenstein would have hated the idea. But the situation which has developed may speak in favour of it none the less. (Rhees to Anscombe and von Wright, 19 July 1973)

At this point, it was von Wright who protested. It is true that he supported a more scholarly approach to Wittgenstein's papers and he was less concerned that scholars would misunderstand or misuse them. But precisely because he thought a complete edition was a most important and needed thing, he did not want to put the task into unexperienced hands:

> The plan of a Complete Edition we have discussed among ourselves before; some day, I am confident, such an edition [will] be produced—but I see no urgency here and the task is in any case enormously complicated and I should feel very hesitant to let the two Italians go ahead with it alone. (von Wright to Anscombe, 2 August 1973)

With this statement, Rhees and von Wright seemed to have found a clear take on Ranchetti and Rosso's proposal. They would support the Italians' work on an index, but not an attempt to produce a complete edition. But while this compromise sounded perfectly innocent, it carried the seeds which grew into the tragedy of the Tübingen Wittgenstein Archive. For it seems that the literary executors' principal rejection of Ranchetti and Rosso's proposal for a complete edition was not clear enough to the two Italian scholars. When they returned to Tübingen, they had reason to believe that the literary executors would support an application for research funding, but unjustified was their assumption that this would mean the literary executors would soon be willing to agree to bolder editorial ambitions as well.

6.2.3   The First Application for a Big Research Grant

The "German-Italian team"—this is what the literary heirs called Ranchetti, Rosso and Nedo from now on—had won general support for the idea of writing a proposal for a research grant. With this achievement, however, the three men were confronted with a very practical matter; according to the regulations of the German Research Foundation, none of them was eligible to submit a proposal for a research grant. Ranchetti and Rosso were merely guest researches at the University of Tübingen, and Nedo lacked the necessary academic degree. What was needed in Germany to submit a proposal for a research grant was a German professor. Now a new character enters the story, a young and successful linguist who had become a professor at Tübingen in 1971: Hans Jürgen Heringer. He seemed suited for the project because he was trained as a philologist and had given lectures on Wittgenstein in cooperation with the philosopher Ernst Tugendhat at the University of Heidelberg. Nedo therefore approached Heringer one day with the idea of submitting a proposal for a grant to do a research project on Wittgenstein's Nachlass. Heringer agreed and became the new organizational kingpin of the endeavour.

With Heringer as the formal head of the research proposal, the project was coined a research project in computational linguistics. Ranchetti's reading circle became the Wittgenstein research group at Tübingen, now working out a six-year funding scheme under the title "Development of a Theory and Methods for Analysis and an Edition of German Texts with the Use of Data Processing".[8] Using the corpus of Wittgenstein's Nachlass, the idea was to develop software to process the similarity of remarks such that, for instance, genealogical trees of remarks across the whole Nachlass could be generated automatically. Although the central research question of the new proposal concerned how to compute

---

[8] DFG-proposal, translation by Christian Erbacher, the German original reads: *Entwicklung einer Theorie und von Methoden zur Analyse und Edition von deutschen Texten mittels elektronischer Datenverarbeitung*, Private Archive Heringer.

the similarities in Wittgenstein's writings, the majority of the work load would be devoted to transcribing the writings with a view towards producing a historical–critical edition. In accordance with Rosso and Nedo's ambition to use data processing to solve editorial problems, the project goal was to create a machine-readable transcription of Wittgenstein's Nachlass that would be more efficient than traditional methods for both searching within the writings and for preparing a critical edition. According to the proposal, such an edition would hopefully initiate a completely new Wittgenstein scholarship. The one who worked out the technical details of this idea was Nedo, who had by this time left the Max Planck Institute (cf. Willkomm 2022). The proposal was submitted to the German Research Foundation as early as in January 1974. Rhees, however, after receiving a copy of the proposal, was not inclined to share the group's enthusiasm:

> I did not get a good impression from the thing which Heringer sent me. The preparation of a <u>concordance</u> perhaps they could do: although there are enormous problems of headings and cross references which they have never discussed in letters to me or conversations with me. Because it will be such a massive thing when it is finished, I do not know whether anyone will ever use it. But I do not have strong feelings here.—The question of the "kritische Ausgabe" is different. And from what they say in their <u>Anhang</u> here I do not think they have much idea <u>at all</u>. They modestly propose to present to the world for the first time (<u>sic</u>) einen <u>unverstellten</u> Wittgenstein. But the one page of the one typescript— mit welchem sie während dieser sechs Monaten hausieren gegangen sind—does <u>not</u> give einen 'unverstellten' Wittgenstein. (Rhees to von Wright, 24 March 1974)

Rhees's misgivings nevertheless receded into the background as the project proposal was subjected to a long-winding review process for several months. In August 1974, the German Research Foundation signalled that the proposal was judged to be eligible in principle. As if to signal that it had already been approved, Nedo immediately forwarded the good news to Rhees (Rhees to von Wright, 19 September 1974). During his subsequent visit to Rhees, Nedo led Rhees to understand that the project would be funded with six million German marks. But to actually receive this funding, the group would need the definite commitment of the literary heirs (Rhees to von Wright, 19 September 1974). Although the envisaged sum had actually shrunk by 60 per cent during Nedo's next visit (there was now the mention of 350,000 GBP), Rhees considered the German Research Foundation's offer "great and amazing" (Rhees to von Wright, 19 September 1974). The literary heirs therefore met with the research group to draft a written agreement. For this purpose, the German Research Foundation financed a trip to Cambridge for Heringer, Ranchetti and Nedo in October 1974 (Notification of approval by the DFG for a trip to Cambridge, October 1974). Rhees, Anscombe and von Wright all got a good impression of the Tübingen research group during this meeting. They agreed that all its members could, without restrictions, use and copy Wittgenstein's papers in the Wren Library. That is, they would also gain access to the hitherto unpublished passages written in Wittgenstein's code (for the story of the coded passages, see Chap. 1 and 5). The agreement reads as follows:

1. The literary executors grant the members of the research group access to all manuscripts and permit them to use the manuscripts scholarly without any restriction during the research project. Likewise, the literary executors have nothing against that the members of the research group get access to Wittgenstein's dictations and the notes of and for his lectures and conversations.
2. The literary executors are principally in agreement with a publication of the materials.
3. Any publication of the materials happens with the consent of the literary executors and in prior agreement with them.
4. The literary executors support the scholarly work on the manuscripts as much as it is possible for them. (Agreement between the literary heirs of Wittgenstein's writings and the research group Wittgenstein, 19 October 1974)[9]

Although the literary executors kept full control over any publication, this agreement was a solid enough foundation for work on Wittgenstein's Nachlass at Tübingen. Just as with the outcome of Rhees's first encounter with Rancetti and Rosso, it was mainly the trustworthiness of the persons and not the prospects of the project that determined why the literary executors signed the agreement, as von Wright explicitly noted: "I think we can trust them; whether they will be able to produce anything very helpful or valuable remains to be seen" (von Wright to Rhees, 23 October 1974). Rhees too remembered that the agreement was based on trusting that the scholars from Tübingen would handle the papers with integrity and discretion (Rhees to University of Tübingen President Theis, 15 November 1980, RBA). After deciding that they could trust the group, Rhees was even willing to pay for a work room for Nedo at Trinity College.

But despite all these prospects in the autumn 1974, the literary executors did not hear anything from Tübingen during the subsequent six months. By spring 1975, they still wondered about the silence because they knew nothing about the project proposal getting stuck in the review process. The members of the evaluation committee had changed and the proposal now involved long-term funding. The evaluation committee was concerned about the large amount of funding being applied for and the composition of the group; in particular, the referees wondered

---

[9] Translated by Christian Erbacher. The German original reads as follows:

1. Die Nachlassverwalter ermöglichen den Mitgliedern der Forschungsgruppe den Zugang zu allen Manuskripten und gestatten ihnen die uneingeschränkte wissenschaftliche Bearbeitung der Manuskripte im Rahmen des Forschungsprojektes. Ebenso haben die Nachlassverwalter keine Einwände dagegen, dass die Mitglieder der Forschungsgruppe Zugang zu den Diktaten Wittgensteins und den Mitschriften und Notizen seiner Vorlesungen und Gespräche erhalten.

2. Die Nachlassverwalter sind grundsätzlich mit einer Publikation der Materialien einverstanden.

3. Jede Publikation der Materialien geschieht mit Zustimmung der Nachlassverwalter und in vorheriger Absprache mit ihnen.

4. Die Nachlassverwalter unterstützen im Rahmen ihrer Möglichkeiten die wissenschaftliche Arbeit an den Manuskripten.

whether scholars who were not trained in the relevant disciplines would be able to successfully carry out this most challenging project (Heringer, Oral History Interview, 23 March 2018). Indeed, one reviewer with a background in philosophy was very critical regarding the chances of success. This was the start of many questions and clarifications sent to and from the German Research Foundation in Bonn and Professor Heringer in Tübingen. Another six months passed before the German Research Foundation finally rejected the proposal in the winter of 1975 (Michael Nedo, A Sketch of the History and the Current Situation of the Research Project by the Wittgenstein Archive, no date).

6.3   Second Act (1976–1978)

6.3.1   Wittgensteinians at Oxbridge

The failure to receive funding for the research proposal could easily have meant the end of the Wittgenstein research group at the University of Tübingen. But this was not the case. Nedo had already devoted himself fully to the project. Spurred on by the enthusiasm of creating the research proposal and by the success of the first meetings with the literary executors, he subsequently obtained a personal stipend from the Thyssen Foundation. This stipend allowed him to travel to Cambridge in March 1976 and to work with Wittgenstein's Nachlass at Trinity College. However, not all of the literary executors were informed that Nedo was doing this. Von Wright was told about Nedo's work at Cambridge only after inquiring about the Tübingen group in late April 1976 (Rhees to von Wright, 29 April 1976). This was why he asked Anscombe—who had become a professor of philosophy at Cambridge after having transferred her part of the Wittgenstein papers to the Wren Library—to find out who was actually working on Wittgenstein's Nachlass and for what purpose:

> One thing worries me a little. I understand from letters from Rhees and from the Senior Bursar at Trinity that the German-Italian team has been working at Cambridge on the Wittgenstein-papers. As you remember, we gave them our "blessings" when we saw them at Cambridge two years ago. Since then I have heard nothing directly from them. But I heard that their project in its original form was turned down by the Deutsche Forschungsgemeinschaft and I understand from Rhees that they are now working according to some different, reduced plan. So what are they doing? Ought we not to keep an eye on them? I am not anxious to have contact with them but perhaps you, being on the spot, could try to find out something about their work. (von Wright to Anscombe, 31 May 1976)

Anscombe summoned Nedo to her rooms. There, he had to undergo a critical examination of his doings at the Wren Library (Nedo, Oral History Interview). His answers, however, satisfied Anscombe, and von Wright too considered it worth supporting what Nedo described as his current work; he wanted to improve von Wright's catalogue of the Nachlass by giving it more detail, and he planned to produce a technically enhanced microfilm copy of the whole Nachlass (Final Report, 31). Since von Wright regarded neither his own catalogue nor the Cornell microfilm as free from flaws, he welcomed Nedo's initiative. Thus, the literary executors trusted Nedo once more, and Nedo's subsequent work would indeed become an important building block for a second proposal for a large research project at the University of Tübingen.

While Nedo was working as a Thyssen stipendiary at Cambridge, he continued to think about the use of data processing for editing Wittgenstein's writings (Nedo, Oral History Interview). He consulted experts at Cambridge and rented (by the hour) unintelligent terminals (i.e., terminals lacking processing capabilities and thus relying on the central computer) and the central computer in order to experiment with digitally transcribing Wittgenstein's manuscripts. No one but Nedo believed in the success of a machine-readable transcription of Wittgenstein's writings at that time. But the fact that he was working on the Wittgenstein papers with the blessing of the literary heirs attracted the attention of other scholars who were interested in a critical re-examination of the hitherto published volumes from Wittgenstein's Nachlass. This was not least because a new Wittgenstein scholarship had emerged at Oxford that incorporated philological, historical and biographical aspects. To mention this new thread of scholarship is important in the present context because Nedo's contact with the 'young Wittgensteinians' contributed to the success of the second grant proposal for a Wittgenstein project at Tübingen.

One might assume that the new Wittgenstein research at Oxford was inspired by Anscombe because she had lived and taught there for many years. It is true that she trained many students at Oxford and conveyed to them much of what she had learned from Wittgenstein (Warnock 1996). But her influence on the philological, historical and biographical Wittgenstein scholarship was rather indirect. In fact, she partly rejected it. Independent of her presence, there had always been an interest in Wittgenstein among Oxford scholars who kept themselves informed about his new philosophy through a "busy Cambridge-Oxford grapevine" (Ryle 1999, 112).[10] Students had copied a dictation that Wittgenstein had prepared for a lecture (published in Wittgenstein 1958), and copies of that copy then circulated in both Oxford and Cambridge. In addition, Friedrich Waismann, who once had cooperated with Wittgenstein in Vienna, moved from Cambridge to Oxford in 1939 in order to lecture there. Paul Grice and Stephen Toulmin, who had participated in Wittgenstein's last lecture in Cambridge in 1947, were also hired to lecture at

---

[10] Email from B. F. McGuinness to Christian Erbacher, 11 April 2018: "Wittgenstein's work was known at Oxford in three stages—study of the Tractatus, led by Ryle—scattered copies of the Blue and Brown Books and lectures by Cambridge immigrants such as Stephen Toulmin and George Paul, leaks by Anscombe pupils such as Frank Cioffi and Dennis Paul—publication and presentation in lectures by Miss Anscombe in lectures from Walton St, the first time most of us had been so far inside Somerville. These were a dramatic performance with Tony Quinton allotted the part of the "spalla" or stooge. Then came Strawson's review in Mind…".

Oxford. All these lecturers made Wittgenstein's new philosophy known, though in a different vein than Anscombe's.

Another of Wittgenstein's conversation partners, Gilbert Ryle, contributed to the rise of a new text-critical Wittgenstein scholarship at Oxford by lecturing on the *Tractatus* shortly after Wittgenstein's death. In these lectures, he and David Pears criticized Frank Ramsey's English translation from the 1920s (Harré 1999, 39–53). This eventually led to a new translation that Pears and another young scholar, Brian McGuinness, produced with the ambition of it being closer to the German original (Wittgenstein 1961). Anscombe was not particularly fond of this translation (Anscombe to McGuinness, undated, presumably 1959).

Despite Anscombe's reservations about McGuinness and other Oxford Wittgensteinians, McGuinness soon cooperated with the other two literary heirs. The reason was that Waismann's own literary executors entrusted McGuinness with the task of sorting out Waismann's papers.[11] Among these papers, McGuinness found notes from conversations between Wittgenstein, Moritz Schlick and Waismann (and other members of the Vienna Circle) dating back to 1929–1931 (Wittgenstein 1967b). When McGuinness was preparing these for publication, he contacted Rhees who was then editing *Philosophische Bemerkungen*, a work containing Wittgenstein's writings from the same period around 1930. Eventually, Rhees added to his edition a couple of essays found in Waismann's Nachlass that illuminate the connection yet also differences between Wittgenstein's thought and that of the Vienna Circle. Starting from this cooperation with Rhees, McGuinness increasingly devoted his studies to historical aspects of Wittgenstein's life and work. It led him to collaborate with von Wright in the latter's editing of Wittgenstein's letters (Wittgenstein 2008) and the *Prototractatus* (Wittgenstein 1971), and it enabled him finally to write a biography of Wittgenstein (McGuinness 1988). In his editorial work, McGuinness was significantly supported by Joachim Schulte, one of his own students and collaborative partners. Schulte studied at Oxford in 1972 and attended Anthony Kenny's lecture on the so-called middle Wittgenstein. Kenny, in turn, had just written an introduction to Wittgenstein's work and was now translating Rhees and Wittgenstein's *Philosophische Grammatik*—exactly the volume he would criticize the editing of in 1977, initiating the text-critical turn in the history of editing Wittgenstein (see Chap. 4).

This is of course a rough and incomplete sketch of some proponents of the new developments in the Oxford-based Wittgenstein scholarship, and each of them significantly influenced the reception of Wittgenstein's thought in the academic world.[12] But the point to mention here is that the scholars at Oxford were naturally

---

[11] Waismann, in his will, appointed Stuart Hampshire (1914–2001), Isaiah Berlin (1909–1997), and Gilbert Ryle (1900–1976) as literary executors; see Erbacher et al. 2017, 105–147; Schulte 1979, 108–140.

[12] Not mentioned here but certainly most influential are, for example, Gordon Baker and Peter Hacker, who consulted Wittgenstein's manuscripts for their analytical commentary (Hacker and Baker 1980–1996).

curious about who this hitherto-unknown Nedo was—this man who was work-
ing with the blessings of Wittgenstein's literary heirs on the papers deposited at
Cambridge. And for Nedo, it was naturally of interest to establish contact with the
English scholarly elite. Thus, Nedo—and Ranchetti and Rosso too—approached
McGuinness, at first mainly to discuss biographical material (McGuinness, Oral
History Interview; Schulte, Oral History Interview; Nedo, A Sketch of the History
and the Current Situation of the Research Project by the Wittgenstein Archive).[13]
But these early ties between Tübingen and Oxford would become stronger with
the prospect of new research funding.

6.3.2 The First Wittgenstein Symposium at the University of Tübingen

Nedo's acquaintance with Wittgenstein scholars at Oxford probably contributed
to the acknowledgement of his work back in Germany. In any case, his progress
in charting the Nachlass seemed promising enough for the Thyssen Foundation
to intensify its funding for Wittgenstein scholarship at Tübingen. The Thyssen
Foundation already funded Rosso and Schulte in their work on Wittgenstein at
Tübingen, and the foundation's manager, Gerd Brand, now wanted to nurture these
early roots of scholarly excellence with a big project. For this purpose, a symposium was organized to deal with editorial problems and the question of a complete
edition of Wittgenstein's writings. Heringer—the official principal investigator
of the first DFG proposal—was able to make this event part of the University of
Tübingen's fifth centenary celebration in April 1977. The symposium therefore
became a prominent event that appealed not only to academic philosophers but to
a variety of scholars from other disciplines.[14] In particular, linguists and computer
experts from Germany, England, Italy, France, Finland and Canada attended and
met with the literary heirs and other philosophers. Representatives of the publishers Blackwell and Suhrkamp also attended in order to find out what leading scholars thought about the future of scholarly editing.

Being the first big public event to deal with editorial questions and problems
connected to Wittgenstein's writings, the symposium at Tübingen heralded a
whole new approach to Wittgenstein's papers. Kenny even thought it was the first
step towards a new level of quality in Wittgenstein scholarship:

> The symposium marked the beginning of a new phase in Wittgenstein studies, by defining
> the extent of the problem and by the realization that the appropriate first step to a com-
> plete edition must be the establishment of a computerized database (the word was still so
> unfamiliar to the general public as to appear in inverted commas in the early reports of the
> symposium). (Kenny 2006, 382–396)

---

[13] This material was used by Ferry Radax for his documentary film (Radax 1974–1975).

[14] Lectures from the symposium are published in Wittgenstein 1979.

Kenny was one protagonist of this new Wittgenstein scholarship that was characterized by a sensitivity to text-critical problems and a willingness to solve them by using computer technology. At the Wittgenstein Symposium, he strengthened his criticism of Rhees and Wittgenstein's *Philosophische Grammatik* by putting forward an interpretation of the chapter "Philosophy" that had been excluded from Rhees's edition (Kenny 1979, 9–34). Though Kenny, in smaller circles, defended the elegance of Rhees's work and the joy of having no learned commentary, his criticism led to more and more people seeing Rhees's procedure as an editorial absurdity.[15] Rhees, who also gave a lecture at the Symposium, must have felt that his intentions were completely misunderstood. He was convinced that the "Big Typescript's" passages on philosophy were not a part but a pre-version of the philosophical work that the *Philosophische Grammatik* was meant to present (see Chap. 4). Furthermore, he was convinced that it was impossible to understand Wittgenstein's passages on philosophy when read in isolation. In his opinion, the chapter "Philosophy" had to be read as part of a discussion that Wittgenstein continued throughout all his life of philosophizing (Rhees to von Wright, 22 January 1976; Erbacher 2017a, 286). Rhees was of course aware of the difficulties of editing a volume that would be adequate to his understanding of Wittgenstein's discussions, and he was aware of the shortcomings of his own editorial work—but he was equally certain that Wittgenstein would have loathed to print his writings in the state they were in when he died. In Rhees's understanding, Wittgenstein had entrusted him with the tasks of making selections and decisions in preparing the writings for publication (Rhees to Kenny, 2 March 1977). Rhees was clear about the fact that his decisions were built on interpretations, but according to him, this was also the case with any other editorial work and any other form of presentation, including a computerized edition. Rhees considered it naïve to think that a complete printing of Wittgenstein's writings in their original state would be a form of presentation free from interpretation. For him, this was a pseudo-argument, the purpose of which was to serve research interests at Tübingen and Oxford:

> I think most of the self- righteous horror of 'interpretation'—both in Tübingen and in Oxford—is confused, and often eine Sophisterei. (Rhees to von Wright, 20 April 1977)

Rhees had no hope of scholars following him as he tracked the complicated genetics of Wittgenstein's remarks in his Nachlass. He regarded the appeal to computer technology as an attempt to avoid the hard work of trying to understand what Wittgenstein wanted to say. Rhees had the impression that the kind of scholarship asked for at the Tübingen symposium mainly served its own purpose of self-preservation; it treated philosophical texts not as being written by humans for humans but as data produced by machines for machines:

---

[15] Remark by Joachim Schulte from a response regarding an earlier version of this text.

It is as though they supposed that some purely <u>external</u> arrangement of the manuscripts, attending to dates which may be written on them, or to the type of ink from which some date may be inferred—but ignoring any other sense in which one manuscript might have bearing on another: as though in this way the manuscripts would be ("for the first time") accessible to those who wanted to study them.—<u>nota bene</u>: I do not say that such an arrangement or cataloging would have no value. I am uncomfortable lest people think that this sort of 'indexing' is so interesting that attention to what Wittgenstein was <u>writing</u> falls into second place, is pushed into the background.

I found Nedo still repeating the <u>Schlagwort</u>: "eine Konkordanz, welche ohne irgendeine Art von <u>Deutung</u> zustande gekommen ist"; and he said this would be <u>guarenteed</u> [*sic*] by the fact that the Konkordanz would be the product of the Maschine.

[…]

I would object, very often, if someone said that his account or presentation of what Wittgenstein was saying in, say, the <u>Untersuchungen</u>, or the way in which the different parts of the <u>Untersuchungen</u> are connected, - that his was the <u>only possible</u> way doing it, die <u>einzig mögliche</u> Deutung. (Here I think of the way Wittgenstein sometimes objected to the suggestion that there was only <u>one</u> way of treating a philosophical problem, or only one possible answer to some question that may be raised in discussion.)

But I think that if a Konkordanz is introduced with the remark that this "must be free from any sort of interpretation, because (<u>sic.</u>) it is all done by computer", - this would itself be a special and a <u>sonderbare</u> Darstellung of all that Wittgenstein has written in these manuscripts: a kind of <u>Gleichmacherei</u>, in which Wittgenstein's mature and sinnige Bemerkungen were strung on the same thread, one after another, with some tentative pencilling, without any sort of Auszeichnung. This itself would be an interpretation, eine Deutung. of the charcter [*sic*] of the body of writings. A "possible" one, if you like. But with little to commend it except its availability for some sort of data processing. (Rhees to von Wright, 20 April 1977)

According to Rhees, the misunderstanding of the philosophical orientation of Wittgenstein's writings could not be better displayed than by the suggestion to feed them through a computer. Rhees thus concluded that those who asked for a machine-readable transcription of Wittgenstein's writings simply did not know about the discussions contained in the writings. What is more, he doubted that a computer could do justice to the complexity of textual interconnections in Wittgenstein's Nachlass. Wittgenstein sometimes developed his views on one and the same topic over years and decades, leading to documents that were philosophically connected even though physically disconnected; and the other way round, physically closely connected remarks could be philosophically disconnected (Rhees to von Wright, 20 April 1977). However, despite his grave doubts, Rhees did not break with the group at Tübingen. He turned to von Wright after the symposium:

I wonder whether you and I each ought to write some sort of 'opinion' or 'report' giving our impressions of the Tübingen project - of what sort of plant or animal it now appears to be (if it is a living thing at all, not just a machine). (Rhees to von Wright, 20 April 1977)

Unlike Rhees, von Wright was not hostile towards academic scholarship. He himself was part of the scholarly establishment and did not consider it his task to save Wittgenstein's writings from the eyes of ambitious researchers. Von Wright thought the writings would take care of themselves. According to him, it was the task of the literary executors to preserve and structure the papers. But he interpreted the signals from the research group at Tübingen with mixed feelings: on the one hand, he doubted that the group would be able to produce a complete edition during the next years or even decades; on the other hand, he considered it necessary that the huge challenge of a complete edition ought to be tackled at some point, and at that time he saw no better alternative to the Oxford-Tübingen network. Hence, to turn down their offer without scrutinizing it was, for him, as irresponsible as to accept it without scrutinizing it (von Wright to Rhees, 14 March 1977; von Wright to Anscombe, 31 January 1977). He therefore saw his main duty as being to keep control over what would happen in Tübingen. He had nothing against a text-critical revision of the volumes he had edited, and he understood Kenny's criticism of Rhees's editorial decisions when making *Philosophische Grammatik*.[16] The use of computer technology to edit philosophical texts was to him as unclear as it was to Rhees, but instead of rejecting it, he was open to finding out how linguists and computer experts might help the literary executors in fulfilling their task. In sum, von Wright came away with a generally positive view of the Tübingen symposium and thought computerization might be helpful for editing new volumes:

> I was present from beginning to end and, although it was trying, I do not regret it. I think I now have a much clearer picture of the "project" of the German-Italian team. I think one must, and can, distinguish sharply between
>   a) the "computarization" [*sic*] of the Nachlass and
>   b) publishing "critical editions" of parts or the whole of the Nachlass.
>   The work of the team, financed by the Thyssen-Stiftung, is limited to a). It will take some 4-6 years. When it is completed it will remain a permanent aid to research on the Nachlass, for example to solving problems of the chronological order of writings. Such research is sure to interest scholars. How important it is to an understanding of Wittgenstein's thoughts and their development, is not easy to know in advance. It seems reasonable to think that it will be of some importance, however.
>   As far as I understand, we—i.e. you and Elizabeth Anscombe and I—have granted the team the access to the sources which will be needed for the work under a). But all decisions regarding b) are still in our hands and we have not committed us [*sic*] to anything so far.
>   The work done under a) will, of course, be relevant to such work which may possibly be undertaken in future under b). But which [*sic*] this relevance will be cannot be decided

---

[16]Von Wright already demanded a text-critical revision some years earlier (Von Wright 1969, 483–503). In March 1982 he wrote to Anscombe: "I shall not send a copy to Rhees. I much respect him and should not like to hurt his feelings. But I cannot help being critical of the way he composed the Philosophische Grammatik. And I am also distressed by his edition of the Philosophische Bemerkungen. A close comparison of the printed text with the typescript is now undertaken by Mr Nyman. It turns out that single sentences and also whole paragraphs were omitted - for no good reason as far as I can see. There are also a number of rather violent interferences with Wittgenstein's style - but it might be that they are not due to Rhees but to somebody at Suhrkamps. A thorough revision is certainly in place if there is going to be a new edition." Von Wright to Anscombe, 15 March 1982.

until a) is completed. "In principle" I would favour a publication of the entire <u>Nachlass</u>, if one can, with the aid of the computer, produce a readable text with illuminating comments and cross-references. But, as said, there is neither need nor opportunity for deciding about this now. (von Wright to Rhees, 26 April 1977)

Just as in his response to Ranchetti and Rosso's original request from 1973, von Wright made a crucial distinction between digitizing and editing Wittgenstein's writings. This distinction was also inscribed into the 1974 agreement with the literary executors and was once again reinforced through the conclusions von Wright drew from the Wittgenstein symposium. But, in fact, parts of the Tübingen group still harboured the idea of producing an edition and not merely doing preparatory work for it. This difference would indeed prove fatal for the Tübingen project.

6.3.3 Approval!

The first Wittgenstein symposium at Tübingen was a great success and fulfilled its main purpose: a proposal for a big research project was submitted to the Thyssen Foundation within a few months. Under the title (in translation) *Securing, Documenting and Indexing the Unpublished Writings by Ludwig Wittgenstein*, the production of a machine-readable version of all of Wittgenstein's writings was proposed (see Final Report). Besides the members who had been part of the first grant proposal, McGuinness and Schulte joined the group as experts on Wittgenstein's writings. The official principal investigator was again Heringer, and thus the project proposal was still situated within the context of computational linguistics with the research aim of programming the automatization of similarities. But, again, the biggest part of the proposal's workload was reserved for transcription work that was meant to be the foundation for a complete historical–critical edition of Wittgenstein's writings. In fact, the proposal promised that Wittgenstein's Nachlass would be documented and reconstructed in its entirety, that it would be transcribed and saved on magnetic tapes. What is more, textual phenomena such as underlinings, revisions and correction signs were supposed to be identified and included in the machine-readable transcription. Software for computerized text analysis was to be programmed, and, last but not least, a way forward—from the transcription to the complete historical–critical edition—was to be found (Final Report, 6). Nothing less than all this was the working package that the research group at Tübingen wanted to tackle with the support of the Thyssen Foundation.

It only took some weeks before the Thyssen Foundation sent out the message in January 1978 that its board, in principle, was willing to finance the proposal. But this good news also contained a drawback, since the proposed budget was reduced by 50 per cent. This meant the total amount of funding on offer was 353,000 German marks—only 6 per cent of the 6 million marks envisaged in 1974. Hence, Heringer, Nedo, Ranchetti, Rosso, McGuinness and Schulte had to discuss how they might deal with the reduction. They met in Pisa on 19 March 1978 (Minutes of the meeting by the members of the Wittgenstein Archive, 19 March 1978). The group decided it would not buy its own 'terminal', that is, a screen and an input device. But there was no way to avoid cutting wages as well. In the end, the project had enough funding for one full-time researcher, one half-time researcher for coordination, one secretary and two consulting scholars. This being the case, there was a clear tension between the reduced resources of the project and the unreduced ambitions promised in the proposal. It was therefore necessary to drum up extra funding from the very beginning of the project. At the outset, further means indeed came from the Thyssen Foundation—three stipends which could guarantee Nedo's post as well as Schulte's and Rosso's membership in the group (Minutes of the Tübingen work meeting, 18–22 November 1978). In addition, Heringer was able to provide a half-time typist and two student workers as well as rooms and support from the computational unit of Tübingen University. In sum, the combined working resources gave the endeavour the appearance of having reasonable chances for success. The project proposal was therefore approved in the summer of 1978.

6.4   Third Act (1978–1979)

6.4.1   Working Efficiently at Tübingen

With approval of the project grant, the research group at the University of Tübingen constituted itself as the "Wittgenstein Archive". The line-up at the archive resulted from the history of the earlier research group: there were two heads, namely Heringer, the official principal investigator, and Nedo, whose position the Thyssen Foundation wanted to secure. This double management of the project was mirrored by the fact that it resided at two locations: while the transcribing was to be done at Tübingen (Heringer convinced the university to give the archive a whole floor in a stately villa in the city of Tübingen), Nedo kept his office at Cambridge to secure access to the original papers and stay in contact with the literary heirs. The two posts for academic consultants were also already set: McGuinness as an acknowledged expert in the scholarly community and Ranchetti as the *spiritus rector* of the original idea. Schulte and Rosso remained associated stipendiaries. The consultants and stipendiaries were supposed to check and correct the transcriptions. The few unfilled positions were for those who did the actual transcribing.

Coordination of the daily work became the task of Reinhard Nowak, a young scholar who had written an excellent dissertation related to both philosophy and linguistics (Nowak 1981). As a student worker for Heringer, he had already proved his reliability and hence was considered the right man for the post (Minutes of the work meeting, 27 June 1978, Cambridge). Indeed, his abilities seemed to have attracted responsibilities: in contrast to the project managers, Nowak had to be physically present at the archive in order to organize the transcription and coordinate cooperation between all members. That the latter was difficult may be seen from the locations of the members: while Heringer held a chair at Tübingen, Nedo had his office in Cambridge, McGuinness lived and worked in Oxford, Ranchetti in Florence and Schulte in Bologna (The use of *EDV* [electronic data processing] in the production of a historical critical complete edition of L. Wittgenstein's writings, 15 December 1979, Private Archive Nowak). In a time of analogue communication, the scattered living arrangements of the members made dialogue and decision-making processes complicated. In addition to coordinating communication between the members, Nowak was to organize communication between the project group and the University of Tübingen, a task which included checking and administering the incoming bills for travel and materials. Besides this, Nowak's main responsibility was to organize the work flow and the technical aspects of the envisaged transcribing process. In other words, Nowak had to look after the whole daily business of the archive; and it seems that it was thanks to his management that the project could produce significant results in a comparatively short time.

The transcribing process at Tübingen began slowly because the texts were both typed in natural language and then prepared for Optical Character Recognition (OCR) processing. But soon it was clear that this procedure would be far too time-consuming (Final Report, 9–13; Schulte, Oral History Interview). This was why, in the winter of 1978, the student workers cut straight to using the OCR-writer. The resulting transcripts were saved on magnetic tapes at the university's computational unit. Under Nowak's guidance, the student workers—Mülder, Moritz, Keller-Bauer and Kulemann—produced 3,500 pages of transcripts and experimented with coding text phenomena, spending roughly 1,000 working hours from the start of the project to May 1979 (Work report, 23 October 1980; Report about the text input from August 1978 to May 1979, 15 June 1979; Work report, 26 March 1979). According to a summary from the summer of 1979—that is, within the first project year—19 manuscript ledgers (in particular Wittgenstein's manuscripts with the catalogue-numbers 104, 116, 117, 118, 135, 136, 137, 139a, 143, 144, 153, 156a, 157a, 157b, 158, 159, 160, 161, 168) and 11 typescripts (in particular Wittgenstein's typescripts with the catalogue-numbers 208, 210, 211, 214a, 215a, 216a, 217a, 218a, 220, 221, 232) were transcribed and saved (Nowak to Ranchetti, 14 August 1979; Minutes of the meeting of the group, 7 July 1979). Based on this, Nowak estimated that the production per week should be 350 pages (Minutes of the meeting of the group, 7 July 1979; Circular to all employees, 18 December 1979). The results of this disciplined work meant that by the time of the Final Report in 1982, more than 10,000 pages had been transcribed—about 60 per cent of Wittgenstein's Nachlass (Final Report, 8–9).

Looking solely at this impressive achievement, one can easily overlook the disruptions that caused the breakdown of the project during 1979–1982. But the number of transcribed pages shows that the breakdown was not due to shortcomings in the transcription work. The reason why none of the 10,000 transcribed pages have entered a scholarly edition seems rather to be a consequence of the project's structural burdens, two of which have already been mentioned: (1) conflicting ideas within the project group as well as between the group and the literary heirs as to what the overall goal of the project was, and (2) a funding policy that necessitated an immediate search for further funding. When the actual transcribing work began, a third burden was added.

6.4.2   Obstacles in Deciding on the Design of an Edition

The ideal workflow at the Wittgenstein Archive at the University of Tübingen was planned thus:

(1) Using the new microfilm that Nedo had produced in Cambridge, paper copies of the Nachlass items should be produced.
(2) The paper copies should be transcribed with an OCR-typewriter and include coding for relevant "text phenomena" (i.e., underlinings, deletions, revisions, etc.)
(3) The transcripts should automatically be read into the computer and saved.
(4) A printout of the saved transcripts should be compared with the paper copies from step (1) or with the original papers at the Wren Library at Cambridge.
(5) The corrected and revised transcripts should then serve as the basis for developing an editorial design for a historical critical edition of Wittgenstein's writings.

This sequence seems fairly reasonable at first glance, but it has an inbuilt conflict resulting from the decision for an editorial design being placed last: there was fundamental disagreement within the project group as to whether it was possible to begin with producing a transcription that should serve as the basis for an edition, and then think about the form of that edition as the work proceeded. Already at a very early stage, computer experts from Pisa advised the project group that if digital tools were being used to prepare an edition, the workflow should be turned the other way round (Minutes of the meeting with Heringer, McGuinness, Nedo, Picchi, Ranchetti, Rosso, Schulte and Zampolli, 20 March 1978, Pisa; Minutes of the work meeting, 27 June 1978, Cambridge). This is because relevant text phenomena must be coded into the transcription, and *which* text phenomena are relevant depends on the form of the edition. But to decide which text phenomena are relevant for a given edition requires knowledge about the text phenomena that exist—that is, one needs to know which markings in the documents have a function. Without this knowledge, one is in danger of coding markings that are irrelevant at the same time as being unaware of the signs that are indeed relevant. Either case would have enormous consequences, given that the Nachlass consists of 20,000 pages. Now, the project work at Tübingen began without consent concerning the form of the future edition, thus also without consent concerning the question of which text phenomena ought to be included in the transcription code. This crucial point of the editorial design remained unclear until the very end of the Wittgenstein Archive at Tübingen. The minutes mention again and again the discussion of prototypes for different editorial designs, and they document very different ideas amongst group members. Presentations of specific models of prototypes are repeatedly announced in the agenda, but they are just as often postponed to some subsequent meeting. In fact, the Wittgenstein Archive at Tübingen never agreed on an editorial design (Heringer to Nowak, 14 January 1982). The Final Report presents a set of text phenomena in Wittgenstein's writings and discusses options for dealing with them editorially. The different options are illustrated by a couple of prototypical designs (Final Report, 42–44). But a decision in favour of one design was never made. There were both internal and external reasons for this.

One external reason was the afore-mentioned attitude of the literary heirs— to await results before making any decision for or against specific publications. Since they were only familiar with editing processes in the world of analogous book production, they saw no problem in withholding consent until they saw transcriptions on paper. But since the computational processing of texts requires decisions about possible uses at the stage of coding, the literary heirs' policy of 'wait and see' was paralyzing for the planning of an edition at Tübingen. Nevertheless, the literary heirs considered the existing agreement with the group as far reaching, and it was completely in line with their established bottom-up working practices; in both their internal cooperation and concerning cooperation with third parties, they always edited a single given volume and then made their new decisions on the basis of what was achieved. Thus, one volume after the other originated from slowly growing trust in increasingly tighter collaborative relationships. The good experiences with this piecemeal policy can explain the literary heirs' cautious attitude concerning cooperation with the project group at Tübingen.

The tension resulting from the literary heirs' piecemeal policy and the project's need for goal-oriented top-down planning of an editorial design were intensified through the respective cultural differences built into the involved institutions. The University of Tübingen's administration championed a systematic top-down organization of the project by asking for a binding agreement for an edition of Wittgenstein's writings. This requirement combined the interests of the group members at Tübingen and the logic of the administrative culture at Tübingen. Thus, within the first months of the project, the head of the administration at Tübingen told Heringer that it would be unacceptable to manage a project of this size based only on the literary heirs' letter of general intent without the university or the project leaders being the copyright holders of the materials for a historical critical edition (Central Administration of the University of Tübingen to Heringer, 20 December 1978). From the university's perspective, securing the copyrights was a necessary condition to access the project budget. But it was just such a legally binding carte blanche that was alien to the literary heirs' working culture. They were therefore irritated when the Tübingen group proposed a new agreement with more rights for the Wittgenstein Archive. Having received a draft of the proposed new agreement, von Wright wrote to Rhees and Anscombe:

> I have studied the "Entwurf" of an amplified agreement with the Tübingen group. (When I was in England last Autumn, Nedo gave me a preliminary version of it to which I did not then react; you presumable got the same paper from him.)
>   Frankly, I do not like this document at all. (Its present form even less than the one of last Autumn.) It seems to me that our agreement of 1974 with the group is from our point of view satisfactory. If it does not satisfy the group we ought to consider very carefully

what further concessions we are willing to make—if any. (von Wright to Anscombe and Rhees, 23 January 1979)

Anscombe consented: "I agree with you we can leave things as they are" (Anscombe to von Wright, 13 February 1979). At this point, the literary heirs had seen no results from Tübingen, not even a sample of how a future edition might look. They therefore saw no reason to transfer further rights to the group at Tübingen. But when some members of the archive insisted on an amplified new agreement, the literary heirs felt the Tübingen group might distrust their intentions as stated in the 1974 agreement. This, in turn, made the literary heirs suspicious about the intentions of those at Tübingen who insisted on being granted more rights (Work report, 26 March 1979):

> There is something obscure about the whole thing which I cannot understand. Our agreement of the year 1974 seems to me to be a clear and good document. We have no interest in adding anything to it. If the Tübingen group wants something more from us they must make it plain what they want and give reasons for why they want it. This has not happened. (von Wright to Anscombe, 16 May 1979)

As the Tübingen project proceeded, it was becoming clear that there was a basic conflict resulting from different ideas about whether or not the Wittgenstein Archive was supposed to prepare a publishable edition of Wittgenstein's writings. This seed of the tragedy now began sprouting. The project group asked for the assurance of eventually getting the rights to publish an edition. But to convince the literary heirs to grant such permission, the group members would have to agree between themselves on the form of the edition they wanted to publish. This was what the group was unable to achieve.

The members had different ideas concerning the use and the users of a future edition of Wittgenstein's writings. Ranchetti thought the production of an edition was the very idea behind the whole project. Rosso proposed an editorial design as early as in the summer of 1978, when the computer experts from Pisa pointed out that one had to know the eventual use of the transcriptions before beginning to code the text (Minutes of the work meeting, 27 June 1978, Cambridge). Schulte too believed the essential editorial decisions ought to be made at the very beginning of the project. However, when discussing the issue within in group and with the project leaders, no agreement could be reached. Heringer considered the main point of the transcriptions to be to code the textual structures so that an automatic processing of similarities would become possible, and this opinion was in accordance with the project proposal. According to Heringer, the transcripts should be integrated into a research platform that would not necessitate any decision about an editorial design. Nedo too thought it was unnecessary to agree on an editorial design at the beginning, though for different reasons than Heringer; Nedo regarded the future edition as the most important aspect of the project, and he did have specific ideas about its form (Minutes of the work meeting in Cambridge from 27 June 1978). Thus, in addition to the lingering question about which design was right for an edition, there was no agreement amongst the archive members that an editorial design should be pinned down at the beginning of the project.

Even if all the members had seen the need to agree on an editorial design at the outset of the project, it seems questionable whether the issue could have been decided successfully. This is because research on text phenomena and markings in Wittgenstein's writings had only just begun. As explained above, decisions concerning editorial designs and thus the relevance of text phenomena require knowledge about the latter. But at the time of the Tübingen project, the text phenomena in Wittgenstein's writings were not yet fully scrutinized. For instance, many pages in his writings contain revision markings in the margins (sometimes called section markings), the specific functions of which had only partly been unravelled at the time; indeed, they are still debated today in specialized research (see, e.g., Rothhaupt 2011, 137–186). Other phenomena in the manuscripts such as the possible functions of different lengths of dashes or differently-sized spaces or gaps were also discussed at Tübingen (Nedo, Oral History Interview; Final Report attachment, 3). Basic research was needed to determine which text phenomena were relevant for the proposed edition and thus ought to be coded in the transcripts. This research had hardly started because the phenomena had been known and discussed only amongst the literary heirs and their closest intimates before the Cornell microfilm had been released in 1969.

At the time of the Wittgenstein Archive at Tübingen, it was probably Rhees who could read the traces of Wittgenstein's writing better than anyone else. But he was convinced that one could learn to read these traces only through long study of the manuscripts. His own extensive studies of the writing traces were tacitly built into the volumes he edited. He did not make this tacit knowledge explicit, so it remained secret until he taught it individually to subsequent editors. He was very willing to share his expertise, for instance with Cora Diamond, who edited notes from Wittgenstein's lectures on the foundations of mathematics (Wittgenstein 1976a). But in most cases of possible editors, he did not see enough interest and motivation to find out what Wittgenstein had really wanted to say and to understand how he had worked. The extent to which he introduced individual members of the Tübingen group to his art of reading Wittgenstein's writing traces is undetectable in the documents of the archive. The protocols of the group meetings, in any case, do not show that Rhees's or other experts' readings of single items and passages played a crucial role. It therefore seems that a rich source of information for deciding on an editorial design—Rhees—probably remained unexploited. But this is not surprising considering the polemics against Rhees's editorial decisions in his *Philosophical Grammar*.

6.4.3 Endless Productivity and Digital Editions as a Research Process

Whatever the exact dynamics between all the above-mentioned factors that led to indecision concerning an editorial design at Tübingen, the result was that transcribing at Tübingen went on efficiently but without a clear picture of which textual phenomena would be needed in a future edition. The production process was thus changed so that the text phenomena such as dashes, underlinings and section markings would be added only in a second step, namely directly at the computer terminal when the transcripts would be compared with the original papers and corrections were made (Minutes of the Tübingen work meeting, 18–22 November 1978). But this change in the workflow was merely a postponing of making the fundamental decision on the editorial design. What is more, as long as there was no agreement about the editorial design and about the relevance of the different text phenomena, the use of computer technology lost one of its main purposes, because a great advantage of a machine-readable transcription in contrast to an analogue transcription is the coding of the text phenomena. By failing to make the decision concerning that coding, one main argument for producing the digital transcription collapsed. Nowak, who had the most contact with the actual transcription work at Tübingen, became increasingly aware of this problem that resulted from the logic of digital transcriptions. He therefore wrote a memorandum in December 1979 stating that the digital transcription would require decisions concerning several codes for text phenomena, but that the then-current state of the work was characterized by the lack of these codes, which nevertheless would have to be created with a view to the form of the final edition (The use of *EDV* [electronic data processing] in the production of a historical critical complete edition of L. Wittgenstein's writings, 15 December 1979).

The described difficulties at the Wittgenstein Archive show that the prerequisites for the reasonable use of digital technology for editorial purposes are not necessarily technological issues that can be solved by technological means. Rather, the prerequisites are epistemic and organizational issues—philological knowledge and editorial decisions—that must be clarified in order to make efficient use of digital technology. Until today, projects on digital editing are complex challenges that must combine organizational management with technological abilities and philological expertise concerning the relevant text phenomena of a given author. The reasonable use of technology depends on editorial decisions, and these decisions must rest on the editors' familiarity with the texts to be edited. But such familiarity is enhanced by the editorial work that involves using technological skills. Both the familiarity and the technologically skilled work lead the editors in making their editorial decisions. Successful digital editing therefore requires circular editorial-hermeneutical-technological processes that cannot be substituted by a sequential workflow. This self-referential and self-informing research process has the best chances of resulting in one final product, that is, if it is carried out by one devoted person who possesses the required skills and faculties, or if it is carried out by experts who are truly cooperating. But true cooperation did not take place at the Wittgenstein Archive at Tübingen—or rather: the cooperation collapsed when the common goal seemed to get closer but the group members lost their mutual trust and realized they did not share the same goal.

6.5   Fourth Act (1979–1980)

6.5.1   The Second Wittgenstein Symposium at the University of Tübingen

According to Heringer, the solid base on which to build the Wittgenstein Archive required three as-yet missing foundation stones: (1) an agreement between the archive and the literary heirs concerning the goal of the current work, (2) adequate funding, and (3) an agreed-upon design for a complete edition of Wittgenstein's unpublished writings—a design which could be used to coordinate the project. The reason for launching a second Wittgenstein symposium at Tübingen was to quarry these three missing foundation stones. Since the first symposium had been a great success, the Thyssen Foundation was willing to support a second event with another 36,000 German marks. This was enough to invite the literary heirs to Tübingen and the 'who's who' of the then-current Wittgenstein research (German department at the University of Tübingen to Nedo, 4 April 1979). The list of participants eventually included Georg Kreisel and Norman Malcolm (both students of Wittgenstein and friends of the literary heirs) as well as Anthony Kenny, Peter Winch, Jaques Bouverese, Barry Smith, David Pears, Kristóf Nyíri, Hans Kaal, Gordon Baker and Peter Hacker. In addition to this representative ensemble of mostly native English-speaking Wittgenstein scholars, the symposium hosted well-known German philosophers, representatives of the Wren Library, the publishers of Wittgenstein's writings Blackwell and Suhrkamp, and last but not least, funding agencies such as the Ministry of Culture of Baden-Württemberg, the German Research Foundation, the Thyssen Foundation and the Heidelberg Academy of Sciences and Humanities. These prominent guests gathered during 1–7 July 1979 in order to listen to evening lectures and to enjoy the finest cuisine of the Black Forest (Agenda of the 2nd Wittgenstein symposium in Tübingen). Of course, the participants knew the gathering's purpose was to build new alliances for further funding, but the set-up was so luxurious and well organized that most of the participants who are still alive today have vivid and enduring memories of this event that some call "a true symposium" (Heringer, Oral History Interview, 18 May 2018).

Just as with the outcome of the first symposium, all the hopes pinned to the second one were fulfilled. After the symposium week, the literary heirs were willing to sign a new agreement with the project group at Tübingen that granted them more rights for future publications. In particular, on 19 July 1979, they gave the Wittgenstein Archive the exclusive right to produce a historical critical edition, promising that this exclusive right would last for the subsequent ten years (Final Report, appendix).[17] In the amplified agreement, the persons working at the

---

[17] The copy of the agreement in the final report is in German:

Wir, die Inhaber der Urheberrechte der zur Zeit seines Todes nicht publizierten Schriften Ludwig Wittgensteins, treffen mit dem Wittgenstein-Archiv Tübingen folgende, den Vertrag vom 19. Oktober 1974 ergänzende Vereinbarungen:

Wittgenstein Archive were mentioned by name (R. Nowak, M. Rosso, J. Schulte, B. F. McGuinness, M. Ranchetti, H. J. Heringer and M. Nedo). However, since the archive itself was not a legal entity, the rights were formally transferred to the project leaders Heringer and Nedo. The agreement made clear that the literary heirs demanded a veto-option in case of negotiations with publishers, and that they demanded a regular report on the project's progress.

With this new agreement, it seemed possible to make a reliable plan for preparing a historical critical edition of Wittgenstein's writings. The group members now were not only assured that the fruit of their labour would eventually be published, but the project leaders could seek further funding. It was obvious that the production of a complete digital edition would exceed the means provided by the Thyssen Foundation. The long-term funding of an editorial project, including funding for employing a sufficient number of staff members, was the formidable task of the academies. Hence, Heringer had already considered transferring the

---

Wir präzisieren die seinerzeit erteilte grundsätzliche Zustimmung zur Publikation einer historisch-kritischen Gesamtausgabe der erwähnten Schriften Ludwig Wittgensteins an das Wittgenstein-Archiv Tübingen, und wir werden dieses Recht für einen Zeitraum von zunächst zehn Jahren niemandem sonst übertragen.

Dieses Recht zur Publikation der nämlichen Schriften Ludwig Wittgensteins schließt ein das Recht der uneingeschränkten wissenschaftlichen Bearbeitung dieser Schriften. Dazu übertragen wir Ihnen die Rechte auf Zugang zum Material des Wittgenstein-Nachlasses, an dem uns das Urheberrecht zusteht. Daß die Publikation nur in Absprache und Zusammenarbeit mit uns, den Urheberrechtsinhabern, zu erfolgen hat, ist bereits in der Vereinbarung vom 19. Oktober 1974 gesichert, d.h. jede Publikation kann nur mit schriftlicher Zustimmung unsererseits geschehen. Diese Publikation soll in der Sprache der Manuskripte, unübersetzt, erfolgen. Über die Verhandlungen mit den Verlagen müssen wir unterrichtet werden, und wir behalten uns hier ein Mitspracherecht vor.

Sowie wir das Recht zur Publikation einer Schrift von Ludwig Wittgenstein einem Verlag unserer Wahl übertragen, werden wir vor Abschluß des Verlagsvertrages das Wittgenstein-Archiv in Kenntnis setzen und den Vertrag gegebenenfalls im Sinne des Forschungsprojekts mit dem Archiv abstimmen.

Wir legen Wert darauf, daß der Personenkreis der Mitarbeiter am Wittgenstein-Archiv uns bekannt ist, und daß Änderungen in der Zusammensetzung der Forschungsgruppe nur nach vorheriger Rücksprache mit uns erfolgen. Wir bitten um eine zumindest jährliche Information über den Fortgang der Arbeiten, nach Möglichkeit in der Form eines schriftlichen Berichts.

Am Wittgenstein-Archiv arbeiten zur Zeit R. Nowak, M. Rosso und J. Schulte als angestellte Mitarbeiter, B.F. McGuinness und M. Ranchetti als beratende Mitarbeiter, und H.J. Heringer und M. Nedo als Projektleiter.

Da das Wittgenstein-Archiv Tübingen für uns keine l e g a l e n t i t y darstellt, übertragen wir die obengenannten Rechte und Verpflichtungen an Herrn Heringer und Herrn Nedo in ihrer Funktion als Leiter des Wittgenstein-Archivs. Wir legen Wert darauf, daß alle Verhandlungen und Abmachungen wie in der Vergangenheit zwischen uns und Herrn Nedo oder Herrn Heringer erfolgen, daß sie uns Rechenschaft schulden, daß sie unsere Wünsche der Forschungsgruppe vermitteln und daß die Forschungsgruppe durch sie mit uns verhandelt.

archive to the Heidelberg Academy of Sciences and Humanities (HASH). Having secured the exclusive rights, he could actually take steps towards realizing this idea. During the second Wittgenstein Symposium, he and the romanist Eugenio Coseriu, who had become a HASH member in 1977, explored options for submitting a proposal to transfer the archive to HASH. (Minutes of the meeting of the group, 7 July 1979). Riding on a tailwind from the symposium, Heringer devoted his next sabbatical to consolidating and extending the archive with a view to transferring it to HASH. The prospects for this were positive because leading German philosophers supported the idea. Hans Georg Gadamer, for whom Heringer and Nowak wrote an extensive personal memorandum, saw the need to secure the materials at the Wittgenstein Archive at Tübingen (Draft of a memorandum to H. Gadamer). With the support of Dieter Henrich, a commission at HASH was set up to coordinate the creation of an editorial project (Heringer to HASH, 17 January 1980). A proposal for the transfer was supposed to be submitted and discussed without delay, that is, still in 1979. Additional support came from the German society for philosophical editions that now included a section for the use of computational processing in editorial projects, a member of which was the creator of TU-STEP, Wilhelm Ott, from the University of Tübingen (Report by the working-group philosophical editions of the Allgemeinen Gesellschaft für Philosophie in Deutschland e.V.).

In sum, it seemed that two of the project's foundation stones—missing at the beginning of 1980—were now supplied. After the exclusive rights for a historical critical edition had been given, the project was on track to be transferred to HASH, which would mean long-term funding and additional positions for staff members (Heringer to HASH, 17 January 1980). In order to conclude the consolidation of the project, the third foundation stone was now sorely needed: the project group's agreement on an editorial design in order to coordinate the member's efforts and ensure that everyone worked towards the same goal. The failure to reach such agreement is precisely what led to the breakdown of the project at the very moment when success seemed so close at hand. By the end of 1980, none of the expectations from the early months of the year remained.

6.5.2   Breaching Trust

There was no clear hierarchy in the Wittgenstein Archive. There were two project leaders, one of whom was a professor of linguistics with the ambition to transfer the project to HASH so it could be embedded in the established structures of a German academy, while the other had paved the way for the project through his self-study and personal devotion. He relied on a personal stipend for his work at Cambridge. Then there were two consultants, one a renowned Oxford Wittgenstein scholar, the other a humanist ecclesiastical historian who understood himself as the *spiritus rector* of the whole endeavour. Finally, there were the two stipendiaries, Rosso and Schulte, who were formally not subordinated to the project management because their stipends were independent of the archive funding. Thus, there was in principle only one clear chain of command at the archive, namely from the leaders to the one scholarly staff member (Nowak) and the transcribing student workers. Yet even this line of instruction was split at its head due to the dual leadership, for any work that exceeded the mere typing of texts had to be accomplished through consensual agreement. Accordingly, the group members had always understood themselves as having equal rights when making fundamental decisions, and this was a principle they had documented at the outset of the project (Minutes of the Tübingen work meeting, 18–22 November 1978). The project was thus constituted as being built on democratic decision making.

The minutes from the time before the amplified agreement with the literary executors show that the group members insisted on being mentioned in the agreement as on par with the project leaders (Minutes of the work meeting, 1–5 October 1979). They were therefore upset when the final agreement gave the exclusive rights for publication solely to the project leaders and not to all the members (Minutes of the work meeting 1–5 October 1979). And their anger turned to rage when they were given a sketch for new working contracts that the University of Tübingen's administration had elaborated on behalf of Heringer (Circular to the employees, 24 July 1979). According to these contracts, all working results were to be delivered to the project management (Draft of the contracts for the employees). Thus, the two new documents—(1) the enhanced agreement with the literary heirs and (2) the revised working contracts—brewed distrust that the archive's transfer to HASH no longer served the interests of any group members other than the two leaders. The other members would have no rights to the future edition, and the project leaders would get all the royalties and the scholarly recognition. This was a "serious breach in collegiality" for the members, leading to an unacceptable state of "serfdom", as they pointed out in a letter of protest (Minutes of the work meeting, 1–5 October 1979; Letter to the heads of the project "Wittgenstein Archive"—from the rest of the members of the research group, September 1979).

Ranchetti was provoked to such an extent that he approached the HASH member Coseriu, who was supposed to support the transfer of the archive (Minutes of the work meeting, 7–10 October 1980; Heringer to Ranchetti, 3 January 1980). This intervention had potential "fundamental consequences" (Minutes of the work meeting, 7–10 January 1980) for the archive's future, so Heringer agreed to champion the other members' demands in his communication with the University of Tübingen's administration. Concerning the contracts, a solution was found according to which individual editors should be responsible for single volumes of the future complete edition; they should receive the royalties and be allowed to make their own editorial decisions, albeit in coordination with the other editors (Minutes of the work meeting, 7–10 January 1980). This solution solved the conflict of interests within the group for the time being, though Rosso actually left the project because of the contract issue (Minutes of the work meeting, 16–18 July 1980). But the compromise once more prevented the creation of a clear hierarchy in project management, and this eventually resulted in even stronger conflicts.

Due to the double management, the two project locations had also evolved: While Nowak in Tübingen coordinated the transcription work with the student

workers, Nedo in Cambridge began working with Isabell Allen-Weiss, a new stipendiary who was financed through the Robert Bosch Foundation. At the beginning of the project, the office at Cambridge seemed crucial for keeping in contact
with the literary heirs and for having access to Wittgenstein's papers at the Wren
Library. But now, with the prospect of transferring the archive to HASH, several
members questioned what the Cambridge office would contribute to the main
objective, if anything.

This question became especially pressing when the transcripts from the two
locations were to be combined and it was discovered that the two different data
formats used at the two places were not entirely compatible: the computation
unit at Tübingen saved the transcripts on magnetic tapes from Telefunken, while
Nedo's office at Cambridge used IBM computers. The data from the latter could
not be transferred into the Telefunken system. This meant the transcripts produced at Cambridge could not be used at the project headquarters in Tübingen;
in fact, the group members at Tübingen never saw them.[18] This primarily technological complication gave rise to some members' doubts as to whether the
work carried out at Cambridge still served the overall common goal. Those who
worked at Tübingen felt less and less informed about what was actually happening
in Cambridge, not least because the project meetings were too rare even though
they were held on a regular basis. At the same time, the Tübingen headquarters
received an increasing number of bills for costs incurred by the Cambridge office.
In particular, the administration at the University of Tübingen became reluctant to pay high service costs for IBM computers at Cambridge when the results
saved on that system could not be used by the Telefunken system at Tübingen
(Correspondence about the agreement to pay bills from Cambridge; Nowak, Oral
History Interview).

Thus, besides the distrust caused by the new agreement with the literary heirs
and the new contracts for group members, there was now a growing distrust
among the members at Tübingen fed by the suspicion that Nedo was carrying out
parallel activities for an edition but not telling them about it (Minutes of the work
meeting, 13–16 April 1980). Ranchetti, therefore, in spring 1980, asked for a special meeting dedicated to discussing the archive's organizational structure (Memo
from the group meeting, 3 March 1980). Nedo's minutes of this meeting, written
from memory, read like the description of a political coup: Heringer, McGuinness,
Nowak, Ranchetti, Rosso and Schulte are said to have entered Nedo's office at
precisely 17:30 on 3 March 1980, putting forward the complaint that the work at
Tübingen was disrupted through Nedo's activities at Cambridge, and that Nedo
could not fulfil his tasks as a project leader because he spent too much time at
Cambridge and too little time at Tübingen (Memo from the group meeting, 3
March 1980). The group demanded the removal of Nedo as one of the project
leaders. By referring to the constitution of the project, Nedo could prevent this

---

[18] In a response to an earlier version of this text, Schulte pointed out that he was not familiar with
any transcriptions that would have been produced in Cambridge.

from happening. But when bills from Cambridge continued to be sent to Tübingen for payment, when it became known that Nedo, after concluding the Thyssen-project, was soon to be funded with a personal stipend from the German Research Foundation (Schulte, Oral History Interview; Heringer to Rhees, 30 October 1979), and when rumour had it that Nedo would not refuse being addressed as "doctor" (even though not holding the degree), the other group members confronted him a second time on 18 April 1980. Heringer, McGuinness, Ranchetti, Rosso, Schulte and Nowak repeated their fundamental criticism of Nedo's uncooperativeness with the rest of the group; it was suspected that Nedo would regard the whole project as his private endeavour and that he would not consult the others when taking new steps; furthermore, the group reproached Nedo for publishing false statements about the project and himself (Minutes of the work meeting, 13–16 April 1980).

At the end of this second confrontation, the members presented Nedo with a letter asking the literary heirs to dismiss Nedo as one of the project leaders. According to this letter, Nedo was supposed to remain a member of the archive, but without any power to make conceptual and organizational decisions. This power was supposed to be given to Ranchetti and McGuinness, who would act as co-leaders along with Heringer. The letter to the literary heirs was supposed to be signed by all members of the archive, including Nedo (Attachment to the work report, 25 September 1980). Nedo refused to sign it and left the meeting. The other members remaining in the room formulated a new letter to the literary heirs. In it, they asked only for Nedo's dismissal:

> We write to you in your function as one of the trustees of the Wittgenstein papers to say that a number of new organizational developments has taken place in our project which make it appear inappropriate that Mr. Nedo should continue to function as one of the leaders of the project. Mr. Nedo would remain an active member of our group but would no longer be responsible for planning or administration. We are aware that this may require some alteration in the contract with you, but of a kind for which provision has been made.
>
> We propose to send you shortly a more detailed account of the present state of affairs and of the form of organization that we wish to propose for the future. It will also be necessary at that stage to define the relation of our project to a number of other bodies such as Trinity College, Cambridge, the University of Tübingen, and the Thyssen Foundation.
>
> We had hoped to send you this letter with the agreement and signature of Mr. Nedo and have shown it to him but we are in the event compelled to send it [*sic*] over the names of the remainder of the group. (Ranchetti, McGuinness, Nowak and Schulte to the literary heirs, 18 April 1980)

This letter was immediately sent by registered mail to the literary heirs.

6.5.3   Mobilization

After the letter was sent to the literary heirs, the Tübingen and Cambridge branches of the project split. Heringer, who tried to explain in another letter to Rhees and von Wright what was going on in Tübingen, spurred on the consolidation of the project in a way that excluded Nedo (Heringer to von Wright, 29 April 1980). By June 1980, he had drafted a conceptual paper stating that the project objectives were still to be met, but without Nedo having any role in the steering of the project (Policy paper, June 1980; McGuinness to Heringer, 24 May 1980). Heringer's conceptual paper regarded the development of an editorial prototype and a respective coding system as most urgent. The technological cooperation with the computational unit at Tübingen was to be strengthened by using the software TU-STEP, which had recently been developed at Tübingen (Work report, 11 June 1980). It seems that Heringer's proposal was implemented immediately because the project's Final Report states that the coding system was implemented in July 1980.[19] Furthermore, the Final Report states that this coding system was built such that it could be used with OCR-A and the editing software TU-STEP. By using this system, the split with Cambridge was manifest and explicit: the coding system would not work with IBM computers, and hence, the cooperative transcription at Cambridge must cease (Final Report, 26). The Final Report also draws the ultimate conclusion from this curtailment of cooperation, namely that the two locations did not work towards creating one and the same edition (Final Report, 28).

The project group's break-up and the work towards creating different editions were facts by July 1980. This development was mediated by the use of different technological formats (Telefunken and IBM), but it cannot be traced back to the technological problem of the two different formats. The use of non-compatable technological systems is instead a symptom resulting from the way the project was set up and the failure to cultivate cooperation. The project's breakdown can thus be understood through many interacting factors in the history and theory of cooperation. The mutually negative feedback of these factors created an atmosphere of distrust that made cooperation impossible. Theoretically speaking, once such a state has been reached, technological or organizational problems can no longer be solved cooperatively. After a group's break-up, the parties may achieve peaceful coexistence if they manage to follow their own goals without interfering with each other. However, if the parties—each of whom has individual ambitions—enter into a situation of competition, everyone will lose out and suffer damage. This is precisely what happened in the story of the Wittgenstein Archive at the University of Tübingen.

While the archive members at Tübingen suspected Nedo was pursuing his own editorial plans, Nedo feared that an edition was in the making at Tübingen but without him as one of the editors. This conflict came to a head when Heringer and Ranchetti wanted to make known their plans for an edition (Heringer to Ranchetti, 4 September 1980). Nedo thought this was not in line with the agreement with the literary heirs and thus demanded that they be informed. He hoped they would not consent to Heringer and Ranchetti's plans. Of course, this strengthened his

---

[19] In a response to an earlier version of this text, Heringer points out that he had drafted a transcription and indexing system that was used in Tübingen.

position and the likelihood of a confrontation because it was still Nedo who had the immediate contact with the literary heirs, mainly with Anscombe and Rhees in England. In fact, Rhees had supported Nedo in connection with a new research proposal shortly before the breakup (Minutes of the work meeting, 16–18 July 1980, Florence). In a written recommendation, he stressed Nedo's trustworthiness, saying that he (Rhees) knew of no other person he would like better to entrust with the editing of Wittgenstein's writings on the foundations of mathematics (Rhees to B. Zimmermann, 14 May 1980). Rhees, it seems, thought Nedo could continue the editorial work in his (Rhees's) spirit and in accordance with his understanding of Wittgenstein's texts. And for Rhees, this was the crucial prerequisite for any editorial work. Thus, for Nedo, it could only be an advantage to draw Rhees into the conflict with the other members of the Tübingen project; and Anscombe too would take sides with Nedo when the conflict reached her ears shortly thereafter.

6.6   Fifth Act (1980–1982)

6.6.1   Collision at Oxford

The literary heirs still took it for granted that they had the last word on any decision for publications from Wittgenstein's papers, even though they had given the exclusive rights for a critical edition to the leaders of the Wittgenstein Archive at Tübingen. After the letter asking for Nedo's removal, they thought there was a power struggle going on and that the Tübingen group members wanted to sell the bear skin before they had caught the bear (Rhees to Anscombe, 24 September 1980). This enraged most of all Anscombe, who was informed of the happenings at Tübingen by Nedo (Anscombe to von Wright, 1980_4). She told Nedo to tell the group that no one but the literary heirs had the power to decide on which parts of Wittgenstein's writings would be published and in which editorial format (Minutes of the work meeting, 16–18 July 1980; therein notification from the literary heirs to the Wittgenstein Archive at the University of Tübingen about Michael Nedo, 11 July 1980). In particular, she assured Nedo that the literary heirs would never consent to an edition with learned commentary from the editors. And while Nedo transmitted this message as the spokesman for the literary heirs, Anscombe stood up for Nedo's interests when contacting von Wright:

> Dear Georg Henrik
>   Thank you for your letter. I am very sorry I did not write as I promised to. I have been puzzling over the Tübingen business.
>   It seems evident that the letter we got was prompted by the agreement we signed last year in Tübingen, and also that there is a sort of power struggle going on.
>   Like you, I have a very disagreeable impression: those people write as if they had acquired rights in a valuable property, and wanted to decide how to divide up the spoils, though it will be long before they produce anything. It certainly needs emphasizing that we have in no way relinquished our ownership of the copyright.

I also feel alarmed at the indications that they think of producing 'historic-critical' editions. This is unacceptable: what we have envisaged was only a transcription with a description of the MS sources. Nedo understands that very well; and it is my impression that they want to get rid of him as Projektleiter in order to be free to make their own decisions. There is talk of dividing the texts up among them as so many provinces. I see signs that they do not believe we shall veto the publication of texts burdened with learned commentary. I certainly intend to do that: what I want to see is a complete transcription of the whole of the texts, and I do not believe in the competence of any of them to produce a commentary.

I don't think that we can be indifferent to whether that project goes on. For if it does, there are all those photographs at Tübingen, with a group of people who think they have a right to work on them. There is no saying what they will do. (Anscombe to von Wright, 1980_4)

Both Anscombe and von Wright thought they had granted access to Wittgenstein's notes written in his private code solely for the transcription work. And both understood their agreement with the archive in Tübingen as a letter of intent—not as empowering the project leaders to make decisions concerning publications without asking them for permission. Like Anscombe, von Wright too was irritated when he received the letter from Tübingen asking to remove Nedo, and he began to doubt that the work at Tübingen was being carried out according to a reasonable plan. He still hoped the archive would produce a publishable manuscript, and he was even willing to agree to an edition with philological references and learned commentary (von Wright to Anscombe, 2 August 1980). But Anscombe's warning about what was going on at Tübingen reached von Wright at the same time as he received worrying signals from other quarters as well. Passages in Wittgenstein's code, which the literary heirs had covered up in the Cornell microfilm, appeared in an essay written by a befriended colleague. These passages were only meant to be seen in the original papers at the Wren Library and in the uncensored microfilm at Tübingen. Since the literary heirs had not permitted access to the originals at the Wren Library, the mentioned colleague must have studied the coded passages at Tübingen. This was why von Wright felt a loss of control concerning the access to the materials at Tübingen (von Wright to Anscombe, 7 May 1980).[20] But two other people—a member of the German Research Foundation and a philosopher from Tübingen—also told von Wright about their second thoughts concerning the archive:

When, last February, I was attending a conference in West-Germany I met Dr Zimmermann from the Deutsche Forschungsgemeinschaft and Professor Bubner of Tübingen University. I was curious to hear their views of the project. I got the impression that both had some doubts about it; in particular, they seem to worry about the fact that neither Heringer, nor Nedo, nor Ranchetti were philosophers.—I know no details about the present financial basis of the project; if asked for an opinion by those who have so far financed it, I should probably refuse to give one. (von Wright to Anscombe, 19 June 1980)

---

[20] This suspicion was later confirmed through the publication of the "Secret Diaries" (see Wittgenstein 1991).

In light of this converging information, von Wright, after June 1980 at the latest, was unwilling to support the project with further recommendations. He asked the other literary heirs to meet soon in order to rethink their relation to the archive and to fulfil their custodial duties in the case of the archive's breakdown (von Wright to Anscombe, 19 June 1980). The meeting was to take place at Cambridge in mid-October 1980. But Anscombe and Rhees went into action a fortnight earlier, on 29 September, the day the members of the Tübingen archive had scheduled a project meeting in Oxford. The group had contacted the two literary heirs living in England, Anscombe and Rhees, in order to present them with the new setup of the archive according to Heringer's conceptual paper (Minutes of the work meeting. 29 September–3 October 1980, Oxford). But both Anscombe and Rhees already knew from Nedo that the project group would be having a meeting, and they were preparing to travel to Oxford anyway (Rhees to Anscombe, 24 September 1980). The two literary heirs showed up at the project meeting the following day. Testimonies differ greatly as to what happened in this meeting, or rather collision, between the Tübingen group on the one hand and Anscombe and Rhees on the other. One thinks readily of the Japanese movie *Rashomon*, in which a story is told from different points of view, all subjective and conflicting. There seems, however, to be a convergence of memories on the point that both Anscombe and Rhees championed Nedo's position (Schulte, Oral History Interview; McGuinness, Oral History Interview; Nedo, Oral History Interview; Schulte, Oral History Interview). The meeting's minutes document that the literary heirs would have considered a change in the project structure as a cancellation of their agreement. Indeed, instead of accepting the proposed restructuring of the archive's management, they presented the group with their own addendum to the agreement according to which only the literary heirs could decide which texts were selected for any edition and that any learned commentary was to be excluded. The minutes thus confirm that the preparation of an edition with learned commentary would be regarded by the literary heirs as a cancellation of the original agreement, and "a discussion of this declaration seemed to them as unnecessary" (Minutes of the work meeting, 29 September–3 October 1980, Oxford).

It is no wonder that such an addendum was resisted by the project group—the members refused to sign it (Nedo, Oral History Interview). Unfortunately, the collision coincided with the fact that just now there was an example for an editorial prototype laying on the table, the discussion of which had been stressed in Heringer's conceptual paper. How else should Anscombe and Rhees interpret this, if not as flagrante proof of their suspicion that the Tübingen group was aiming to produce an edition without informing the literary heirs? All subsequent attempts to explain the situation were in vain. Anscombe had decided that the Tübingen group could not be entrusted with the task of producing an edition and that it was the duty of the literary heirs to get Wittgenstein's writings "out of Heringer's hands" (Anscombe to von Wright, 13 November 1980; Anscombe to von Wright, 30 December 1980; Nowak, Oral History Interview). For this purpose, she listed several points against Heringer that made it impossible for her to support him further (see Anscombe to von Wright, 13 November 1980; Anscombe to von Wright,

30 December 1980). Thus, when the project's Final Report states that the meeting at Oxford was "without result" (Final Report, 3), this is true concerning the fact that no further agreement was signed, but the meeting did indeed have disastrous results: the breaching of trust within the project group had spread to the literary heirs. Heringer now demanded that all Wittgenstein materials from Nedo's office be handed over, while Anscombe demanded that all Wittgenstein materials from the archive at Tübingen be handed over. The situation became an open confrontation.

6.6.2 Showdown at Cambridge

Rhees probably spoke less strongly than Anscombe during the meeting at Oxford. But he too was very disappointed about what had happened. He asked himself how the literary heirs could still fulfil their duty—one which to him was sacred. In one of his many notes to himself, we can observe how he tried to achieve clarity about his responsibilities after the confrontation at Oxford:

> They have spent 6 years trying to decide which shoes to wear and how they should clean them—and they have not stepped even into the vestibule of understanding what sort of manuscripts they are, or how their characters might be shown vis-à-vis one another.
>
> It is wearisome trying to follow them in their interest in shoe brushes, and deadly wearisome to follow their quarrels with one another.
>
> But we shall neglect the MSS entrusted to us—we shall make it harder for other philosophers to see how the MSS may be important—if we
>
> a) shrug our shoulders when a different group claims and uses that unrestricted access which we allowed then to Nedo, Heringer and Ranchetti; (a different group might be better, or it might do things with which we could not agree at all);
>
> b) if we do not care in what sort of show-case the Fg [Forschungsgruppe] finally exhibits them. (Note by Rhees to himself, 13 November 1980, RBA)

Rhees often cogitated his practical decisions in such written discussions with himself. And it was typical for him that once he came to a conclusion, he acted without compromise. Straightaway, he wrote to President Adolf Theis of the University of Tübingen, informing him that the literary heirs were withdrawing permission for the members of the group led by Heringer to access the Wittgenstein materials, and that they would legally intervene with any attempt by the group to publish any parts of the writings transcribed at Tübingen (Rhees to Theis, 15 November 1980). Naturally, this message alarmed the university's president Theis. He replied to Rhees by saying he was sure that the accusations against Heringer resulted from misunderstandings (Theis to Rhees, 15 December 1980). The university, said Theis, supported the restructuring of the archive, and that it was impossible for the administration to agree that anyone without a doctoral degree—like Nedo—could be a leader of such a big project. Later, Nedo would argue that he had become one of the project's leaders due to his previous achievements and his contact with the literary heirs, not in order to carry out administrative tasks; such tasks were part of Heringer's responsibilities as project manager (Nedo to Theis, 27 January 1981). Anscombe accepted this line of argumentation; she thought the accusations against Nedo were exaggerated and would not affect his services to Wittgenstein's writings. Hence, both she and Rhees reiterated to Theis what they expected from the University of Tübingen:

Dear President Theis,
    We must repeat what we have stated in our previous letters, namely that our permission to Professor Heringer and to other members of the Wittgenstein Forschungsgruppe (Wittgenstein Archive), granting access to the Wittgenstein Nachlaß, is now withdrawn.
    We therefore request that all those films, photocopies or transcripts of the Wittgenstein manuscripts which Professor Heringer and the Wittgenstein Archiv now have, be locked up; that any keys be in your custody; and that nobody be allowed access to the material unless he presents a written permission signed by all the members of the committee of the Nachlaßverwalter; but that you do grant access to anyone who does produce such written permission. (Anscombe and Rhees to Theis, 3 January 1981)

Thus, from being given exclusive rights for a critical edition and the prospect of establishing a long-term project at the Heidelberg Academy in early 1980, the project group was now locked out. And yet another difficulty emerged; the issue became a "*causa Wittgenstein Archive*" that affected the University of Tübingen itself when the state court of auditors became aware of it. The university was duty-bound to justify its use of the project budget to this highest financial control. In interviews and investigations, the state court of auditors noticed significant "irregularities" in the travel expenses and therefore confiscated the project documentation (Work report, 9 April 1981; Nedo, Oral History Interview). The university was now required to explain what was going on at the Wittgenstein Archive. This was part of the reason why the university supported Heringer's ambition to consolidate the project's organizational structure with legally watertight contracts. With the hope that this would still be possible, both the chancellor and the president of the university asked for a hearing with the literary heirs.

Before meeting the literary heirs in Cambridge, the senior representatives of the University of Tübingen's administration supported Heringer's plans for the future of the Wittgenstein Archive. Heringer informed Chancellor Sandberger and President Theis about the details of his ideas for a restructuring in order to equip them to negotiate with the literary heirs. Heringer built on the amplified agreement from 1979, which he considered a legal document granting him exclusive rights for a historical critical edition. He hoped to make a fresh start based on transferring the archive to the Heidelberg Academy (Heringer to Theis, 19 February 1981). Gadamer, in a telephone call, had meanwhile advised Heringer to leave the whole project, but Heringer thought that given the university's support, there was still a good chance that the project's objectives could be met (Heringer, Oral History Interview, 23 March 2018). For him, however, it was necessary that Nedo be removed and a scholarly committee be set up to control the use of funds. If these requirements were met, he was willing to continue leading the project, though with an increased number of staff members. This was roughly the concept of negotiation for Chancellor Sandberger and President Theis's meeting with Anscombe and Rhees. Convinced that the legal rights were his, Heringer told the members of the Tübingen group on the evening before the envisaged negotiation that the new concept would get the whole project out of the mist and make it worthy of its task (Heringer to the employees of the Wittgenstein Archive, 16 February 1981).

Chancellor Sandberger and President Theis met with Anscombe and Rhees in Cambridge on 2 March 1981. The course of the discussion is documented in a protocol written by Miss Allen-Weiss, Nedo's assistant at Cambridge. In the protocol, she at first tried to summarize the conversation; as the discussion continued, however, she began recording the direct speech of the participants (Minutes of the meeting between Anscombe, Rhees, Theis, and Sandberger, 2 March 1981, Cambridge). This is a fascinating document. Though possibly biased, it presents the showdown between the Tübingen group and the literary executors. It shows that Sandberger and Theis indeed wanted an agreement for a new setup of the archive in accordance with Heringer's concept. They began the discussion with matters of copyright and the question of access to the materials at Tübingen. Even though Anscombe and Rhees had withdrawn permission to access these materials, Sandberger and Theis insisted that all results from a German research project must principally be accessible to German researchers. Otherwise, the university would not be allowed to pay out the funding means. But the two literary heirs were unimpressed with this argument: they had granted access only to those members of the project who were actually working on the writings. Since they had lost trust in the integrity of these members, they were adamant in their decision to withdraw such permission. Sandberger replied that according to German law, a new copyright was established through the production of a transcription, namely the transcribers' copyright on their transcriptions. Yet, when Anscombe asked whether the mere copying of texts would constitute a new copyright in Germany, Theis had to concede that this was only the case if the transcribers had created a new work through the editorial processing of the transcribed text. But precisely this type of editorial processing had not yet taken place. Thus, Sandberger and Theis's first attempt to get a new agreement failed. They then turned to the question of the project's future.

Theis said the project found itself in a devastating situation: there were all sorts of personal and financial problems and no documents according to which the hitherto carried-out work could be judged. This was why Theis was convinced of the need for new project management. But the project now had such a bad reputation in German academia that no qualified German scholar would be willing to step in. Since no one else was in sight, Heringer would be the only acceptable option. At this point, Anscombe made it clear that for her, the project could only have a future if Nedo was part of it. According to Anscombe, Nedo had invested a lot of work and had been successful in his applications for funding. This statement must have vexed Sandberger and Theis, for from their point of view, it was impossible that someone without a doctoral degree would have a leading role in such a project. Anscombe said that according to her information, Nedo had carried out all the studies necessary for a doctoral dissertation and all that was missing was for him to submit and dispute it. She went on to declare that it was unthinkable for her to cooperate further with Heringer because he would not respect the interests of the literary heirs. This, she said, was demonstrated by his refusal to sign the literary heirs' addendum to the agreement during the meeting in Oxford.

The two parties' opinions concerning which positions Heringer and Nedo should have in the future were incompatible, and there seemed to be no chance for any agreement at this meeting. Theis made another attempt by saying that two professors were needed to lead the endeavour, namely one philologist and one philosopher. Anscombe asked why a philologist was necessary. Sandberger replied that this necessity resulted from the fact that the project had been reviewed by philologists in Germany. Anscombe asked whether the question of the future project leader should depend on the fact that the project had once been coined a philological project. Sandberger and Theis conceded that the evaluation of the work must be carried out by a philosopher. They mentioned some German philosophers who might act in a scholarly committee to evaluate the project work. Yet, even on this point, the ideas from Tübingen did not have the slightest chance when Rhees commented on the proposal for an evaluation committee:

> These are supposed to be the people who can judge the quality of the transcriptions? The last three people you mention have not done any particular study of the manuscripts in question. I would not have therefore thought that they would be qualified to judge. (Minutes of the meeting between Anscombe, Rhees, Theis and Sandberger, 2 March 1981, Cambridge)

Now Anscombe took the lead: Would it matter from which university the professor came who would lead the project? When Sandberger and Theis said no, Anscombe suggested that she herself could lead it. At this point, the protocol reads "prolonged silence" (Minutes of the meeting between Anscombe, Rhees, Thesis and Sandberger, 2 March 1981, Cambridge). Theis seems to have tried to fend off Anscombe's suggestion by saying that he himself could not deal with the details of the project, and that he needed someone residing at Tübingen who controlled the work. Anscombe replied in a way that brings to mind a Socratic dialogue:

> You say it does not matter where the professor you want is. But then you contradict this by saying he must be there where a lot of the work is being done. Well, that I am, as work is being done in Cambridge. (Minutes of the meeting between Anscombe, Rhees, Thesis and Sandberger, 2 March 1981, Cambridge).

This was but one of many dead ends in the negotiations at Cambridge. Obviously, Sandberger and Theis could not accept the idea that *no work* would be done in Tübingen while Nedo's work in Cambridge would have to be paid by the University of Tübingen. After all, they had come to Cambridge to create a solid foundation for the work in Germany. Rhees then said there was no way the project could continue without Cambridge—the place where everything had begun. The discussion therefore ended without a conclusion.

Reading the protocol of this meeting, the chances for any consent appear low from the beginning. Part of the problem was that the two parties argued from very different starting points. Theis and Sandberger argued based on the institutional necessity to construe, top-down, a project structure that would get the university out of the current problems. By contrast, for Anscombe and Rhees, the starting point was the interest in Wittgenstein's writings and the motivation to be loyal to their principles as literary heirs. These divergent starting points for the negotiations come to expression in the proposal for project leaders: Nedo was unacceptable to the University of Tübingen for formal reasons, yet in the eyes of Anscombe and Rhees, he was the one with the requisite motivation; by contrast, the University of Tübingen judged Heringer to be formally qualified, but Anscombe and Rhees no longer trusted him. There was therefore no concord between the two parties in the meeting on 2 March 1981, not even a pathway to further cooperation. Disappointed, Rhees wrote a note to himself:

> I want to try to understand what Wittgenstein said and what he has written; and, if I can, to make it possible for others to see and understand what he was saying. Chiefly by making it possible for others to <u>study</u> what he wrote. Each of us has his own ideas of how best to do this. What he tried to teach us was "<u>a way of investigating</u> certain questions". If I wanted to get this across to someone in some measure, I should not devote the greatest time and effort to describing the condition of the manuscript pages. I should pay attention to these pages myself, and I should take another to them if his question led that way. But I would keep my attention on thinking about what he said there, and discussing it.
>
> Theis mentioned the "Hegel Ausgabe" and the "Hölderlin Ausgabe", which I understand are in some sense being produced within the University of Tübingen. There had been various editions of Hölderlin's works and of Hegel's before these editions were begun. Those who are making the new editions are familiar with the already published as well as the unpublished writings. Perhaps there have been differences between the already published editions, and for this reason those who are interested feel that there ought to be an 'authoritative text'.
>
> It is possible that, after a century and a half, such an edition will help to remove certain misunderstandings of Hegel. (<u>nota bene</u>: the new edition does not pay attention simply to the manuscripts. It pays attention to the earlier editions, and at times, I suppose, to commentators.)—With the Wittgenstein manuscripts just now it would be different.
>
> It would enable scholars to adorn themselves with the <u>finery</u> of learning, without trying understand what is written there.
>
> Who will the 'scholars' be? At some later time there may be people for whom the publication of "a Wittgenstein edition" would be [a] labour of love. But not now. (Rhees, with reference to the conversation with Theis and Sandberger on 2 March 1981, recorded on 3 March 1981)

6.6.3   Breakdown and Moratorium

It is very likely that Sandberger and Theis returned to Tübingen in a mood *as* pessimistic as Rhees's. The minutes of the next meeting of the Wittgenstein Archive members put the sad state of affairs into words by saying that none of the parties involved—the University of Tübingen, the funding institutions, the Wittgenstein Archive, and the literary heirs—wanted the work that had already been done to be lost, but that each party drew different conclusions from that shared goal (Minutes of the work meeting, 10–1. April 1981, Florence). However, the project group stuck to the idea of publishing a book containing their work despite the failed negotiations at Cambridge, and it wanted to consult an expert on the legal conditions (Minutes of the work meeting, 10–15 April 1981, Florence). Even so, the idea collapsed: the president and the chancellor of the University of Tübingen, the computational unit, Heringer, representatives of the Heidelberg Academy of Sciences and Humanities and members of a possible scholarly committee decided to drop the plan to restructure the archive. The leaders of Tübingen University wanted to prevent any further public discussion of the issues connected with the project management and accounting (Minutes of the meeting between Anscombe, Rhees, Theis and Sandberger, 2 March 1981, Cambridge). Furthermore, the university feared there would be a legal conflict with the literary heirs if a publication was produced and if English copyright law was applied (Theis to Heringer, 8 July 1981). The university administration therefore informed Heringer in July 1981 that the Wittgenstein Archive would be closed down after the official project period and that Heringer should immediately hand over all materials (Theis to Heringer, 8 July 1981; Minutes of the work meeting, 2–4 July 1981).

In this way, the university could limit the damage to its reputation and prevent further complications or lawsuits. Understandably, Heringer felt his university had deserted him in the conflict with the literary heirs. His trust in the institution and in the binding nature of written agreements was damaged. He thus accepted an offer for a professorship at the University of Augsburg and began working there in the winter semester of 1981. It was in Augsburg that he drafted the Final Report for the project together with Nowak, who was struggling to get another job at the University of Tübingen (Nowak to Sandberger, 26 May 1981). In the spring of the following year, the Final Report reached Rhees. He browsed it superficially and felt a deep regret:

> I wish that the whole 'project' had been strangled at it's [sic] birth in 1973/74. At the time
> I said "We may as well let it breathe, and see what happens". This was criminally stupid.
> (Rhees to von Wright, 9 May 1982)

The chance had been lost to incorporate Wittgenstein's writings into the canon of scholarly German philology. All that remained in German academia from the Wittgenstein Archive at Tübingen were legends and rumours, and there was no increase in interest in Wittgenstein's thought. This may be one reason why Wittgenstein was never read in Germany as intensively as in the English-speaking world, despite the fact that he had always written in German. However, even in English academia, the failure of the Wittgenstein Archive at Tübingen had ripple effects. The editing of Wittgenstein's writings was blocked for almost a decade. This was not because of the contracts made with the archive, but because the erosion of trust that emanated from Tübingen spread to the relationship between the three literary heirs and affected the cooperation that was so crucial to all editorial activities: von Wright was vexed that he had not been informed about Anscombe's and Rhees's steps against the archive until after they had been taken. He was certain he would not have exclusively championed Nedo's position, and he would have liked to see a scholarly edition of Wittgenstein's writings made in Germany. This remonstrance resulted in the first serious disruption in the literary heirs' routines of cooperation: von Wright demanded that if all permission concerning the Nachlass was to be decided unanimously, any withdrawal of permission should be decided in unanimity as well. Anscombe replied by appealing to the hardness of logic: if the consent of all three of them was needed for something, it would only take one of them to withdraw consent in order for the permission to be nullified (Anscombe to von Wright, 22 May 1981).

To reject von Wright's demand by referring to logic must have been a provocation for one of the leading analytical philosophers of the time. However, von Wright argued that the withdrawal of permission is a positive decision. He therefore held a different view on the logic of their cooperation:

> I repeat my proposal that we must be unanimous not only when giving permissions but also when changing them (for example cancelling them partly or totally). It is certainly not a point of logic that if a permission, in order to be given, requires the consent of three persons then one of the three can, without the consent of the other two, nullify the permission given. What is required for nullification must be agreed upon. And my proposal is that nullification or any other change in the nature or scope of the permission should have the consent of all the three of us. This proposal appears to me very "logical" and adopting it might be a safeguard against the sort of chaos in which we are now. (von Wright to Anscombe, 3 June 1981)

Rhees also held the opinion that the literary heirs had been drawn into state of chaos. But for him, the chaos began when they gave scholars access to the Cornell microfilm: "The trouble started from the Cornell film of the manuscripts" (Rhees to von Wright, 3 April 1981).This opinion became further entrenched when, after negotiating with Sandberger and Theis, he was approached by yet another group of scholars:

> At the end of March I had a telegram from a Professor Gunner, in Melbourne, Australia, and probably you had one too. He said the University had purchased a copy of the Cornell film, and they had a project (sic) for working on the manuscript copies. He wanted to know what they could rightly do and what they could not. (Rhees to von Wright, 3 April 1981)

In the midst of the ruins resulting from the tragedy of Tübingen, it seems unlikely that any one of the literary heirs was interested in another 'project'. And this was maybe one of the few points the three could easily agree on at the time. After the breakdown of the Tübingen archive, they supported different lines of editorial work on Wittgenstein's writings: Von Wright championed scholarly principles of critical editing in his own work and cooperated with McGuinness and Schulte.[21] Anscombe did not trust McGuinness after the Tübingen affair and did not want to see any edition with his learned commentary (Anscombe to von Wright, 1977_1). She and Rhees supported new funding proposals for Nedo's work, and it eventually led to the volumes of the *Vienna Edition*. Until the first volume of this edition was ready for print, Anscombe insisted on her veto right and blocked further publication from Wittgenstein's Nachlass, even with the home-publisher Blackwell (the blockade stopped only in the 1990s with publication of Wittgenstein 1993). These struggles and troubles around the publication of Wittgenstein's papers were the beginning of what von Wright called the 'via *dolorosa*' in his life (Von Wright 2001, 163). The three literary heirs could not find consensus for almost a decade. Rhees hit the nail on the head when he commented that the 'triumvirate' had become an impossible object: a "triangle whose interior angles will never equal 180°" (Rhees to von Wright, 4 December 1982).[22]

6.7   Scholarly Epilogue

Although many questions remain unanswered and some contradictions still exist after the account presented here, a main motif of the story of the Wittgenstein Archive at Tübingen seems to be clear: trust as the constitutive factor for academic cooperation and the loss of trust as the root of breakdown in cooperation. This holds even for the whole history of the media practices and publication processes as regards Wittgenstein's writings. Trust is fundamental not only for reading Wittgenstein's writings as a cooperative process between reader and text, but also for Wittgenstein's way of 'entrusting' three of his students with the task of publishing from his papers what they thought fit; indeed, Wittgenstein performed the delegation of the task with the words: 'I trust you completely' (see Chap. 2). The same trust remained paramount in the consensual coordination of the editorial work among the literary heirs.[23] Thus, the first two phases in the history of editing Wittgenstein were characterized by trust as a basic factor around which cooperation on Wittgenstein's texts was constituted. The story of the archive at Tübingen is the very moment in that history when this trust could no longer be taken for granted. As mentioned above, the very questions that the shift to digital media evoke are connected to a distrust of human judgement. A remarkably different trust emerges in the story of the archive at Tübingen when the binding nature of interpersonal trust within a small cooperative community (i.e., the literary heirs)

---

[21] Thanks to this cooperation, critical editions of Wittgenstein's main works were eventually published: Wittgenstein 1989, 2001.

[22] This seems to be an allusion to the Penrose triangle, cf.: Penrose and Penrose 1958, 31–33.

[23] The mentioned categories 'delegation' and 'coordination' were part of the discussion with Carlos Spoerhase in the *Werkstatt Praxistheorie* of the SFB1187 in the summer of 2018; I am grateful to Sebastian Gießmann for initiating this discussion; see Gießmann 2018, 95–109.

is replaced by trust in results produced by computational algorithms and the binding nature of institutional rules and written agreements.

The tragedy of Tübingen can be understood as a process through which a stable culture of trust is replaced by a regime of distrust, thus becoming a giant 'breaching experiment' in the sense described by Harold Garfinkel (1963, 187–238). His by-now classic studies of breached trust show how collaboration collapses when trust disappears. In the history of the Wittgenstein Archive at the University of Tübingen, this takes place not only in the manner of one of Garfinkel's ethnomethodological quasi-experiments but in the reality of highly interdependent, scholarly and cooperative relationships. The effects were therefore not locally limited but caused a chain reaction that emerged at many levels and ultimately altered the overall structure of the literary heirs' cooperation. From Garfinkel's experiments, we also know that the breakdown of trust means that a previously-existing common worldview can no longer be taken for granted. When trust is lost in a cooperative community, a previously-assumed common reality breaks down into many realities. This is also the case in the story presented in this chapter, and it is why any single account or form of storytelling will not do justice to all points of view. Hence, the whole drama told here could just as well be arranged in the form of a 'Rashomon movie', with conflicting stories told by the literary heirs and the members of the Wittgenstein Archive at Tübingen.

Acknowledgements   This essay is dedicated to Erhard Schüttpelz. It was written as part of the research subproject *P01: Wissenschaftliche Medien der Praxistheroie: Wittgenstein und Garfinkel* of the Collaborative Research Centre 1187 "Media of Cooperation" (SFB 1187 Medien der Kooperation) at the University of Siegen. I thank Julia Jung and Anne dos Santos Reis for their help in formatting, and I thank Hans Jürgen Heringer, Michael Nedo, Reinhard Nowak and Joachim Schulte for commenting on an earlier version of the essay.

Archival Documents

Letters written by Elizabeth Anscombe are quoted with permission from Mrs M. C. Gormally (Dr Mary Geach). Letters written by Rush Rhees are quoted with permission from Volker Munz. Rhees's letters and notes dated 14 May 1980, 14 and 15 November 1980, 3 January 1981, 3 March 1981, and the protocol of the negotiation on 2 March 1981 are quoted with additional permission from the Richard Burton Archives at the University of Swansea. Letters written by Georg Henrik von Wright have been quoted with permission from Anita and Benedict von Wright. Hans Jürgen Heringer gave permission to quote from the project's Final Report, and Reinhard Nowak gave permission to quote from the minutes of the project group at the Wittgenstein Archives at the University of Tübingen.

List of Archival Sources

Abbreviations:

NLF = National Library of Finland

RBA = Richard Burton Archive

WWA = Von Wright and Wittgenstein Archives at the University of Helsinki

Agenda of the 2nd Wittgenstein symposium in Tübingen, Private Archive Heringer.

Agreement between the literary heirs of Wittgenstein's writings and the research group Wittgenstein, 19 October 1974, Private Archive Heringer.

Anscombe and Rhees to Theis, 3 January 1981, WWA, WWA documents\ Wittgenstein's Nachlass\Filing cabinet\Rush Rhees III (1975–1998)

Anscombe to McGuinness, undated [presumably 1959], kept at McGuinness's private archives, published in Erbacher, Christian. 2015. Editorial Approaches to Wittgenstein's Nachlass: Towards a Historical Appreciation. *Philosophical Investigations* 38(3): 165–198.

Anscombe to von Wright, 1972_1, NLF, COLL.714.11-12.

Anscombe to von Wright, 1977_1, NLF, COLL.714.11-12.

Anscombe to von Wright, 13 February 1979, NLF, COLL.714.11-12.

Anscombe to von Wright, 1980_4, NLF, COLL.714.11-12.

Anscombe to von Wright, 13 November 1980, NLF, COLL.714.11-12.

Anscombe to von Wright, 30 December 1980, NLF, COLL.714.11-12.

Anscombe to von Wright, 22 May 1981, NLF, COLL.714.11-12.

Attachment to the work report from 25 September 1980, Private Archive Nowak.

Central Administration of the University of Tübingen to Heringer, 20 December 1978, Private Archive Heringer.

Circular to all employees, 18 December 1979, Private Archive Nowak.

Circular to the employees, 24 July 1979, Private Archive Heringer.

DFG [German Research Foundation] proposal: Development of a Theory and Methods for Analysis and [an] Edition of German Texts with the Use of Data Processing, 1974, Private Archive Heringer.

Draft of a memorandum to H. Gadamer, Private Archive Nowak.

Draft of the contracts for the employees, Private Archive Heringer.

Final Report of the Project—Securing, Documenting and Indexing of the Unpublished Writings of Ludwig Wittgenstein, no date, Private Archive Heringer.

German department at the University of Tübingen to Nedo, 4 April 1979, Private Archive Heringer.

Heringer to Nowak, 14 January 1982, Private Archive Nowak.

Heringer to Ranchetti, 3 January 1980, Private Archive Heringer.

Heringer to Ranchetti, 4 September 1980, Private Archive Heringer.

Heringer to Rhees, 30 October 1979, Private Archive Heringer.

Heringer to the employees of the Wittgenstein Archive, 16 February 1981, Private Archive Nowak.

Heringer to Theis, 19 February 1981, Private Archive Heringer.

Heringer to von Wright, 29 April 1980, Private Archive Heringer.

Letter and portrayal of the Wittgenstein Archive by Heringer to the Heidelberg Academy of Sciences and Humanities, 17 January 1980, Private Archive Heringer.

Letter to the heads of the project "Wittgenstein Archive"—from the rest of the members of the research group, September 1979, Private Archive Nowak.

McGuinness to Heringer, 24 May 1980, Private Archive Heringer.

Memo from the group meeting, 3 March 1980, RBA UNI/SU/PC/1/2/11/2.

Michael Nedo, A Sketch of the History and the Current Situation of the Research Project by the Wittgenstein Archive, no date, RBA, UNI/SU/PC/1/2/11/2.

Minutes of the meeting between Anscombe, Rhees, Theis and Sandberger, 2 March 1981, Cambridge, 1981, RBA, UNI/SU/PC/1/2/11/2.

Minutes of the meeting of the members of the Wittgenstein Archive, 19 March 1978, Pisa, Provate Archive Nowak.

Minutes of the work meeting, 7 July 1979, no location mentioned, Private Archive Nowak.

Minutes of the meeting with Heringer, McGuinness, Nedo, Picchi, Ranchetti, Rosso, Schulte and Zampolli, 20 March 1978, Pisa, Private Archive Nowak.

Minutes of the Tübingen work meeting, 18–22 November 1978, no location mentioned, Private Archive Nowak.

Minutes of the work meeting, 1–5 October 1979, Tübingen Private Archive Nowak.

Minutes of the work meetings, 7–10 January 1980, no location mentioned, Private Archive Nowak.

Minutes of the work meeting, 13–16 April 1980, no location mentioned, Private Archive Nowak.

Minutes of the work meeting, 16–18 July 1980, Florence, Private Archive Nowak.

Minutes of the work meeting, 29 September–3 October 1980, Oxford, Private Archive Nowak.

Minutes of the work meeting, 10–15 April 1981, Florence, Private Archive Nowak.

Minutes of the work meeting, 2–4 July 1981, no location mentioned, Private Archive Nowak.

Minutes of the work meeting, 27 June 1978, Cambridge, Private Archive Nowak.

Nedo to Theis, 27 January 1981, RBA, UNI/SU/PC/1/2/11/2.

Note by Rhees to himself, 13 November 1980, RBA, UNI/SU/PC/1/2/11/2.

Notification of approval by the *DFG* [German Research Foundation] for a trip to Cambridge, October 1974, Private Archive Heringer.

Nowak to Ranchetti, 14 August 1979, Private Archive Heringer.

Nowak to Sandberger, 26 May 1981, Private Archive Heringer.

Oral History Interview with Brian McGuinness, 20–23 October 2013, Siena, Project Archive Erbacher.

Oral History Interview with Hans Jürgen Heringer, 23 March 2018, Herrsching am Ammersee, Project Archive Erbacher.

Oral History Interview with Hans Jürgen Heringer, 18 May 2018, (by telephone) Hersching-Siegen, Project Archive Erbacher.

Oral History Interview with Joachim Schulte, 20 April 2018, Tromsø, Project Archive Erbacher.

Oral History Interview with Michael Nedo, 22–24 July 2015, Cambridge, Project Archive Erbacher.

Oral History Interview with Michele Ranchetti, by Alois Pichler, no date, Wittgenstein Archives at the University of Bergen.

Oral History Interview with Peter Hacker, 11 August 2014, Kirchberg, Project Archive Erbacher.

Oral History Interview with Reinhard Nowak, 16 May 2018, fernmündlich Schwäbisch-Gmünd-Cölbe, Project Archive Erbacher.

Policy paper, June 1980, Private Archive Heringer.

Ranchetti, McGuinness, Nowak and Schulte to the literary heirs, 18 April 1980, Private Archive Heringer.

Report about the text input from August 1978 to May 1979, 15 June 1979, Private Archive Nowak.

Report by the working group philosophical editions of the Allgemeinen Gesellschaft für Philosophie in Deutschland e.V., 11 July 1979, Private Archive Heringer.

Rhees to Anscombe and von Wright, 19 July 1973, WWA, WWA documents\Wittgenstein's Nachlass\Filing cabinet\Rush Rhees II (1972–1974).

Rhees to Anscombe, 24 September 1980, RBA, UNI/SU/PC/1/2/11/2.

Rhees to Kenny, 2 March 1977, WWA, WWA documents\Wittgenstein's Nachlass\Filing cabinet\Rush Rhees III (1975–1998); published in an edited form in Rhees 1996.

Rhees to Theis, 15 November 1980, RBA, UNI/SU/PC/1/2/11/2.

Rhees to von Wright, 19 September 1974, WWA, WWA documents\Wittgenstein's Nachlass\Filing cabinet\Rush Rhees II (1972–1974).

Rhees to von Wright, 24 March 1974, WWA, WWA documents\Wittgenstein's Nachlass\Filing cabinet\Rush Rhees II (1972–1974).

Rhees to von Wright, 22 January 1976, WWA, WWA documents\Wittgenstein's Nachlass\Filing cabinet\Rush Rhees III (1975–1998).

Rhees to von Wright, 29 April 1976, WWA, WWA documents\Wittgenstein's Nachlass\Filing cabinet\Rush Rhees III (1975–1998).

Rhees to von Wright, 20 April 1977, WWA, WWA documents\Wittgenstein's Nachlass\Filing cabinet\Rush Rhees III (1975–1998).

Rhees to von Wright, 3 April 1981, WWA, WWA documents\Wittgenstein's Nachlass\Filing cabinet\Rush Rhees III (1975–1998).

Rhees to von Wright, 9 May 1982, WWA, WWA documents\Wittgenstein's Nachlass\Filing cabinet\Rush Rhees III (1975–1998).

Rhees to von Wright, 4 December 1982, WWA, WWA documents\Wittgenstein's Nachlass\Filing cabinet\Rush Rhees III (1975–1998).

Rhees to Zimmermann, 14 May 1980, RBA, UNI/SU/PC/1/2/11/2.

Rhees, with reference to his conversation with President Theis and Chancellor Sandberger on 2 March 1981, 3 March 1981, RBA, UNI/SU/PC/1/2/11/2.

The use of *EDV* [electronic data processing] in the production of a historical critical complete edition of L. Wittgenstein's writings—content-related, organizational and personnel aspects, 15 December 1979, Private Archive Nowak.

Theis to Rhees, 15 December 1980, RBA, UNI/SU/PC/1/2/11/2.

Theis to Heringer, 8 July 1981, Private Archive Heringer.

Von Wright to Anscombe and Rhees, 23 January 1979, WWA, WWA documents\Wittgenstein's Nachlass\Filing cabinet\Rush Rhees III (1975–1998).

Von Wright to Anscombe, 7 January 1972, NLF, COLL.714.11-12.

Von Wright to Anscombe, 2 August 1973, NLF, COLL.714.11-12.

Von Wright to Anscombe, 31 May 1976, NLF, COLL.714.11-12.

Von Wright to Anscombe, 31 January 1977, NLF, COLL.714.11-12.

Von Wright to Anscombe, 16 May 1979, NLF, COLL.714.11-12.

Von Wright to Anscombe, 7 May 1980, NLF, COLL.714.11-12.

Von Wright to Anscombe, 19 June 1980, NLF, COLL.714.11-12.

Von Wright to Anscombe, 3 June 1981, WWA, WWA documents\Wittgenstein's Nachlass\Filing cabinet\Rush Rhees III (1975–1998).

Von Wright to Anscombe, 15 March 1982, NLF, COLL.714.11-12.

Von Wright to Rhees, 1 August 1973, WWA, WWA documents\Wittgenstein's Nachlass\Filing cabinet\Rush Rhees III (1975–1998).

Von Wright to Rhees, 14 March 1977, WWA, WWA documents\Wittgenstein's Nachlass\Filing cabinet\Rush Rhees III (1975–1998).

Von Wright to Rhees, 26 April 1977, WWA, WWA documents\Wittgenstein's Nachlass\Filing cabinet\Rush Rhees III (1975–1998).

Work report, 26 March 1979, Private Archive Nowak.

Work report, 11 June 1980, Private Archive Nowak.

Work report, 23 October 1980, Private Archive Nowak.

Work report, 9 April 1981, Private Archive Nowak.

References

Bloor, David. 1983. *Wittgenstein: A Social Theory of Knowledge*. New York: Columbia University Press.

Bloor, David. 1992. Left and Right Wittgensteinians. In *Science and Culture*, ed. Andrew Pickering, 266–282. Chicago: University of Chicago Press.

Erbacher, Christian. 2015. *Formen des Klärens. Literarisch-philosophische Darstellungsmittel in Wittgensteins Schriften*. Münster: Mentis.

Erbacher, Christian. 2017a. "Gute" philosophische Gründe für "schlechte" Editionsphilologie. In *Textologie—Theorie und Praxis interdisziplinärer Textforschung*, ed. Martin Endres, Axel Pichler, and Claus Zittel, 257–298. Berlin: DeGruyter.

Erbacher, Christian. 2017b. "Among the omitted stuff, there are many good remarks of a general nature"—On the Making of von Wright and Wittgenstein's Culture and Value. *Northern European Journal of Philosophy* 18(2): 79–113.

Erbacher, Christian. 2019a. Das Drama von Tübingen: Eine Humanities and Technology Story. *Working Paper Series des SFB* [collaborative research center] *1187* No. 13, Siegen, 1–44.

Erbacher, Christian. 2019b. Ways of Making Wittgenstein Available: Infrastructures and Publics in the History of Editing Wittgenstein. In *Medien der Kooperation /Media of Cooperation— Infrastructuring Publics*, ed. Matthias Korn, Wolfgang Reißmann, Tobias Röhl and David Sittler. 265–284. Berlin: Springer.

Erbacher, Christian, Julia Jung, and Anne Seibel. 2017. The Logbook of Editing Wittgenstein's "Philosophische Bemerkungen". *Nordic Wittgenstein Review* [S.l.] 6(1): 105–147.

Garfinkel, Harold. 1963. A Conception of, and Experiments with, "Trust" as a Condition of Stable Concerted Actions. In *Motivation and social interaction: cognitive approaches*, ed. O. J. Harvey, 187–238. New York: Ronald Press.

Gießmann, Sebastian. 2018. Element einer Praxistheorie der Medien. *Zeitschrift für Medienwissenschaft* 19: 95–109.

Groddeck, Wolfram, Gunter Martens, Roland Reuß, and Peter Straengle. 2003. Gespräch über die Bände 7 & 8 der Frankfurt Hölderlin-Ausgabe. *Text. Kritische Beiträge*, 8(1): 1–55.

Hacker, Peter M. S., and Gordon P. Baker. 1980–1996. *Volume 1–4 of an Analytical Commentary in Philosophical Investigations*. Hoboken, NJ: Wiley-Blackwell.

Harré, Horace R. 1999. Gilbert Ryle and the Tractatus. *The Liacre Journal* 3: 39–53, http://www. linacre.ox.ac.uk/facilities/library/gilbert-ryle-collection. Accessed: 25 September 2018.

Hintikka, Jaakko. 1991. An Impatient Man and His Papers. *Synthese* 87(2): 183–201.

Isaac, Joel. 2012. Kuhn's Education: Wittgenstein, Pedagogy, and the Road to Structure. *Modern Intellectual History* 9(1): 89–107.

Jones, Steven E. 2016. *Roberto Busa, S. J., and the Emergence of Humanities Computing: The Priest and the Punched Cards*. London: Routledge.

Joyce, James. 1984. *Ulysses: A Critical and Synoptic Edition*. Prepared by Hans. W. Gabler, Wolfhardt Steppe and Claus Melchior. New York/London: Garland.

Kaal, Hans, and Alastair McKinnon. 1975. *Concordance to Wittgenstein's Philosophische Untersuchungen*. Leiden: Brill.

Kaufringer, Heinrich. 1972 and 1974. *Werke*. Vol. 1: Text and Vol. 2: Indices, ed. Paul Sappler. Tübingen: Niemeyer.

Kenny, Anthony. 1977. From the Big Typescript to the *Philosophical Grammar*. In *Acta Philosophica Fennica—Essays on Wittgenstein in Honour of G. H. von Wright*, ed. Jaakko Hintikka, 41–53. Amsterdam: North-Holland Publishing Company.

Kenny, Anthony. 1979. Wittgenstein über Philosophie. In *Schriften. Beiheft 3. Wittgensteins geistige Erscheinung*, 9–34. Frankfurt a. M.: Suhrkmap.

Kenny, Anthony. 2006. A Brief History of Editing Wittgenstein. In *Wittgenstein: The Philosopher and His Works*, ed. Alois Pichler and Simo Säätelä, 382–396. Frankfurt a. M.: Ontos Verlag.

Kermani, Navid. Deutschlands Schicksal. *Die Zeit* 44, 23 October 2008. https://www.zeit. de/2008/44/L-Hoelderlin-Kermani. Accessed: 25 September 2018.

Kuhn, Thomas. 1962. *The Structure of Scientific Revolutions*. Chicago: University of Chicago Press.

Lyas, Colin. 1999. *Peter Winch*. Teddington: Acumen Press.

Lynch, Michael. 1992a. Extending Wittgenstein: The Pivotal Move from Epistemology to the Sociology of Science. In *Science as Practice and Culture*, ed. Andrew Pickering, 215–265. Chicago: University of Chicago Press.

Lynch, Michael. 1992b. From the "Will to Theory" to the Discursive Collage: A Reply to Bloor's "Left and Right Wittgensteinians". In *Science as practice and culture*, ed. Andrew Pickering, 283–300. Chicago: University of Chicago Press.

Lynch, Michael. 1997. *Scientific Practice and Ordinary Action. Ethnomethodology and Social Studies of science*. Cambridge: University Press.

McGuinness, Brian. 1988. *Young Ludwig. Wittgenstein's Life, 1889–1921*. London: Duckworth.

Media of Cooperation, 2015. Official proposal to *DFG* [German Research Foundation] for *SFB* [collaborative research center] 1187. Siegen: University of Siegen.

Nowak, Reinhard. 1981. *Grenzen der Sprachanalyse: ein Beitrag zur Klärung des Verhältnisses von Philosophie und Sprachwissenschaft.* Tübingen: Narr.

N. N. 1993. Schlaucherls Triumph, Der riesige Nachlaß des Jahrhundert-Denkers Wittgenstein soll vollständig gedruckt werden—als Pfründe eines dubiosen Herausgebers. *Der Spiegel Online*, http://www.spiegel.de/spiegel/print/d-13682916.html. Accessed: 27 September 2018.

Osterle, Kurt. Die Editions-Operette. *Die Zeit*, 8 January 1993, https://www.zeit.de/1993/02/die-editions-operette. Accessed: 27. September 2018.

Pacioni, Marco, and Rita Romanelli. n.d. *Archivio Michele Ranchetti*, https://www.vieusseux.it/inventari/ranchetti.pdf. Accessed: 27 September 2018.

Penrose, Lionel S., and Roger Penrose. 1958. Impossible Objects: A Special Type of Visual Illusion. *British Journal of Psychology* 49(1): 31–33.

Pichler, Alois, and H. Hrachovec ed. 2008. *Wittgenstein and the Philosophy of Information.* Frankfurt a. M.: Ontos.

Popper, Karl. 1935. *Logik der Forschung, Zur Erkenntnistheorie der modernen Naturwissenschaft.* Wien: Springer-Verlag.

Radax, Ferry. 1974–1975. *Ludwig Wittgenstein.* WDR Köln.

Rawls, Anne W. 2011. Wittgenstein, Durkheim, Garfinkel and Winch: Constitutive Orders of Sensemaking. *The Journal for the Theory of Social Behavior* 41(4): 396–418.

Rothhaupt, Josef G. F. 2011. Wittgensteins Kringel-Buch als unverzichtbarer Initialtext seines "anthropologischen Denkens" und seiner "ethnologischen Betrachtungsweise". *Wittgenstein-Studien* no. 2: 137–186.

Ryle, Gilbert. 1999. The Genesis of 'Oxford' philosophy. *The Liacre Journal* 3, http://www.linacre.ox.ac.uk/facilities/library/gilbert-ryle-collection. Accessed: 25 September 2018.

Schulte, Joachim. 1979. Der Waismann-Nachlass. *Zeitschrift für Philosophische Forschung* 33: 108–140.

Schulte, Joachim. 1987. *Erlebnis und Ausdruck.* München: Philosophia.

Sismondo, Sergio. 2009. *An Introduction to Science and Technology Studies.* Hoboken, NJ: John Wiley and Sons.

Star, Susan L. 1999. The Ethnography of Infrastructure. *American Behavioral Scientist* 43(3): 377–391.

Von Wright, Georg H. 1969. Special Supplement: The Wittgenstein Papers. *Philosophical Review* 78 (4): 483–503.

Von Wright, Georg H. 2001. *Mitt liv som jag minns det.* Helsingfors: Söderström.

Warnock, Mary. 1996. *Women Philosophers.* London: J. M. Dent & Sons Ltd.

Willkomm, Judith. 2022. *Tiere—Medien—Sinne. Eine Ethnographie bioakustischer Feldforschung.* Springer.

Wittgenstein, Ludwig. 1958. *Preliminary Studies for the "Philosophical Investigations". Generally Known as The Blue and Brown Books.* Oxford: Basil Blackwell.

Wittgenstein, Ludwig. 1961. *Tractatus Logico-Philosophicus*, Translated by D. F. Pears, and B. F. McGuinness, International Library of Philosophy and Scientific Method. London: Routledge and Kegan Paul.

Wittgenstein, Ludwig. 1964. *Philosophische Bemerkungen.* Edited by R. Rhees. Oxford: Basil Blackwell.

Wittgenstein, Ludwig. 1965. A Lecture on Ethics. *The Philosophical Review* 74: 3–12.

Wittgenstein, Ludwig. 1966. *Lectures and Conversations.* Edited by Cyril Barrett. Oxford: Basil Blackwell.

Wittgenstein, Ludwig. 1967a. *Lezioni e conversazioni sull'etica, l'estetica, la psicologia e la credenza religiosa.* Mailand: Adelphi.

Wittgenstein, Ludwig. 1967b. *Ludwig Wittgenstein und der Wiener Kreis.* Edited by B. McGuinness. Oxford: Basil Blackwell and Frankfurt a. M.: Suhrkamp.

Wittgenstein, Ludwig. 1969. *On Certainty / Über Gewißheit.* Edited by G. E. M. Anscombe, and G. H. von Wright, translated by D. Paul and G. E. M. Anscombe. Oxford: Basil Blackwell.

Wittgenstein, Ludwig. 1971. *Prototractatus. An Early Version of Tractatus Logico-Philosophicus.* Edited by B. McGuinness, T. Nyberg, and G. H. von Wright, translated by D. F. Pears, and B. F. McGuinness, historical preface by G. H. von Wright and a facsimile of the author's manuscript. London: Routledge and Kegan Paul.

Wittgenstein, Ludwig. 1976a. *Wittgenstein's Lectures on the Foundations of Mathematics.* Edited by C. Diamond. Cambridge, 1939, Ithaca, NY: Cornell University Press.

Wittgenstein, Ludwig. 1976b. *Osservazioni filosofiche.* Introduction and translation by M. Rosso. Turin: Einaudi.

Wittgenstein, Ludwig. 1978. Wittgensteins Vorlesungen über die Grundlagen der Mathematik. Cambridge, 1939. In *Schriften* Vol. 7, ed. C. Diamond, translated by J. Schulte. Frankfurt a. M.: Suhrkamp.

Wittgenstein, Ludwig. 1979. *Schriften. Beiheft 3: Wittgensteins geistige Erscheinung.* Frankfurt a. M.: Suhrkamp.

Wittgenstein, Ludwig. 1989. *Logisch-philosophische Abhandlung. Tractatus logico-philosophicus.* Edited by B. McGuinness, and J. Schulte. Kritische Edition. Frankfurt a. M.: Suhrkamp.

Wittgenstein, Ludwig. 1991. *Geheime Tagebücher 1914–1916.* Edited by W. Baum. Berlin/Wien: Turia & Kant.

Wittgenstein, Ludwig. 1993. *Letzte Schriften über die Philosophie der Psychologie. Das Innere und das Äußere. 1949–1951.* Edited by G. H. von Wright and H. Nyman, text newly proofread by J. Schulte. Frankfurt a. M.: Suhrkamp.

Wittgenstein, Ludwig. 2001. *Philosophische Untersuchungen. Kritisch-genetische Edition.* Edited by J. Schulte in cooperation with H. Nyman, E. von Savigny, and G. H. von Wright. Frankfurt a. M.: Suhrkamp.

Wittgenstein, Ludwig. 2008. *Wittgenstein in Cambridge. Letters and Documents, 1911–1951.* Edited by B. McGuinness. Malden, MA: Blackwell.

The Happy Afterlife of a Testament

7

Passing the Baton

Does the tale of editing Wittgenstein's writings end with the tragic collapse of the research project at Tübingen?—Of course not. The tale takes a happy turn in its next episode. But since my decade of research has come to an end, chapter seven can only be a short story about the Wittgenstein Archives at the University of Bergen (Norway): When four Norwegian universities shared the cost of buying the Cornell microfilm, von Wright, in 1980, encouraged the young scholar Viggo Rossvær to formally apply to the Norwegian Research Council for funding a "Nordic Wittgenstein Project" (NWP). The NWP initially had no ambition to produce publishable transcripts of Wittgenstein's writings. It simply aimed to study Wittgenstein's manuscripts. However, dealing with the Cornell microfilm turned out to be cumbersome. The project leaders therefore tried to improve the retrieval catalogue by matching the microfilm volumes with von Wright's catalogue of the *Nachlass* and by developing a system of keywords. Later on, the NWP hired students and conscientious objectors to actually make some transcriptions, but these were still only meant for the Norwegian researchers' own purposes. However, when Rossvær got to know Reinhard Nowak of the Tübingen Wittgenstein Archive during conferences in Dubrovnik in 1981 and 1982, he received first-hand information about the collapse of the archive in Tübingen. This was the moment when several people began to wonder: Could the NWP build on the work that had been done at Tübingen? Indeed, Professor Heringer sent a researcher to Bergen in 1984, and he carried with him a magnetic tape with transcriptions from Tübingen. But the transferred material became a very problematic present: Anscombe, being only afterwards informed about the transfer, demanded that the NWP hand the magnetic tape over to Michael Nedo. But this was precisely what the NWP had promised Heringer it would not do. Consequently, Anscombe refused to grant the NWP permission to do any further work on Wittgenstein's *Nachlass*. The NWP had been

C. Erbacher, *The Happy Afterlife of Ludwig W.*, Beiträge zur Praxeologie / Contributions to Praxeology, https://doi.org/10.1007/978-3-662-66155-0_7

drawn into the conflicts resulting from the fall of Tübingen and found itself stuck in the impasse during the years of the moratorium in editing Wittgenstein.

This was roughly the situation Claus Huitfeldt faced when he became the leader of the NWP in 1985. Huitfeldt had been one of the conscientious objectors who was involved in transcribing the Wittgenstein manuscripts, and he had finished his civil service around the same time as the NWP needed a new leader. He seemed suited for the post since, along with having a *magister* degree in philosophy, he had experience with computational transcription, which was the methodological focus of the NWP. By this time the project had moved to the University of Bergen, where a unit for computing in the humanities planned to create a system for computational transcriptions of literary texts.

When Huitfeldt arrived to lead this project, he learned about the predicament of the magnetic tape. There was only one rational conclusion for him to draw: winning the permission of all three literary heirs was a prerequisite for any further work on Wittgenstein's *Nachlass* in Bergen. Resolving the conflict with Anscombe thus became Huitfeldt's first priority as the NWP's leader. In this ambition he was supported not only by von Wright but by professors at the University of Bergen and several internationally-influential Wittgenstein scholars who signed an official petition in 1987, asking the literary heirs to consent to the production of a transcription of the Wittgenstein papers at Bergen. These efforts failed. In Huitfeldt's diplomatic journey to England in 1988, he consulted with Anscombe, Rhees and Nedo in personal conversations, but again failed to reach an agreement that would allow the NWP to continue its work. Anscombe would not give in unless the tape was transferred to Nedo, and she even threatened the NWP with lawsuits. In effect, the NWP shut down in 1989.—But fortunately, it could be revived shortly thereafter.

In 1990, after Rhees's death, the triumvirate of the literary heirs became a consortium of literary executors, now involving Anscombe and von Wright, Peter Winch as Rhees's successor and Anthony Kenny as von Wright's future successor. In this new constellation, it was possible to agree to a truce. Being respected by both Anscombe and von Wright, Kenny could act as a mediator. After inspecting Nedo's work, he negotiated a compromise according to which the Wittgenstein Archives at the University of Bergen (WAB) was allowed to create a complete machine-readable transcription of Wittgenstein's *Nachlass*—something von Wright always thought the Tübingen archive was meant to do. With this concession, the WAB could be constituted in 1990. By 1990 too, Huitfeldt had found a way to deal with the magnetic tape affair: the tape was donated to the University of Bergen Library under the condition that no one would be allowed to look at it—and indeed, it has never been looked at to this day. From this time onwards, the WAB continued the editorial work on Wittgenstein's writings that the three literary heirs had begun forty years earlier.

It took another decade of hard work before the WAB managed to present a complete machine-readable transcription that then served as the 'mother version' for a complete electronic edition—the *Bergen Electronic Edition* published on CD-ROMs by Oxford University Press in 2000. Since then, the WAB's new director Alois Pichler has been active in updating the electronic *Nachlass* and making it freely available online. Wittgenstein's writings have thus found their way into the public domain with the greatest possible transparency, and as far as we can see today, the tale of the papers which Wittgenstein left to posterity must be called a happy one.

The story of the WAB is a counterpoint to the story of the archive at Tübingen in many respects. I refer not only to it having successfully produced a product; it still exists and inspires many scholarly activities connected in some way to Wittgenstein's *Nachlass*. Its whole set-up, the way it has grown, the way it has been embedded in an international network of Wittgenstein scholars, the way the leadership has been shared and transferred to different directors at different times—all this reads like a cooperative antithesis to the complex drama of Tübingen. But this does not mean the story of cooperation at the WAB is uncomplicated. As of today, the WAB itself has a history of more than 40 years. This history contains a vast wealth of scholarly threads dating back to von Wright and Knut Erik Tranøy's friendship at Cambridge in the 1930s (see Chapter 2 in this book). In addition, the story of the WAB is a fascinating technological tale of finding an adequate mark-up format for transcribing complex literary texts, and it stretches from the first days of standardizing computing in the humanities to the cutting edge of today's digital humanities. In other words, telling the story of WAB is a project in its own right, and it would fill at least another volume. Most of the relevant archival material for telling this success story of cooperation during the period of the early digital humanities is ready to be studied. The WAB has established its 'Archive's Archive' with thousands of documents from its own history as well as oral history interviews on tape. Re-listening to them and remembering what Professor Heringer once told me after he had read "The Tragedy of Tübingen", I imagine that of all the adequate literary formats for the contrapuntal story of the WAB, my favourite would be a modern one-act comedy: Viggo Rossvær, Claus Huitfeldt and Alois Pichler would meet under the old lime tree during a Wittgenstein Symposium at Kirchberg in Austria and share their memories from forty years of Norwegian *Nachlass* work, larding their recollections with many amusing but respectful anecdotes. Other adequate literary formats will of course spring from the minds of other authors. I would like to encourage them, for I would love to read their accounts of the happy afterlife of Wittgenstein's testament.

The manufacturer's authorised representative in the EU is Springer
Nature Customer Service Centre GmbH, Europaplatz 3, 69115 Heidelberg,
Germany. If you have any concerns regarding our products, please
contact ProductSafety@springernature.com

Printed and bound by CPI Group (UK) Ltd, Croydon, CR0 4YY
24/04/2026
02096360-0002